ADDITIONAL PR

"Like watching a great stage drama enacted on a meticulously designed set in which all of the principal players surprise us with the deep register of their flaws and fortitude."

—Kathleen Finneran, author of *The Tender Land*

"A testament to the power of art, literature, and ideas."

—Rabbi Susan Talve, Central Reform Congregation

"This 'Remembrance of Things Past' is neither 'sweet' nor 'silent,' and I cite that sonnet because Henry Schvey's mother quotes Shakespeare frequently and his father is a character straight out of one of the tragicomedies: tempestuous, driven, hateful and hate-filled yet kind. Their son's memoir is closely watched and keenly heard: a riveting account of childhood and young manhood from the wounded adult who survives."

—Nicholas Delbanco is the author, most recently, of *The Years*

"With chilling accuracy, Henry Schvey reveals the cruelty that simmered beneath the seemingly placid surface of 1950s America. With artistry and skill, wisdom and compassion, Schvey exposes not only his complicated relationship to his highly successful but sadistic father, but also the ways in which literature, art, and love can save a young man's soul."

—Eileen Pollack, Professor, MFA Program in Creative Writing, University of Michigan

"Wickedly funny and heartbreaking in turn, this incisive and ironic sweep of his family's foibles and the America of the 60's 70's and 80's makes for compulsive reading. This is writing from a master of the genre which deserves a wide readership. Hugely enjoyable and compelling."

—Jane Lapotaire, Royal Shakespeare Company Hon Associate Artist, Tony Award, Helen Hayes and Olivier Award winner

THE POISON TREE

a memoir

January, 2017

HENRY I. SCHVEY

For Paige and Panmill,

Dear colleagues, and warm friends — who bring such a wonderful grace and inspiration to the PAD. You add so much to our students and faculty!

Yours,

Henry

Walrus Publishing | Saint Louis, MO

Published in the United States by Walrus Publishing
St. Louis, MO

Walrus Publishing is an imprint of Amphorae Publishing Group, LLC.
4168 Hartford Street
Saint Louis, MO 63116

The material in this book reflects the author's recollection of events. Some names, locations, and identifying characteristics have been changed to protect the privacy of those depicted. Dialogue has been re-created from memory.

Cover by Kristina Blank Makansi
Cover art from Shutterstock

10 9 8 7 6 5 4 3 2 1

Library of Congress Control Number: 2016938148
ISBN: 9781940442167

This book is dedicated with love to my wife Patty, my children Aram, Jerusha and Natasha, and to my grandchildren Evan, Julian and Livia. Each day they remind me of what a loving family can be.

THE POISON TREE

a memoir

Demand me nothing, what you know, you know.
From this time forth I never will speak word.
—Shakespeare, *Othello*

So we beat on, boats against the current,
borne back ceaselessly into the past.
—Fitzgerald, *The Great Gatsby*

I.

Christmas morning, and my father and I are camped underneath a lavishly decorated Christmas tree. Dozens of opened presents lie strewn all over the floor, and they're all for me. Scraps of blue paper and silver ribbons fly through the room. I have just opened an amazing gift: a Joe Palooka punching figure—it's huge! Taller than I am. The rubber base is filled with sand, so I can stand and punch him and he pops right back up, smiling, daring me to punch him again. I am five years old. I sit on the floor with my legs crossed Indian style, dressed in Superman pajamas. My father wears a green flannel bathrobe, the color of Gerber's peas. I love that bathrobe and find it strangely comforting.

I dump a small wooden box of toy figures on the floor, and Dad and I divide them up into Good Guys and Bad Guys. We call the game Cowboys and Indians, but the "cowboys" are really a motley assemblage of G.I.s and cavalry officers; the Indians are mixed with some metal German soldiers left over from my father's own childhood. As they face across one another waiting for the signal to attack, the two armies shimmer and glow green and red from the lights on the Christmas tree. Dad and I pepper one another's forces with marbles. First I shoot—then Dad—then I again. The marbles, too, are divided up like the Cowboys and Indians. A ragtag bunch of cat's-eyes and onionskins; even the occasional chippie, big as a walnut. Our duel lasts for hours, and only ends when one of the two of us has defeated the other's men by knocking them all over on their sides. I'm happy to have cavalry soldiers and cowboys on my side, since men on horseback are almost impossible to knock down. Germans fire at cowboys from the prone position and offer miniscule targets. What I have to do is hit a Kraut at just the right angle with one of the smaller marbles, in the crease between his cocked left elbow and the rifle. Only then can I kill him by successfully turning him over on his side. Indians are easier to kill, but there are so many they wear you down. Germans and G.I.s are made of cast iron, so that even a perfectly placed shot sometimes bounces off and does no damage. You need a really big marble fired at maximum velocity—and a lot of luck.

In this memory, my mother is absent. She floats in and out at odd intervals, a woman in a Chagall painting, wearing a snowflake apron. She appears, serves her men hot chocolate, and floats away.

For hours, my father and I are transported into another world. At some point, we agree to a ceasefire while he toasts Aunt Jemima frozen waffles. I drown my buttered waffle with maple syrup—but he says nothing. Not one word. Later, we break for Mrs. Paul's fish sticks, Swanson TV dinners, and *The Lone Ranger* on television. The day flashes by in seconds.

Those early images of joy on Christmas morning, however precisely remembered, feel fraudulent, surreal—too good to be true. I angrily part the curtain which separates me from my past, and peer into that glowing room where, on my RCA Victrola, Burl Ives is always singing "Big Rock Candy Mountain." I watch the turntable slowly meander around in circles. The forty-five rpm record skips a bit, then continues on its way. For a moment, time has stopped.

Four decades later, I am standing outside my father's apartment, a key in the palm of my hand. My father's initials—NIS—are cut deep into the metal. I wonder how it must have sounded when the letters were forcibly etched into the brass. I have returned home from the Netherlands where I have been teaching English literature for several years now. My father is in the hospital being treated for lymphoma, and I have come back to New York to visit him. I don't know if he will survive. After our brief visit, he sent me to his apartment at 405 East 56th Street to pick up an address book from his desk.

Just who is he, I wonder? A combination of steely resolve and intense charisma, Dad was the personification of 1950s suave. He was Don Draper decades before Don Draper existed: manicured, handsome, powerful. That's how he appeared to me as a boy, and how he appears to me today. He could also be cruel and vindictive. And even now, I was, and still am, desperate for his love. Decades after leaving New York, years after leaving the United States, I am still confused. I still want to know, *who is he?* I am a child at a crosswalk, waiting for a signal, a nod that it is safe to cross the street alone.

I unlock the door and enter his apartment. Immediately, his cologne rushes at me. Not Old Spice. Something much more expensive. It is on everything. Musky, masculine, intoxicating. Even the furnishings—a large yellow kimono hanging on one wall; two black, lacquer Chinese chests, one decorated with jade green birds, the other with flowers—radiate his scent.

As I stand there revisiting the phantasmagoria of his things, I feel strange. Instinctively, even after all these years, his posessions evoke a sense of danger. I want to walk away, no—run. Forget the elevator; just race down the ten flights of stairs, not look back. Never look back. Panic overtakes me. My heartbeat escalates; my palms sweat. But, really, it's hardly appropriate for me, a grown man in my forties—an adult myself, married with children and a mortgage—to turn and run. I'm a reasonably successful professor teaching in the Netherlands and lecturing all over Europe. I am not only a son, I'm a husband and father, with three young children of my own. But, here, in this room again, my other identities melt. I'm his son—Norman Schvey's son. I breathe in deeply, shut my eyes, and wait for this wave of irrational panic to subside. I know it will. It always does. Besides, what could I possibly say to the doorman if I ran into him in the lobby? That I was standing in the entryway of my hospitalized father's apartment, took a look around, and concluded that I was too afraid to stay up there alone? I smile at this feeble joke at my own expense. Anyway, I'm here for a purpose—I'll find his address book and return to the hospital.

My eyes open again, and there I see an eighteenth-century English grandfather clock across from a lithograph of a bare-breasted Indian girl, a cheap work he picked up at a flea market in the Village for a hundred bucks after flirting with the artist. A brilliantly colored, hand-woven Turkish carpet lies beneath a seven-foot-tall tennis racket he didn't knew what to do with, so he leaned it against the wall. Permanently.

The things around me have nothing to do with him, or his taste, but I recall that furnishings don't, or least didn't, really matter to him. Unlike his wardrobe, they don't have to be precisely coordinated. Upon his desk is a bag of colored balloons with his face on them. I blow up a green one and watch my father's head expand to grotesque proportions, then shrivel to nothing. Beside the balloons is a carved mahogany Merrill Lynch bull with its "We're Bullish on America" inscription. Beside the bull is a rough-hewn, marble paperweight I have never seen before. Inscribed with Gothic lettering, it reads:

"I Don't Hold a Grudge—I Get Even."

However ill-matched, each object is in its proper place. The only thing not in perfect order is a single, white coffee cup and saucer resting on the rubber rack beside the sink. They've been washed and rinsed, and are ready to be wiped and placed on the shelf when he returns.

There is a vast collection of overcoats in the front hall closet. I try on a bowler hat. When did my head grow bigger than his? I draw my fingers along a green Loden coat from Austria; its fur prickles like the pelt of a wolf. Nothing fits. His coats are all way too wide on me; his hats too small. I watch myself twirl an antique English walking stick with a silver head in the hall mirror. I swing the stick and the handle comes loose. There is a dagger hidden within.

I stumble into an oversized walk-in closet enveloped by a cornucopia of suits, shirts, and ties. Everything is in pristine condition. Everything hangs neatly. Even suits and sport coats he hasn't worn in twenty years look new. The array of suits and jackets, arranged on hangers according to season and coordinated by color, remind me of a row of obedient dogs, panting, waiting for their master's return. I see, too, he has cut out all the sizes from the inside of his jackets and suit pants. Why? Is he vain about his weight?

Even living alone, my father wanted, and was in "need of more space," as he said. So he recently acquired the neighboring apartment and smashed through the adjoining wall. The apartment previously belonged to a group of four British Airways stewardesses, and over gin and tonics, he managed to get the women to divulge their plans to move. He snapped up the place and tore down the adjoining wall before the superintendent could stop it. His apartment is now twice as large as before, but the floor is uneven in the kitchen where the two floors have been patched together.

In the bathroom, I pick up a 100% boar-bristle hairbrush. The brush is immaculate—not a single gray hair. I unscrew the tiny green cap of Pinaud aftershave and sniff. I pour the aftershave into my palms, rub them together, and slap my cheeks with his scent. I slide open the medicine cabinet: Preparation H, Bayer Aspirin, traditional Colgate toothpaste, an old-fashioned glass eye cup. There is also a burgundy leather travel kit. Everything so clean and tidy that by the time I enter the bedroom and inspect his dresser, it doesn't surprise me to find that his socks are color-coded—crew-length divided from calf-length—and that his jewelry chest is divided into a collection of tiny velvet compartments, all perfectly organized with shirt stays, tie clips, tuxedo studs, and cuff links. Beside the lavish chest rests a smaller leather chest I brought back from Florence from one of my lecture tours. I gave it to him for his birthday twenty years earlier. Plainly, it has never been used.

The phone rings, but I don't answer. After several rings, the machine finally snaps on. "This is Norman Schvey speaking," it shouts; the volume is set way too high. "If you wish to leave a message, do so after the beep. Speak properly and distinctly. I will try to call you back as soon as possible. Thank you."

The message is unexceptional and one I have heard many times before when I've called from abroad and left a message, but the tone: "Speak properly and distinctly!" can be no one else's. There is the suggestion that he may not return the caller's message, even if it is distinct; he will merely "try" to do so. I note for the first time, the absence of a discernible pause between "possible" and "thank you," making the courtesy sound perfunctory in a way I'd never noticed.

Sifting through papers and account books stacked neatly on his desk, I notice something odd: a cream-colored invitation to my parents' wedding in 1946, printed on thick vellum. The invitation is perfectly preserved, and does not smell like a musty, antique document. Why has he saved it after all these years? I wonder. On the cover of the invitation are two entwined hearts with my parents' initials, RL and NS. Inside, a pair of silver embossed doves are perched on the exact midpoint of a leafy branch, the doves so close together that their breasts touch, the twin points of their beaks kiss. The larger dove spreads its wings, protecting the smaller. The invitation has a braided tassel knotted along its spine.

Mr. and Mrs. Jay Lerner
request the pleasure of your company
at the marriage of their daughter
Rita Kay
to
Mr. Norman Irwin Schvey
Sunday, the thirtieth of June
Nineteen hundred and forty-six
at six o'clock
Hotel Pierre
New York

I've never seen this before and am stunned by its elegance. I'm also amazed it has been saved in such pristine condition, considering my parents' divorce. I find the menu for their wedding dinner, and each dish reads more elegant than the one before: Canapes Favorite, Compote of Melon Tricolor, Paillette d'Orre, and Asparagus Mimosa. I wonder what they tasted like, and what it must have been like to be present at the Pierre for the union of two of New York's most prosperous Jewish families; both so successful, each patriarch had an office in the Empire State Building.

My mother told me the man she married was different than the person I knew as my father. She said he had been an accomplished dancer with perfect manners until their wedding night when, she said, everything changed. In the photo on his desk, both dressed in their wedding finery, they are on the brink of it. In a few short hours, they will have spent their first night together in the sumptuous bridal suite of the Hotel Pierre. One thing I did learn, much later, is that whatever happened that night set the tone for everything to come—including me. In my imagination, and in my gut, I know one thing to be true. That was the night I was conceived!

For some reason, as I stare at the wedding photograph, Longchamps, that long-departed restaurant on 34th Street which used to be a fixture on the ground floor of the Empire State Building, invades my memory. I have no idea why I am there or why that image insists on infecting my thoughts.

I am a little boy, and we are about to order lunch. My grandmother, looking beautiful and far more youthful than I can remember, wears a pale blue suit with velvet trim and gray, calfskin gloves. I wear a navy sailor suit with shorts and matching blue cap.

She turns away from me, and I am immediately slapped hard across the face by my father for not saying "Thank you" to the white-gloved waiter who has just laid a cloth napkin across my lap. Before I can begin to comprehend this, I am whisked from my chair and told to smile by a photographer who, for some reason, takes my picture as a souvenir. I do as I'm told. I smile as hard as I can, which actually, is a horrible grimace, and looks nothing like a smile. I hold this pose until I am told to stop. My jaw hurts. My cheeks burn.

After this sudden reflection, I pick up everything I have touched and place it all carefully back in its proper place. Then I remember exactly why I am there—to run an errand, to retrieve his address book, not lose myself in the past. Yet I cannot move. I sit down on my father's bed.

My father's bed is a huge California King elevated two feet off the ground. The bed of an emperor. My feet do not touch the floor. First, slowly, then faster, I kick my legs against the wooden slats, an unruly child knocking his feet underneath his movie seat. I am that child. I don't want to walk through the streets of Manhattan or turn on the news, or look for his damn address book. I don't want to investigate anything or look through his things anymore. I just sit there narcotized, banging my legs against the slats of his bed as hard as I can.

I want to remember another time when I was happy, and it comes back.

Uncle Leon. Uncle Lee. He treated me like his special pal … his only pal. We spent nearly every Saturday morning together. He stuttered around grownups, but never with me—except for that one time I would rather forget, even now, nearly forty years later. Uncle Lee taught me to drive, bought me chocolate frozen custard, and he taught me "prestidigitation." Each Saturday we drove to Nedicks for hot dogs and orange drinks. I drank too fast and accidentally burped one time, so Uncle Lee burped, too. After that, a burping contest was a regular feature of our Saturday mornings.

We drove through Central Park in his shiny black 1956 Cadillac, and went to Central Park to ride the huge carrousel decorated with monkeys wielding sticks of dynamite, threatening to blow up the merry-go-round, and everything else. Those laughing monkeys almost took even my child's sense of anarchy a bit too far; their crazed expressions both drew me in, and frightened me. But Uncle Lee was there when I got scared, sitting on a park bench nearby, watching. He had his own charmed, black-mane horse called Lucky, and Lucky seemed to smile every time I passed him and stretched up for a brass ring. Uncle Lee tipped his grey homburg towards us.

Afterward, we drove to Gramsie Lerner's on Central Park West, and I played with Gramps. We played Pisha Pasha, and watched *Charlie Chan* and *Bulldog Drummond* movies. Then, after Gramsie made me a snack, I spent the night in Uncle Lee's room on the twin bed right next to his, and the next morning, we watched the sun rise together. I saw him hang his toupee on the phrenology head beside his bed, and remove his truss. We showered together the next morning in the steaming glass stall, which felt like a space capsule, and we sang "The Bear Went Over the Mountain" together as loud as we could. In the steamy shower stall, I felt safe, and completely invisible to the rest of the world. Our screaming voices reverberated like thunder against the glass as the song built to its inevitable, but wonderful conclusion:

Oh, the bear went over the mountain ...
To see what he could see.

On Thanksgiving morning, I got up at 5:00 a.m. to watch the Parks Department men set up wooden horses to control the crowds along Central Park West during the Macy's Day Parade. Watching from Gramsie's second floor window as they set up in the dark was almost more fun than the parade, although nothing beat the time Woody Woodpecker slammed right up against Gramsie's window. Around five-thirty or six, Gramsie made breakfast: a tuna fish sandwich stuffed with O&C Potato Stix on white bread, sliced into quarters with the crusts cut off. I drank my milk out of a shot glass and zoomed around the living room in a special red car with pedals. No rules.

Gramps treated me like a young prince. (He used wonderful, old-fashioned words like, "dast" and "dassent.") "You dassent touch that knife, Henry; it's much too sharp!" Even eating an apple with Gramps was magic. He peeled an apple without ever breaking the skin—not once. I watched the skin of the apple curl like a snake sunning itself, slowly wrapping around into a circle in the ashtray alongside one of his big cigars. When finished, he folded his golden pocketknife with the initials JNL, and put it in his vest pocket. I wanted to peel my own apple, but Gramps said, "You dassent, Henry." So, I listened. But, when Gramsie went out shopping, Gramps relented. He covered my hands with his huge peasant ones, and tried to teach me to peel an apple like he did. The operation had to be kept secret, he said, because Gramsie would be "mad as hell" if she found out. But no matter how hard I concentrated, my peel always broke, usually four or five times on a single apple. Even so, when he put the pieces of my skin in the ashtray alongside his, my failed attempts looked like baby snakes curled up beside their grandfather. Now, looking back, those times with Uncle Lee, Gramps, and Gramsie, they were my safe haven. There, I was loved and spoiled, like all grandchildren should be.

Gramps cheated at cards, too. When I caught him looking at my hand in the beveled edges of the mirrored card table, I started crying. But Gramps told me he only did it so that I would catch him! He did it to teach me an important lesson—that the world is full of shysters and cheats. "You dassent ever gamble," he told me. We didn't use money; we used a special stash of red poker chips Gramps kept in an old cedar box that still smelled like his huge cigars.

After dealing the cards and playing poker, Gramps' fingers hurt, so he lit a candle and dripped molten wax on them. He said it helped his arthritis better than any medicine you could buy from the drugstore. I sat beside him, transfixed, as he dripped hot wax from a long, white candle onto his thick fingers. He never complained or cried the way I would have done when the wax dropped on his fingers. After the medicinal wax coated his fingers, he peeled it off slowly and then let me play with the remains. I rubbed it between my fingers until the wax was soft; and when Gramps wasn't looking, I popped it into my mouth and chewed it like Juicy Fruit gum.

I remember the exact moment I heard about Gramps' death. I was ten. It was on a Saturday night and I was sitting at home with Margaret, our maid, watching *The Invasion of the Body Snatchers*. The phone rang and Margaret screamed. So I raced to the phone ahead of her and answered it. Mrs. Lopez, one of my parents' friends, wished me "Condolences" in her heavy Puerto Rican accent. I hung up and had no idea what she was talking about. To me, "Condolences" sounded like "Congratulations." And strangely, both words reminded me of those big red delicious candy apples coated with hard, red candy I would eat while ice skating at Wollman's Rink in Rockefeller Center. So I thought it must be good news.

That night, my parents came home late, and they told me that Gramps had died of stomach cancer. Cancer! It was the first time I had even thought of death. My mother, although intelligent and with a Master's Degree from Columbia University, told me that her little boy should only think "happy thoughts." I guess that's why she never said a word to me about Gramps' disease. Finally, I knew why I hadn't been allowed to stay over at Gramps and Gramsie's house for weeks! And why Uncle Lee had not come to pick me up that morning like he promised. I cried and thought of my little pieces of apple skin alongside his unbroken, perfect one.

As long as Gramps lived, it hadn't mattered what happened at home. But when Gramps died, he left a void that even Uncle Lee couldn't fill. For one thing, watching movies or playing cards with Uncle Lee wasn't the same. He couldn't stay awake during Humphrey Bogart films, and he wouldn't cheat me at poker, even when I begged him to. The best he could do was watch *Abbott and Costello* with me. And Gramps, he had thick fingers, smoked cigars, and wore double-breasted suits, which to me, made him look almost like Sidney Greenstreet, or George Raft. But Uncle Lee, his hands were pale and ivory white, and unlike my conversations with Gramps, talking to him was like talking to another boy my age. Or even younger.

Uncle Lee had actually been married once, to a Southern belle that Mom said came from a state that began with the letter "A," but it didn't last more than a week. Since then, he'd lived with Gramsie, and worked at MacLaren's, the Men's Wear business that Gramps owned in the Garment District.

As I grew older, I felt sorry for Uncle Lee with his truss, bicarbonate of soda, and ExLax (which I insisted on trying once, and found it didn't taste nearly as good as advertised). I knew, too, that Lee had once been admitted to Harvard Law School, but was forced to drop out in his first year to help with the family business during World War II. He never went back. Mom did tell me, though, that Uncle Lee's grades were even higher than Judge

Brandeis's, and his exam paper was still on display at Harvard, right next to that of the famous judge.

Sometimes when I stayed over at my grandparents', I went to work with Uncle Lee the next morning. I helped cut trousers (Gramsie told me never to use the word "pants" in her house—it was the only thing that could make Gramps angry). I marked pieces of fabric with tailor's chalk. I liked the feel of the soft, greasy, white chalk between my thumb and forefinger; it wasn't at all like the dry, brittle chalk they used in school. That chalk squeaked and left a mess on your hands. This chalk was soft and smooth and shiny, like a baby seal's fur.

For reasons I couldn't understand, my father hated Uncle Lee. Once at breakfast, he spooned up a big mess of scrambled eggs from the bowl and held it above his plate. Then he dumped the eggs down on his plate, and announced that this was what his brother-in-law's brains looked like. More awful still, he then shoveled a big forkful of eggs into his mouth and swallowed them all. After that, Uncle Lee became known at home as Scrambled Eggs.

My father asked if I could remember my younger brother's bris. When I told him I couldn't, he laughingly told me the story of how Uncle Lee was afraid of blood. So, when the Moyle's knife bit into the foreskin of Bobby's penis, he keeled over and collapsed right there in front of everybody. Lee's toupee dislodged and no one wanted to touch it, so the maid had to pick it up—with silver ice tongs—as they carried him to a couch. That story made me tear up—I couldn't bear to think of Uncle Lee on the ground with his toupee off and everyone laughing. I decided it was probably not true, but since it was one of the few times my father laughed, I pretended it was funny, and I laughed, too.

Uncle Lee picked me up at seven o'clock every Saturday morning, but never set foot inside our house until after my father left. He fingered the brim of his hat between his hairless hands, standing by the little table in our hallway, which was twisted into the shape of an enormous fish encrusted with real seashells. One particular Saturday, Uncle Lee announced it was "high time" I learned to drive. Where he grew up in Pennsylvania, all the boys drove tractors by the time they were eight, and girls knew how to drive by the age of ten or so. Girls! So, at age nine, I wasn't really surprised to be sitting on Uncle Lee's lap holding the steering wheel of his big, black 1956 Cadillac, whizzing through the deserted streets of midtown Manhattan.

A thin sheen of rain covered the streets, and I remember being a little scared—I wasn't one of those daredevil kids who embraced danger—but it felt completely natural for me to be behind the wheel of Uncle Lee's Cadillac. I was locked securely between his legs, clutching the bulky, scalloped ridges of the steering wheel, unable to reach the pedals as he helped steer. Then we stopped. He told me to wait outside in the car while he went into a novelty shop on Broadway and Times Square. He came back fifteen minutes later with something hidden behind his back. He had a surprise for me, he said, and unfurled a newspaper which read:

HENRY SCHVEY ELECTED PRESIDENT IN LANDSLIDE!

As he handed the paper to me, a thrill and feeling of absolute confidence and power shot up my spine. I knew I would be elected president someday. It was inevitable. That was how things were supposed to be. That's how I felt around Uncle Lee.

At least until I ruined everything.

We'd driven all the way to Coney Island to ride the roller coaster. The minute we exited the coaster, Lee ran straight to the men's room and threw up. There was a little blue feather tucked in the band of Uncle Lee's homburg, and I remember him rubbing it between his thumb and forefinger, moaning as he ran to the men's room as soon as we were allowed off the coaster. But after his stomach settled, we still went to Nathan's for hotdogs and went to a penny arcade where I played skeeball for hours. Uncle Lee sat watching, like he did at the merry-go-round, tapping his capped, too-perfect teeth with one forefinger while I played. Sometimes he whistled, but more often he emitted a strange sound through his front teeth with no discernible tune.

Then it happened. We visited a magic shop on West 43rd Street on our return to the city. We'd been there together before; the owner knew Uncle Lee and even addressed him deferentially as "Mr. Lerner." Uncle Lee said I could pick out several tricks. I found a whoopee cushion, and a plastic ice cube with a fly inside so it looked like a dead fly was in someone's drink. I also found plastic vomit, which I would use on Margaret on a Saturday night after eating fudge and watching *The Blob*. But Uncle Lee liked different kinds of tricks, tricks that involved "prestidigitation" and "legerdemain," words so odd I was certain he had invented them. While the man behind the counter showed me disappearing ink, Uncle Lee stood at the other side of the store, passing steel rings back and forth, forming a chain. Now the rings were separate, now they were linked again—how had he done it? Uncle Lee liked the magic store, probably more than I did. He never seemed to stutter there, even talking with grownups. As we were about to leave, I asked him for a pen that wrote in disappearing ink. But when he looked at his watch, he said, "Uh-oh, we're late."

"Late for what?" I asked. There was no such thing as late. Uncle Lee had taken me to a doubleheader at Yankee Stadium the previous year and we stayed through both games—even when the second game went into extra innings. I knew he was bored, but I pretended not to notice. I ate eight hot dogs. Eight! The game ended with Yogi Berra hitting a home run, and we celebrated by drinking Yoo Hoos, which had Yogi's smiling picture on the bottle.

"Your p-p-parents might be worried."

Of course, I knew exactly what he meant. My father might have returned from playing tennis, and would wonder where I was. When he found out I was with Scrambled Eggs, there might be a problem. I knew this, but told him I just wanted to look at more tricks. Uncle Lee said there was no time.

"But I really want to see that one, just that one. Pleeease." Uncle Lee hesitated, shrugged his shoulders, and was about to relent just like I knew he would. Then, looking down at his Bulova, said, "We need to leave now."

This made me furious. "What do you care? It's Saturday."

"We're late."

"You're afraid, aren't you?"

"Of what? Of course not."

"Of *you know who*," I spat. "If you're not, why do you always wait outside our front door when you come to pick me up?"

"I don't."

"Yes, you do. You always wait out in the hallway by the fish table and never come in."

"I don't."

"Yes, you do. Uncle Lee, why do you have to be such a fairy?"

As soon as I said it, God, I wish I hadn't.

Uncle Lee grabbed the tricks, but one of the steel rings fell and bounced off the glass counter top, and rolled along the floor. He retrieved it and then grabbed my wrist hard and stomped out of the magic shop, his size thirteen wing-tipped shoes slapping the sidewalk.

When we reached the Cadillac, and even though I knew what the answer was going to be, I asked if I could drive home like he promised. Uncle Lee's mouth opened, but no sound came out. Then he opened my door and said, "Get in." Just like any other grownup. We drove home without a word.

I wanted to die. So, I banged my head, first softly, then harder and harder, against the window, thinking maybe the door would pop open, I'd fall out and get run over. I'd heard all sorts of stories from my grandparents about careless boys who drowned in rowboats in Central Park; people who fell to their deaths through the grating in front of grocery stores; or people who were tossed from moving cars because they had left their doors unlocked. I'd been warned not to step on manhole covers, or on the steaming grills above where the subway churned below. Things like that happened all the time to people in New York. Only now, when I wanted something really terrible to happen to me, it didn't.

2.

After losing myself in dreams for hours in my father's apartment, I decide to walk through the neighborhood of my youth. The air tastes of ashes. Somehow, the streets still smell like the inside of his apartment with its residue of Montecristo cigars, but it feels better to be outside. I circle the apartment building where I grew up at 86th and Madison, but can't make myself go in. So I turn around and walk south along Madison Avenue. The first thing I see is the old Croydon Hotel, which is no longer called the Croydon. But this is where I used to buy myself tuna fish sandwiches and sour kosher dills, and where I bought a half-pound of head cheese for Gramps just days before he died. Most important, this is where I once punted a football so high it actually bent back the first letter O in the brass Croydon sign and remained that way for years, a testament to my unrecognized athletic prowess. That sign is gone now, leaving no trace of my achievement; but it makes me happy to see it anyway.

Gone too is the Madison Avenue Deli opposite our apartment building on the corner of 86th. I went there after tennis with my father, Dr. Friedman, and his son, Alex. I ordered stuffed derma with thick brown gravy and Cel-Ray soda, just to be like my father. I couldn't believe they made soda that tasted like celery, or why anyone would want to drink it; but since he liked it, I wanted to try it. The soda tasted awful, but I liked the taste and grainy texture of the stuffed derma with its thick brown gravy, until Alex came over to me and whispered, "Don't eat that—derma is skin! Intestines! You're eating guts, half-wit!"

My father ate thick slices of tongue dotted with tiny papillae, or chicken schmaltz with seeded kosher rye bread and unsalted butter. Once I watched him smear bright yellow chicken fat over pale yellow butter at Grandma's; I must have looked horrified, because Grandma said it was a special treat, and asked if I wanted some. My reply, thick with a thirteen-year-old's sarcasm, "I'd rather have a plutonium sandwich on rye." Nobody laughed.

I wander down Madison Avenue, and locate the buildings where my school friends, Pete and Ephraim, lived. Pete was a big, sturdy kid who swam breaststroke on the varsity swim team, but hurt his knee swimming and was diagnosed with Osgood-Schlatters disease. Pete's parents were psychiatrists, and suddenly, I again hear my mother screaming at Pete's mom when she discovered that Mrs. Amsterdam had taken us to see *Psycho* for Pete's thirteenth birthday. The year was 1960. I was not yet twelve; a year younger than the rest of the guys. My mother cried when she found out. She yelled on the phone for half an hour that Mrs. Amsterdam had ruined my life. There was one scene, where Norman Bates dresses up like an old woman, that did give me nightmares, but I never told my mother about it. Oddly, the thing that frightened me most was that the killer's name—Norman—was the same as my father's. Of course, there was nothing Mrs. Amsterdam could have done about that.

Two blocks further down on Madison at 83rd Street is where Ephraim lived. I spent even more time there than I did at Pete's. Ephraim's parents spoke with heavy Austrian-Jewish accents, and had escaped Hitler's Germany just before it became impossible for Jews to get out. I recall that his parents looked and smelled different from mine. I don't think they bathed as often, and their house had a different feel. They talked about art and classical music all the time, and never allowed television during mealtimes. I felt sorry for Ephraim having to live like that, but at least he was able to have friends over to his house, whereas I never could. He had rigged a kind of basketball hoop out of a wire hanger in his bedroom so you could actually play basketball there, even though the ceilings were low and you had to use a tennis ball or a rolled up pair of socks. Our games always included tackling and fighting, and usually ended up with someone on the floor, crying. But we kept on doing it, and loved it.

Once, I ate dinner over at Ephraim's, and they had boiled beef with red cabbage, which stank up the entire hallway. The whole time we ate, his parents kept muttering something in a disgusting, guttural language, saying "shit" this and "shit" that, back and forth to one another. I figured they were

16

cursing at one another like my parents always did at dinnertime. It was only later that I learned from Ephraim that his mother had attended a retrospective of the sculptor Jacques Lipchitz at the Guggenheim a few blocks away, and that they were having a discussion about art in Yiddish, not hurling insults at one another like my parents did.

Even in an apartment that stank of boiled beef and cabbage, Ephraim had his friends over to visit. I never could. Dirty laundry—mostly silk stockings, girdles, brassieres—were in almost every room, along with toys and books. When my father saw these traces of "Lerner filth," he flew into a rage. Often he emitted an actual growl, then a terrible smile. Sometimes the police were called in to intervene, although no one was arrested, and nothing ever changed as a result. Two or three friendly officers in uniform would come inside, and the shouting or beatings would stop, but never for very long. The condition of our apartment was usually the reason for these altercations, although I would not have invited anybody over even if the apartment had miraculously become spotless. At any moment, it might happen. He'd whip out his belt and chase me around our dining room table. Usually this was because he caught me in some lie or other. I lied about everything: Where were my rubbers? Why was I late? Why did I flunk the Math test? Why were my shoes untied? Why did I forget to walk Blackie?

My lies would be exposed and the chase would begin—terrifying, but oddly exhilarating. I ran in circles around a dining room table large enough to seat ten, barely eluding the gold buckle on his belt until I could escape! I became an expert at beating my father, racing just ahead of the tongue of his belt as he chased me like a panting dog. Dashing down the hall, I slammed the door and twisted the bathroom lock in a single, precisely timed flick. Then I sat on the tiled floor in the tub, my heart pumping a mile-a-minute as the combination of danger, flight, and (usually) narrow escape flooded through me. Safe in my porcelain cave with the shower curtain drawn around me, I sometimes sat for hours, alert to any possible sound outside. Then suddenly it was over. Tired out from the chase, he lay on his bed in the next room, and I'd hear the flick and click of his Dunhill lighter and smell his Kent. The signal for all clear.

But these visits back to my friends' apartment buildings were simply a way of avoiding the inevitable—going back to our old apartment at 25 East 86th.

Slowly, I approach the squat, white 1920s building with the familiar black iron bars on the second floor windows. The bars are decorative, but their graceful arabesques suggest the possibilities of keeping strangers out, people locked within. I approach the doorman, and ask him if I can visit my old apartment, knowing full well he won't let me inside. I make up an outrageous lie about researching a book about Art Nouveau architecture in New York. I'm pretty sure the doorman realizes I'm not telling the truth, but politely he says he is not permitted to let strangers in. That's the job of the doorman, he says with a smile. I understand, grateful to be denied access. But before I happily scurry away, having at least tried to revisit my past, he invites me to enter the lobby if I wish. Which I do. And which is more than enough.

Entering the dimly lit parlor on the way down along the cavernous corridor, past the first bank of elevators and countless sconces, each emitting their peculiar, weird orange glow, I am home again. I am fourteen, and my parents are now separated. But there I am, standing between the two adults screaming at one another in the middle of the lobby on a beautiful crisp spring morning. My father has come to pick me up. His silver Lincoln Town Car is double-parked right outside with the motor running.

Mom shrieks at me, "If you take one step outside—to him and his red-headed shiksa whore—I swear to God you'll find me lying here dead when you come home!"

I believe this threat and spin around to face her.

Drivers outside honk. "Move your goddamn car, you sonofabitch!"

My father is completely indifferent to the chaos and yelling outside, which makes me tremble. He turns calmly to my mother, and says, "Get in the car, Henry." Then to her, "I'll see you dead, you and your entire family of Lerner scum."

"You bastard! You're not paying any alimony, so what do you expect? I have custody of him!" Standing and refereeing this blood sport is George, the pliant, good-natured doorman, who, I think, must be a distant ancestor of the current doorman. George wears a starched uniform with a stiff hat perched on his head like a pale blue wedding cake with white frosting. He bites helplessly on a silver whistle as my parents hurl invectives back and forth. All I see is a funhouse mirror of disconnected objects and sounds: grotesquely distorted mouths, horns honking, a black moustache suspended in air above me, blonde hair puffed up in a cotton candy bouffant, the sound of an ambulance, strange echoing laughter.

At this point, two different memories appear. Both are true.

One has me racing out of the lobby and up the back stairway. Since we are on the second floor, I never use the elevator. At the bottom of this back stairway is a small, dark area used by the doormen for smoking, and inhabited only by a collection of sad, broken umbrellas huddled together in an empty Crisco can. The umbrellas, stacked together, remind me of a klatch of broken-down senior citizens. I run upstairs into my room, not forgetting to chase my brother out, and punch him in the biceps just for good measure; he runs away screaming. I slam the door to our room and lie face down on my bed, and cry. A few minutes later, my mother softly enters the room. She hands me a five dollar bill for my good deed in refusing to go with my father; I tear the money into bits, throw the pieces at her, and slam the door after her.

The second memory has me climbing into my father's Lincoln, and being whisked away in tears to my Grandma Schvey's house. My father circles, for what seems like hours, looking for a parking place near The Eldorado at 300 Central Park West. When he finally finds one, it is too small. So, he slams the back end of the massive Lincoln against the car behind us, then accelerates and smashes into the car in front of him, and wedges us into the space. We are parked.

As we walk into the ornately mirrored Art Deco lobby of The Eldorado, I look for myself in one of the long Deco mirrors; however, I am distracted by my father's uncharacteristically pleasing smile at Stanley, the red-faced elevator man he has known since he was a boy growing up in this same building. Stanley, whose bald head is ringed in gray, is perpetually sour and apoplectic. This makes him look exactly like Grumpy in the Disney movie of *Snow White and the Seven Dwarfs*. My father presses the slightly tarnished enamel doorbell, and upon Grandma opening the door, he hands her his laundry. Without a word, he retires into Grandpa's dark bedroom and closes the door. I wonder, why did they close themselves off in his room? What are the two men whispering about? But I don't wonder long.

My grandmother takes one look at me and says, "You're so thin! Here, take my heart, my liver, anything you want! Just eat something!"

As I walk behind her into the kitchen, she picks up her coffee in a tall

19

glass, adds a drop of Sealtest, and gives it a quick stir with an ice teaspoon. I watch the dark brown liquid grow lighter and lighter as she stirs. I don't like coffee, but I want a taste. But I don't ask. Cold water is running over an uncooked chicken in the sink. The chicken is kosher and Grandma is making sure she drains all the blood out.

Then, out of the blue, she says, "Divorce is wrong. Wrong."

"I know, Grandma."

"So do something! They're your parents! No one else can do it for you."

Next, I find myself walking back to the car with Dad. I'm holding a sack of kreplach in waxed paper with a rubber band around it. We stroll silently back to his car where he is required to smash into the cars again to extricate his. We return to his apartment on Sutton Place. After he has his J&B and soda, and I have a soda, and Fritos and French Onion dip, we join his younger brother, Malcolm, at one of the French bistros along 2nd Avenue. Malcolm is an ear, nose, and throat specialist, who chain-smokes unfiltered Pall Malls all during dinner. He has a habit of wrinkling his nose and sniffing before he speaks, and drinks glass after glass of Coca Cola in chipped ice. He complains about his wife, who he claims drinks too much and drives "with a heavy foot," like a "real shiksa." My father laughs and proceeds to flirt with the pretty young waitress who tells us she is an actress and has just moved to New York. My father asks for her phone number and offers to help her get settled. She writes it down. Malcolm smiles and orders another Coke.

My father's father, Grandpa Schvey, as opposed to Gramps, was an austere, self-made man, who grew up in Riga (now Latvia), and came to the United States with nothing. He began dressing windows at Macy's, and, despite frail health, managed to retire as a millionaire at the age of fifty. He brought his younger brother, Henry, over to the New World and paid for him to go to medical school. However, Henry enlisted in the army and died of typhoid fever treating soldiers during World War I. There was another brother who came over and became a rabbi in Philadelphia, but I never heard a word about him until long after Grandpa Schvey's death.

Like some Jews of his era, Grandpa Schvey hated anything that smacked of being too Jewish. The idea of being accepted at a country club or hotel that disallowed Jews delighted him. It was a source of special pride to him that his eldest son was such a huge success on Wall Street, in an industry where Jews had been fiercely discriminated against a mere half century earlier. Grandpa lived long enough to see his eldest son become Vice President and Managing Director of the Unit Investment Trust Division at Merrill Lynch. My father ultimately was more than a successful financier. During the decades of the 1970s and 1980s, he acquired true celebrity status, wielding enormous power as chairman of the most financially successful division of the most important brokerage firm in the world. And he did so with a unique combination of maverick individualism, generosity towards subordinates, and authoritarianism.

Grandpa spoke with a heavy Russian-Jewish accent, but there was nothing Old World about him. Quiet and precise, he dressed like a banker and bore himself modestly. Outside his El Dorado apartment building on Central Park West, I never once saw him without tie and jacket. Despite the accent, his words were always precise, grammatically correct, and he spoke in complete sentences. His office in the Empire State Building, too, was more than just an office; it was a statement of having made it as a successful businessman.

But in all his great success, he had a cruel streak and a mordant wit, which he wielded against my grandmother like a scalpel. Grandma Birdie was a native New Yorker, and in her youth, a great beauty. I still have a signed photograph of her around the time of her high school graduation, wearing only a fur coat and smiling coquettishly at the viewer. Why I wondered, was this glamorous picture taken and at whose behest?

The youngest of five daughters, Grandma was one of only two born in America. And she was smart. She not only graduated from high school, but was admitted to study law at N.Y.U. Instead, she left school to marry my grandfather. She loved him deeply even though Grandpa mocked her at every turn. He treated her as though she were the Greenhorn, not he, and imitated her taste ("Ah, she's heard about that from people who know ..."), and love for strange *tchotchkes* at the thrift store, which were the only things she could afford with the tiny weekly allowance he provided. He hissed the words, "Bitch ... bitch ... bitch" under his breath incessantly as she ladled out his chicken soup and Ritz crackers. She never showed that it bothered her.

Grandpa's bedroom was dark and austere. He ceded the rest of the house to Grandma. His coarse green bedspread literally hurt your fingers to the touch. His room was monastic and disciplined. A set of cast-iron bookends embossed with a likeness of Napoleon sat atop a single, glass bookcase. There was a biography of Lincoln, along with both the regular and large print editions of *The Reader's Digest* and *Esquire*. On Sundays he watched *Meet the Press*, and that program's dour, saturnine host, Lawrence Spivak, seemed a mirror image of Grandpa.

I still often wonder how much of my father's behavior was based on what he saw at home.

The day after my tenth birthday, I went to see Grandma Schvey. I knew she would have something to give me for my birthday—Grandma always gave disappointing presents like socks or handkerchiefs—so I wasn't expecting anything much. But that wasn't why I went to see her.

As soon as I arrived, she kissed me, and, before I could say anything about why I had come, she pressed a ten-dollar bill into my hands and disappeared down the long hallway to her bedroom. Ten dollars! My reasons for visiting fled from my mind as I stared at the bill, studying Alexander Hamilton's face. I followed Grandma to her room to tell her thank you. As I entered, I caught my reflection in the mirror and thought of Mickey Mantle and all his terrible injuries, and began to imitate Mantle's left-handed batting stance. I could do that better than all my friends, just like his home run trot.

"It's your tenth birthday," Grandma said. "That's a big one, isn't it?"

"Yeah," I said.

"Tell me all about it," she said.

"I don't want to right now, Grandma." I looked down at the ground, and tried to control a sudden impulse to cry. I wanted to tell her the real reason for my visit, but now that she asked me, I couldn't speak.

"Did you do anything special yesterday?"

"Mom took me bowling," I answered sullenly.

"And then what?"

"Nothing." I looked up at her. But before I said another word, she vanished.

"Where are you, Grandma?" I looked around, but didn't see her.

"I know it's here somewhere," I heard her mumble, clearly to herself. "Just a minute."

"But where are you!" Anxiety, out of proportion to the danger of the moment, bloomed in my chest.

"Keep your pants on, young man, I'm in here. In my closet." Then I heard her say, "Is he crying? Goodness, silly boy. I'll be right out after I've found what I'm looking for."

The door to her closet was closed, so I stood there stranded, with nothing to do but wait. I hated that. I knew nothing would happen, but I grew frightened nonetheless. What if she died in there? She was old, after all. What would I do? Unlike Gramsie Lerner's house, which smelled like chicken soup, roast turkey, and kasha, Grandma's house, and particularly her closet, smelled of mothballs and cedar. The closet was where she kept my father's old things: books like *Bomba the Jungle Boy*, *Tarzan*, and *Hans Brinker and the Silver Skates*. There were letters in a funny script Grandma said was the Russian language; there was an old, dented lemon wafers cookie tin which contained an assortment of things including jacks, marbles, an old passport, ration cards, a purse full of Indian Head pennies and buffalo nickels, a thank-you note from her nephew, Stanley (exactly my age, only smarter), whom I had never met, and a fountain pen with a golden tip that didn't work. I had never been inside the closet without Grandma, but I knew everything in there, because whenever I visited, Grandma came out with some bizarre curiosity or treasure. Once she brought out my father's elementary school class picture, which had a really tall kid in it who was completely bald! His name was Andrew, and he had contracted scarlet fever and lost all his hair. He sat there in the picture of sixth graders looking like a sad old grandpa among a group of smiling children. It always made me shiver with excitement and curiosity to see Andrew. Grandma thought I wanted to see it because my father, with his thick head of wavy hair was in the first row, and smiling, but it was really Andrew, the bald kid who never smiled, who I wanted to see.

"It has to be here somewhere, so be patient, young man."

"I will, Grandma." While I waited, I metamorphosed from Mantle into Bob Cousy in his black, high-topped sneakers, dribbling once behind my back before banking a lay-up off the top of the hall closet. Somehow the ball rolled off the rim and came back out, but fortunately, Bill Russell was waiting for the rebound. He grabbed Cousy's miss and stuffed it in over Wilt the Stilt for a basket.

Grandma rustled through what sounded like a thick forest of dresses. Her voice sounded like it was coming from a million miles away.

"It's in this box … no, it isn't. Wait! I've got it!"

She emerged with something in her hand: an old framed photograph of a boy feeding a squirrel on a wooden perch. The boy had dark hair, a round face, and a friendly smile. I had seen this photo twice before. Grandma must have forgotten.

"Ups-a-daisy," she said, pulling me onto her lap.

"I'm too old for that, Grandma."

"Suit yourself, smarty-pants. Do you know what this is?" Of course, I knew what I was supposed to say, but I didn't want to, so I quickly grabbed an imaginary bat.

"An old picture."

"Of course it's an old picture, but what is it a picture of?"

"A boy and a squirrel."

"Correct, Mr. Einstein. But who's the boy?"

"I don't know."

"It's your father. It's your father when he was just your age."

As if I cared. I creamed a Pedro Gomez fastball out beyond the Yankee Stadium Monuments in deep center field, 456 feet away. Jimmy Piersall went way back, but Mel Allen, the Yankee announcer, shouted, "That ball is going, going … it is *gone!*" The crowd went absolutely nuts. I watched the flight of the ball, and, realizing it was a home run, began my slow trot around Grandma's room, almost knocking over a lamp.

"Stop that!" she snapped. "The child can't stand still. And he's still biting his nails—disgusting!" She sounded exhausted. As I trotted past third base, she reached out a hand and grabbed my arm, arresting my stride. "Now look at me. When your father was a little boy, just your age, he found a baby squirrel under a tree in Central Park—pay attention; have I told you this before? We knew it wouldn't live, your grandfather and me. But your father, he brought that squirrel home and begged us to let him keep it. Now your grandfather was very strict in those days (he still is, in some ways), and he said the squirrel was an unsanitary thing, a rodent. But your father begged and cried and pleaded, until in the end, he was allowed to keep it for a few weeks. And you know what?" Her voice dropped: fierce, intense. "Your father nursed that helpless squirrel back to health. He fed it milk every day with a little eyedropper. See his expression there in the picture, smiling?" I nodded. "Good. That's your father. And one month to the day after he found it, that squirrel was healthy enough to take back to Central Park and be released. Now, what about that?"

"That's a good story," I said. She let my arm go, and I lashed a single to left. I was now batting right handed, where Mickey had less power, but hit for a higher average.

"It's not a story. It's the truth, the truth about your father. So don't ever say anything bad about him, because he isn't bad."

"But he hits me." I didn't look at her as I said this, but I knew exactly how she looked, and that she'd shaken her head once, firmly.

"I won't hear that. If he does things that seem bad, it's because she doesn't make him feel like a man. You're too young to understand such things. He comes home to that filthy apartment, awful food. Don't think I don't know what it's like up there; I do. No man would put up with that. A man needs to have a warm meal on the table when he comes home from a hard day at the office. Your father works hard, you know that. Did you hear me? I said, do you know that?"

"I know that."

"Good. I know you do. You're a good boy. But a child should never say anything bad about his father. Remember the Ten Commandments? Honor thy—"

"I know the Commandments by heart. I memorized them on Saturday at Rodeph Sholem." There was something thick and heavy in my throat, but I forced myself to prattle on around it.

"Really?"

"Yes. They made us learn five of them, but then Mr. Brilliant got sick and had a nervous breakdown, so we got a new teacher who forgot to make us learn the rest. But I memorized all ten anyway."

"Well, that's good. Now give me a kiss."

Reluctantly, I kissed Grandma, but as I pulled away, the pressure in my chest broke, and I started crying.

"But he is bad. He is! I hate him!"

For a second she hesitated. Then she said, "Don't you say that! Don't you ever say that! What did I just tell you?"

"A stupid story about a stupid squirrel."

"No! Not about a squirrel, about your father. How he rescued that squirrel and fed it milk every day with an eyedropper. Didn't you hear a thing I said, or were you too busy swinging that stupid imaginary blue baseball bat?"

"How do you know it's blue, Grandma?" I tried to get her to stop talking about my father.

"Uh, I don't know. You must have told me, or something. Anyway, don't change the subject. I asked if you heard what I was saying."

"I heard."

"Well, if you *really* heard, you wouldn't say things like you hated your father, would you? Bad men don't rescue defenseless little squirrels, do they? Well, do they?"

"I guess not."

"You guess not?"

"They don't."

"So, it's all settled now, isn't it? Well, isn't it?"

When she wasn't looking, I gouged a thin piece of wood out of the cedar closet door and jammed the splinter into my thumb.

3.

It is late afternoon before I turn and go back to his apartment. Whenever I touch something that belongs to my father, however insignificant, I make certain to return it to its proper place. I feel like a detective. I imagine I've come to "case the joint," solve a crime. Then it occurs to me—that's not who I am at all. I'm not Hercule Poirot; I'm the thief. At least that would explain why I'm sweating, snooping, trying things on, tracing my finger along the black lacquer finish of his thick Mont Blanc fountain pen, compulsively unscrewing and screwing on the cap, resting a sterling silver ashtray in my palm, feeling its impressive heft. What is it I am looking for? It's like I'm trying to crack a code of some kind, trying to answer a question. It feels too late in the day for that. At my age, you're supposed to know these things.

Despite my knowledge that I'm alone, I keep looking up, expecting him to burst in at any moment and tell me to put his goddamn things down. I feel I should wipe my fingerprints off everything I've touched. I feel that this is absolutely forbidden, a violation of some unwritten, unspoken law. I remember suddenly what it was I came to find: an address book. Then I see something interesting, a single 8x10 photograph, and I am again distracted from my quest.

In the picture, my parents, dressed in their wedding finery, are walking down the aisle on their way out of the ceremony. Young and innocent, they are perfectly framed by candles, decorative candelabra, and gorgeous bouquets. My mother's hand rests gently on top of my father's, but his hand seems barely to tolerate hers. His dark brown eyes (so different from my own blue ones) bore straight ahead at the photographer, looking right through him. My father is remarkably young and handsome with surprisingly delicate features, graceful hands, and arched eyebrows. But there is something disturbing, possibly cruel, in the eyes, the tight, unsmiling mouth, and the sleek, black hair combed straight back. My mother, on the other hand, is rapturous. Her face is round; she has not yet had her nose fixed, or begun to bleach her dark hair platinum blonde. The shape of her face still looks just a bit like Gramps' and Uncle Lee's; it won't when those cosmetic alterations are made. Radiant in her white satin wedding dress with its enormous train, and elaborate, turned-back veil, my mother carries a huge wedding bouquet. She is not looking at my father. She is smiling vacantly at someone in a pew just off the edge of the photo to her left. This couple looks lovely, but I can't help thinking that despite appearances, they have already begun moving—literally, as well as figuratively—past one another. Or rather, it is clear that my father's forward motion does not include his young bride.

Although she might seem flighty, my mother is highly educated; she began her undergraduate degree at Cornell, and finished at the University of Pittsburgh. She completed her M.A.T. at Columbia University's Teacher's College while pregnant with me. There she studied with some of Columbia's great luminaries, in particular Lionel Trilling and Joseph Wood Krutch, with whom she studied Shakespeare and the classics. Shakespeare was quoted regularly in our house, and references to his work were sprinkled throughout her conversation, particularly in later years as she became filled with remorse for the blows that she had been given by life.

Two nights before my tenth birthday, a noise wakes me from a sound sleep. I hear the front door being unlocked, and a few moments afterwards I hear screams and a thump. Moments after that, a tiny sliver of light slithers across my face like a worm. The light tickles and I almost sneeze, but manage to keep my eyes closed and pretend to sleep—I instinctively know this is not a good time to be awake. I am pretty used to my parents' fighting, and usually just block things out. I have my own peculiar ritual of getting myself to sleep when I am frightened: I recite every member of the New York Yankees' twenty-five-man opening day roster, by number and position. If that doesn't work, I remind myself of the players' heights and weights, which I have memorized from the back of their baseball cards:

Mickey Charles Mantle, No. 7, Center Field; Born October 20, 1931, Spavinaw, Oklahoma—5'11"—198 lbs.

Lawrence Peter ("Yogi") Berra, No. 8, Catcher: Born May 12, 1925, St. Louis, Missouri—5'8"—194 lbs.

William Joseph ("Moose") Skowron, Jr., No. 14, First Base: Born December 18, 1930, Chicago, Illinois—5'11"—200 lbs.

And so on.

The players' numbers bore a special significance, just as their individual batting stances did. Number 8 was more than a numeral draped across Yogi's stooped, broad back, making him look like Quasimodo carrying his beloved Esmeralda across the rooftops of Paris in *The Hunchback of Notre Dame*. No, those uniform numbers were the simple bedrocks of existence for me. They represented the curtain that I pulled down to block out the strange, terrifying reality around me.

If my mumbled recitation of the Yankees failed, I listened to "Cousin" Bruce Morrow on the transistor radio hidden under my pillow. These were the tricks I used to dampen the animal sounds and screams that, at odd intervals, invaded my sleep from my parents' bedroom down the long, thin hallway. But on this night nothing worked; I was excited about my birthday, and worried about the screams. So when my other tricks failed, I threw the covers off. I heard something like sobbing down the hall, and got up and followed the sobs like the breadcrumbs in "Hansel and Gretel." My brother, Bobby, slept through everything; he cradled a toy Cadillac in his arms like a baby. As I stole down the hallway, I saw my father in his familiar green bathrobe with a towel draped over one of his shoulders like a prizefighter, holding our silver ice bucket in his arms. I recognized the ice bucket right away, since it was something I was warned not to play with. It was a silver wedding gift to my parents from Tiffany's. It was also just the right size to catch a pair of balled-up white sweat socks lobbed from the dining room. I taught Bobby how to lob socks with just the right amount of arc, like I did, or to bank them off the wall. But his efforts were feeble, even allowing for his age. He was a spazz. I knew it was inevitable that he would get picked for right field if I didn't straighten him out fast. My theory was that boys who couldn't throw properly were destined to fail. My ambition was to get to the point where we could play catch without him utterly humiliating himself. It never happened. He was oblivious to his glaring inadequacy; he apparently thought baseball was just a game. I knew better—it was life itself.

Beside my father, there was another man who was short and stocky with black, shiny shoes and squeaky soles. He was wearing a policeman's uniform. Both men disappeared into my parents' bedroom, and then I heard more whimpering. It sounded like a child, or a dog, but I knew it wasn't either one. Then it stopped and sounded exactly like a baby who's been crying so long he can't catch his breath.

The sight of the uniform terrified me, and I wanted to yell, "What's going on around here?" But I couldn't make a sound. So I crept back to my bedroom. My brother was still asleep, still caressing the Cadillac, but it was a long time before my ears stopped straining to hear each pitiful noise from beyond my parents' door.

The next morning was my birthday, and I woke up to the smell of Joy, Mom's perfume. I still smell it today, though now, it makes me sick. I loved it then, and loved how that morning she entered the room brushing right by Bobby's bed, carrying a birthday tray just for me. She balanced the tray carefully, resting it on his bed, before hugging and kissing me. Usually, I pretended to ignore such shows of affection; not today. The tray had scrambled eggs, hot buttered toast, and a cup of cocoa with seven miniature marshmallows floating on top. My mother winked at me as if to say, "Get it?" and I started laughing. Seven was Mickey Mantle's number, of course, and she had arranged the marshmallows in the shape of a seven, just for me. The number was still recognizable despite her walk from the kitchen to my room.

"Happy Birthday, sweetheart! Time to get ready. Doc has the alley all reserved for you." Doc's was the name of the bowling alley.

"Why does Henry get all those marshmallows, and why do they look like that?" Neither of us paid any attention to his question. How could anyone not know what the number seven signified in New York in the 1950s?

"Thanks, Mom," I said. "Hey, where is he?"

"Tennis." That one word said it all.

"Oh."

I was so happy about the seven marshmallows and the bowling that I barely noticed a blue swelling above her eye, or that she was wearing the

30

same dress she had on the night before. Or maybe I noticed it and ignored it. That's possible. After all, it was my birthday, and little else matters when you're ten.

At Doc's, there was a pinsetter named Jimmy, who Doc said averaged 185 per game, and almost made it as a professional bowler. Now he stood behind the pins as a pinspotter, perched up on a tiny shelf with only his shoes visible, waiting for the explosion of balls and the pins. Then he would slide down from his perch and set the pins up again after each ball. Jimmy could bowl as many free games as he wanted after hours. He only made an appearance if something broke or if a ball got stuck. Otherwise, he was invisible; no one knew he was even there. It seemed like a great way to earn a living.

I returned home, anxious to tell my father about my accomplishments. The nightmare of waking up in the middle of the night and seeing a policeman inside our house was just that—a nightmare that had vanished. I had bowled a 168, and wanted to report it to Dad. Mom saw the whole thing, but as a girl she was unable to ascertain the importance of the event. She smiled when I threw a strike, but she'd also smile if I threw a gutter ball. She didn't even know you got two extra balls after you got a strike in the tenth, or that three strikes in a row was called a "turkey;" Dad knew these things.

He woke up with a sleep-creased face. He always looked that way after his nap. I had the feeling that he didn't want me to actually see him asleep, as though it made him seem weak. He wiped his mouth and yawned, filled a tall glass full of ice, added J&B, and filled the rest of the glass with Canada Dry Club Soda, stirring it with a red swizzle stick, the exact color of my new water pistol. Then he rubbed his eyes with his knuckles, which made him look like a sleepy child, and which was almost comical. He walked over to the TV and snapped it off without a word. Bobby was watching *Mickey Mouse Club*, and when it was suddenly turned off, he whimpered, "That's no fair!" Dad simply raised his hand above his head, and the threat was enough to send him scurrying.

Mom came in from the kitchen, smiling. She hadn't seen my father raise his hand to Bobby.

"Guess what we're having for dinner, Mister Birthday Boy?"

"TV dinner?" I said. I liked TV dinners much better than my mother's cooking, and the tiny individualized compartments with dried mashed potatoes, shriveled peas, and Apple Brown Betty provided a sense of security and order, which our dinners never did. Mom shook her head.

"Hamburgers?"

"Of course not, it's my First Born's special day; my Number One son; my Hen-yee!"

"Then I don't know." I was disappointed; I wanted that TV dinner. But I couldn't let on.

"Keep guessing!"

"I don't know, Mom."

She then produced a huge stainless steel platter of steak from behind her back. The steaks were thick and bloody, and marbled with fat, and I felt immediately nauseous. But I smiled anyway.

"Voila! Porterhouse steak with baked potatoes and sour cream. Corn on the cob! How's that sound? Good?"

"Great, Mom!" I lied.

She left and went back to the kitchen, humming "You Could Be Swinging on a Star," leaving my father and me sitting there in front of the blank TV screen. It was August, and our Christmas game with the Good Guys and Bad Guys was so far in the future it might as well have been a hundred years away.

We sat there in silence. Finally, I said, "The Yankees won today, Dad."

"Umm."

"Yeah, Mantle hit one." Silence. Then I said what I longed to say. "Guess what, Dad? I bowled a 168 in my last game at Doc's."

"Oh."

Another long pause followed. My bowling exploits weren't getting me anywhere, either.

"How was tennis?"

"Umm."

"You played with Sy?"

"Yup."

"Did you win?"

"Huh?"

"I said, did you win?"

"I don't know."

"You don't know if you won or not?" I couldn't imagine playing any sport or game without keeping score or knowing who won, and by exactly how much.

"No."

"Oh."

"Can I turn on the TV?"

"I just turned it off."

"Oh."

From the kitchen Mom's song wafted in along with the aroma of broiling meat. "A pig is an animal, with dirt on his face..." She had a nice singing voice in those days, but here she was singing about dirty pigs with terrible manners. Loud enough so that my father could hear. As she cooked, she went on breathlessly humming bits from "You Could be Swinging on a Star."

"What the hell is that she's singing?"

"Just some song by Bing Crosby."

"Oh."

She must have noticed how quiet it was, because she said from the kitchen, "Let him turn on the television, Norman. It's his birthday." Dad said nothing, but he took a swallow of scotch and soda, and grunted something that I figured out meant it was okay to watch. *The Honeymooners* was on, and Mom set the table. Setting the table meant she took a bunch of silverware and flung it on the table in a pile. For some reason, that was how she always set the table, throwing the silver down like that; she never realized how this made my father's blood boil. I noticed his moustache twitch, as it always did when he was simmering and about to explode, but Mom never saw it. Neither could she hear another telltale sign; a faint whirr like a hum which he emitted when he was about to storm. Mom cheerfully called Bobby in. He said, "Hey—I thought we couldn't watch TV!"

"It's my Hen-yee's birthday today," Mom sang. She brought out individual shrimp cocktails in glistening crystal sherbet cups. These cups were wedding gifts and were almost never used.

"Where's the cocktail sauce?" Dad asked.

"There's lemon and there's ketchup," she said. "You want ketchup?"

"What for?"

"For the shrimp cocktail, of course. You just said—"

"I like ketchup!" chirped Bobby. No one listened or cared.

"Don't bother," Dad said. He took a large shrimp, pulled off the tail and devoured the meat. Then he sucked the tail to make sure nothing was left. It made a slurping sound.

"I'm sorry, but I've been out all day with my Birthday Boy; that's why there's no cocktail sauce, Norman."

"What else is there?"

"Porterhouse steaks comin' right up!" she sang in a falsetto, clearing the shrimp cocktails and exiting towards the kitchen as she sang about moonbeams in jars and swingin' on stars.

"Shaddup, Rita!"

She either ignored, or didn't hear this, and returned with four huge steaks, gurgling in their own blood with blobs of curdled brown fat .

"Look at this! Did you ever see meat like this? Special for Hen-yee!" Mom always talked baby talk when she was in high spirits. I usually hated it, but today, for some reason, it didn't bother me.

"How do you expect me to cut this, Rita?" My father was sorting through a dense thicket of knives and forks looking for a carving knife. To illustrate, he actually bit into one of the steaks, holding up one end in the air with a fork. Always immaculately dressed and supremely careful about his appearance in public, my father deliberately allowed steak juice to trickle down his chin and onto his plate.

"I'll find us some sharper knives."

"Don't worry, we can eat it with our teeth," he said, winking at Bobby.

"Yeah, we'll eat it with our teeth—right, Dad?" Bobby squealed with high-pitched laughter.

"Stop imitating your father, Robert!" Mom said, as he reached for one of the steaks with pudgy fingers.

"Look what you've done, Norman!" she said, and scurried over to the breakfront, rummaging around for a carving knife. "See—the boy's imitating you."

"What I've done?" my father said innocently, grabbing one of the knives, and trying to slice the meat. "These won't cut, either!"

"Sorry."

"Sorry, my ass."

Mom didn't respond, but left and promptly returned with a set of gleaming, sterling silver steak knives, still in their Tiffany blue box.

"Do you know how hard I worked on this, Norman? All you've done is play tennis, sleep, drink Scotch, and criticize. How, after the day I've had, can you criticize me? Cocktail sauce? I took him bowling all day long—five games! What did you do? Play tennis? Where's a boy's father on his son's birthday?"

On the black and white television in the room behind us, Ralph Kramden balled his fist and held it up in the air dangerously close to his wife's face. "To the moon, Alice, to the moon!"

"Go ahead and try!" Alice said, defiantly.

"Bang zoom!"

"You don't like it?" Dad challenged.

"No, Norman, I don't like it. Not one bit." Mom put her hands on her hips.

"Fine, I'll eat out with Sy." Dad rose from the table, scraping the parquet floor.

"I mean it, Alice!"

"What do you mean, you're eating with Sy? It's Henry's birthday! You're certainly not eating out with Sy!"

"Go ahead, Ralph! I'd like to see you try!" Alice said again.

"One of these days, Alice, one of these days—*Pow*, right in the kisser!" The TV audience laughed.

I turned my neck to see the TV screen, but when I turned back, Mom was rubbing her cheek, even though Alice Kramden was unscathed.

"Bastard! You filthy bastard," she growled, eyes bright. My father was already halfway down the hall, wallet and keys in hand. "Children, do you realize your father is a filthy bastard? Well, now you know, and you can imitate him some more. How dare you, Norman!" she shouted after him. "And on his birthday, too!"

The front door slammed, and my mother got up slowly and walked away from the table. After a few minutes, she returned. She reached for the bowl of steaming baked potatoes, each one wrapped in its own tinfoil jacket, with crystal dishes for sour cream and butter beside them. Mom slit a cross in the foil of one of the potatoes, added plenty of sour cream and butter and salt, and mashed it all together in one delicious goop. Then she did the same thing to another potato, then a third, until all four potatoes were fixed that way. Although my stomach started hurting from the moment they'd begun fighting, those baked potatoes looked good, and I could imagine eating one as Mom mashed the soft insides of each one with a fork. But she didn't offer either Bobby or me a baked potato. Instead, we just sat there watching her smash the potatoes with the tines of her fork, frantically, over and over again for a long time. Then she returned to their bedroom, and emerged with the oblong bag Dad used for tennis. She carefully removed the rackets from their wooden presses, and, with a sterling silver spoon, scooped out all four potatoes and slathered the mixture all over his Slazengers. Then she took his shorts, shirt, and jockstrap, and packed them up in the tennis bag, and ladled the rest of the mess in with the clothes, and zipped it up again. She continued to sing "You Could Be Swinging on a Star" as she worked.

When she was finished, my mother announced she was leaving.

"Where ya' goin', Mom?" Bobby asked.

"I don't know."

"What do you mean, you don't know—when are you coming back?" I asked, voice cracking.

"I don't know if I'll ever come back," she said, "or where they might find me." Bobby began howling, "*Noooo!*"

"I want you to know if I don't return, or if they find me somewhere dead, I've always loved you both, and none of this is your fault."

"Mom! Don't go! Please!" Bobby and I said in unison. I thought about standing in front of the front door, but was frozen to the spot.

"Farewell, my children, goodbye!" She waved and put a pink silk scarf over her head, shrugged into a light topcoat, and slammed the door.

Bobby sat with his back to the door, rocking back and forth, Indian style, sucking his thumb. I told him she didn't mean it; she would be back soon. But of course I wasn't sure. She had done this before and always returned, but I couldn't really be sure this time. Not after the mashed potatoes on my father's rackets. This was something new and dangerous.

After a while I wandered into their bedroom. In my father's drawers, everything was perfect: his laundered shirts folded and stacked neatly, back to front, so they formed neat, symmetrical piles, each wrapped with a thick blue strip of paper like a birthday present. He used to fold his handkerchiefs so they had five little points like a king's crown, and tuck them carefully into the breast pocket of his suit. I took one of the monogrammed handkerchiefs and inhaled its rich fragrance. It smelled like pine trees in Maine or someplace hours from the city. In a box, I saw an assortment of gold collar stays and cuff links, each tucked away in its own neat compartment. Ordered, like a Swanson's TV dinner. I walked into the bathroom and saw my mother's nylons splayed out over the radiator, panties in heaps on the floor, a girdle slung over the shower rod like a flayed carcass. The contrast couldn't have been more marked.

I went back to the dining room to make sure Bobby wasn't doing something stupid, but he was in our bedroom, reading a *Richie Rich* comic out loud, laughing. As I passed the TV, I noticed *The Honeymooners* was still on, and heard Ralph taking Alice in his arms.

"Baby, you're the greatest!"

I turned the set off.

That night, my parents must have come home separately. They kissed and made up, sort of like on TV. She called him "Normie." She did that when they were affectionate. Then Dad laid out his tennis things for Sunday's game, and discovered the mashed potatoes and went crazy. He slapped her and we watched him drag her body through the dining room by her hair. He ordered us to stay in our room and shut the door. We obeyed. We heard our mother screaming "You pock-faced prick!" daring him to lay another finger on her. We listened as he threw her bodily out into the hallway outside the apartment, slamming the door. Bobby and I sat on our beds holding hands in silence as Mom banged on the door and screamed for the police. The police never came, and after what seemed like hours, the banging stopped. Robert fell asleep. Later, I heard the door open softly. Then there was silence.

And this was what I had been foolish enough to tell Grandma when she handed me that ten dollar bill on my birthday.

Now, everything I have touched so far on or near my father's desk, I have put back in its proper place. I'm about to leave, key in hand, and suddenly recall why I've entered his apartment in the first place. I've been sent to find a small leather address book and bring it back to him in the hospital. It's there, just as he said it would be, in the left-hand drawer of his desk, on top of a stack of business cards and legal pads. I open the book and check for Fionna Bingley's address, just to be sure it's there. The address is written in her own sophisticated British handwriting.

I close the drawer again, but it jams. After more futile attempts to return it to its proper place in the desk, I lift out the drawer and compare it with its twin on the other side. They do not seem to match. I stick my hand inside the dark hole and feel around with a twinge of unreasonable fear. Will my hand get bitten or lost in there? I press on and touch something odd, a piece of wood, and another drawer springs open—a secret compartment! I open it and shudder. I am cold, feverish. I am relieved that this second drawer is empty; empty that is, except for a slim cream-colored leather portfolio trimmed in gold with initials embossed: NIS. I hold it in my hand, wondering whether to open the clasp. I start to put it away, like I have with the rest of the photos and menus and invitations, but I can't.

I release the clasp and open it. What I find inside is an assortment— no, not an assortment—a collection of twenty-eight, 4x6 inch, black and white Polaroid photographs, most going back more than fifteen years, each precisely dated and numbered. My breath catches in my throat, and my chest cavity is invaded with a burning sensation. A corrosive heat seeps into my stomach and begins to spread. All the Polaroid photos are in black and white, and all have the same delicately scalloped edges. They remind me of his white porcelain cup sitting politely on its wire rack in the kitchen.

I pick up the first photograph. It is of a woman. I think I recognize her. But I'm not sure. She is on all fours in the middle of my father's bed, the same bed I am sitting on now. She is naked and bound by rope, but the rope does not seem like it has been drawn especially tight. It feels like it's part of a ritual, rather than a crime. The woman smiles a goofy, embarrassed grin. Her smile is what most disturbs me. It suggests participation in a sexual game, rather than violation. Yet the look on her face indicates the game may have gone on too long, or she no longer wants to play, or maybe, does not want this photograph taken. Maybe she is ashamed and wants this whole thing to stop. Maybe the photographer says just one more picture. Just this last one.

I turn over the photo and see there are several more of the same woman in various poses. In one there is a red whip; in another a dildo. As I sift through them, I realize that there are a great number of women, most bound, most in similar poses, all with similar smiles. They are smiles of resignation and humiliation. I am trembling and feel afraid in a way I have never been since early childhood. This is not simply discovering a secret stash of pornography. This is something else. These pictures remind me of something crucial about me, of my father's treatment of me; they make me feel a sense of personal shame in a way that is clearly disproportionate to the vulgar photos themselves. What could that be?

I phone my wife in the Netherlands. Patty is still home where we live with our three small children in a 19th century canal house in the sleepy, university town of Leiden, The Netherlands, population 150,000. I teach English literature at Leiden University, one of northern Europe's oldest universities, founded in 1575. I relish the sense of European history and culture that touches me each day on my walks to and from the Pieterskerk, or biking along the Witte Singel to work. My office at the university is minutes from the house where Rembrandt was born, and a bust of Leiden's most famous citizen greets me each day as I cycle past. That is why I have stayed in Holland for more than a decade now, and why my children have been born there. It is a world that feels solid and stationary, so different from the violent sounds and smells of the New York in which I grew up.

Patty realizes instantly that I have not called to ask about her or the kids. She knows this as soon as she hears my voice.

"What is it?"

"It's nothing. I'd like to speak to the kids."

She puts my son on the phone. Then I ask to speak to the two girls. Jerusha is five; Natasha barely three. I need to hear their voices. Remember the difference between my present there in Holland and my past in New York.

She returns to the phone and pointedly asks, "So, what is it?"

"Nothing," I say, but of course she knows I'm lying. I just can't tell her yet because I don't yet know myself. But her superior knowledge makes me feel that much more defensive.

"Can you send the children upstairs?"

"Why? Why should I send them upstairs?"

"I don't know."

"Well, what is it?" she asks again, impatience creeping into her voice. "I know you didn't call just to find out how I'm doing."

I'm nervous. This phone call, which I hoped would act as a sedative, is instead increasing my anxiety. My throat constricts. I'm angry. About to say something nasty, something I'll regret. I choke down the impulse.

"I came up to my father's apartment to find something, an address book—and instead, I think, I think …"

"What did you find?"

"Look, let me tell it! Stop interrupting! I've been looking through … old photographs, and papers, and things."

"What things?"

I don't feel comfortable talking to her anymore. This phone call has been a terrible mistake. I called to ask for help, but the problem is mine, and I'm unable to face it. I don't really want to talk about my father, or my parents—or anything else. Anyway, I realize there's really nothing to say.

I change the subject. "You remember Fionna … Fionna Bingley? Well, she just had a child in London. And my father wants to write her, so I had to come up here and look for his—"

"Well, that's really very interesting," she says. There is profound sarcasm in her voice. I know she remembers the string of miserable vacations we had with my father and his girlfriend in the south of France, Portugal, and St. Martin. Fionna Bingley was my father's mistress in those days, and although several years younger than me, she treated me with condescension, correcting me on my French, and pointedly remarking on my inability to drive the little stick shift Renault they rented in Provence. The power dynamic was strange, and those vacations, which seemed to promise luxury, sun, and relaxation, were filled with scenes of raw anger and suppressed tension as my father repeatedly questioned the priority I unaccountably gave to my children's meals or bedtimes. The worst part was how I transformed myself back into my father's son. No matter where we were, I reverted to a frightened little boy in his presence.

"What did you mean by 'interesting'?" I ask, angry now, turning against her. Why?

"It just is. Interesting, isn't it?"

"Listen. I can't talk right now." The next thing out of my mouth, I know, will be ugly.

"I knew it," she said.

"Knew what? What the hell are you talking about?" I shout.

"I knew it!" she repeats. "He's disgusting—your father."

"How—? What do you know about it?" I respond, awkwardly. What has she intuited, over there on the other side of the world where our cozy, Dutch home looks out on a sleepy canal? She is in the Netherlands, thousands of miles from New York. Yet she knows that something ... something has transpired ... something about which I am still ignorant.

"How can you *not* know about it?" she says mysteriously.

I hang up the phone.

I am in New York City, the city of my birth, my childhood. There should be countless people to speak to, myriad places to visit. But there is no one; everyone is either dead or has moved away. I should have destroyed those photos immediately. But I have not done so. I put them back in their secret hiding place, and for some reason I feel almost as though I'm in hiding myself. I wonder, what if he should return from the hospital and find the photos missing? What if he somehow discovers that I have seen them?

I make my way through his apartment. As I walk out the door, I slam it behind me. I emerge on 2nd Avenue still holding the key in my hand.

I walk to the Eldorado where Grandma once lived. I need to forget about what I have seen, immerse myself in something different. During junior high, and well into high school, I visited Grandma all the time. She was my refuge and sanctuary, and always had a meal and a strange, compelling story to tell. Besides, I knew the walk would do me good. But I stopped and recalled the one thing I was absolutely forbidden to do as a child. Her words came to mind.

"Walking through Central Park, especially at sundown, is the most dangerous thing you can do," she warned. "Remember, in Central Park at night there are gangs of Puerto Ricans and Blacks who roam freely. You'll

41

be robbed, maybe murdered." When I shrugged this off as crazy, she said: "Good, go get yourself killed. Be my guest."

So now, as an adult, I find myself following her advice. I walk uptown to 86th Street, then hop in a cab rather than walk through the park.

I had been held up on two occasions by the time I turned ten. The first time was when I was only four. My mother gave me a dollar bill, and I held it clenched in my fist as I rode the mechanical bucking bronco outside Prexy's on 115th Street, right next to Columbia University. Prexy's was "Home of the Hamburger with the College Education," and featured a sign with a grinning hamburger wearing a mortarboard tilted at a rakish angle. It was autumn, and I had on a light blue suit with matching cap. My mother deposited a nickel in the bronco's flank, and left me peacefully rocking back and forth waving the dollar while she went into the drugstore. That's how safe it was in 1953. Then two kids, maybe fourteen years old, came over and one of them told me to show them my dollar. I handed it to him, of course. The boy wasn't really menacing—he probably just thought he might as well try, since I was stupid enough to sit there rocking, waving money for the whole world to see. The other kid asked how I liked the ride, and I started crying as soon as I realized he wasn't giving the money back.

Mom came racing out to see why I was crying, and when I told her they had taken my dollar, she grabbed the kid nearest me, and seeing his comrade take off, shouted, "You watch this one, Henry; I'll get the other!" While she ran down the street to chase the other boy, the criminal in my care simply smiled at the absurdity of my "guarding" him and walked slowly away, leaving me howling louder than before. About fifteen minutes later, my mom came back holding a dollar bill in her gloved hand. I always assumed she had nabbed the crook and made him hand it over. She was Supermom. "All's well that ends well," she said, citing Shakespeare. It never occurred to me that she might have taken another dollar from her purse to stop my bawling, or how strange it was that she assumed I could safely manage to corral the fourteen year old she had entrusted in my care.

The second robbery happened a few years later. A bunch of us kids were in a nearby playground playing baseball. The playground had been almost deserted by the mothers and baby carriages because it had begun to rain. As the rain continued, we played with a kind of ritualized intensity that was unique in the annals of playground baseball. The reason was simple: our game was enclosed by an iron fence. For city kids, there was no Little League, and that fence gave our game the heightened feel of Yankee Stadium. It was in that game that, for the first time, I hit a home run over a real fence. As soon as it sailed over the iron railing, I went into my Mickey Mantle trot for the first time in public. I remember the wonderful soft thud as ball met bat, as though I were swinging through air. I slowly circled the bases with everyone watching, except Richie, who had the demeaning task of fetching my home-run ball on the other side of the fence. It was a game for the ages; even Jimmy—uncoordinated, bespectacled, and eternally relegated to right field—somehow managed to smack a double that one-hopped the fence that day.

While we were in the field, a small group of Puerto Rican kids congregated on the periphery of the playground—a sure sign of trouble. They had a small Scottish terrier with them who yapped and snapped at the raindrops. The rain came down harder and harder, but as it was only the seventh inning, we had to finish. After all, we might never get another chance to play ball in an enclosed yard ever again. If it had been nice weather, there would have been moms and kids around, and we could never have played unfettered. So we played on, ignoring the downpour, and the ring of nasty-looking kids outside. Slowly and almost imperceptibly, during the eighth inning, the gang of Puerto Ricans entered the playground. I was nervous, but didn't want to show it for fear of being called "Faggot!" and ridiculed for weeks, if not years.

Rain was coming down in sheets now, and I could barely see. Someone else finally shouted we should stop, which was fine with me, as long as it wasn't me who initiated the stoppage. But, as we gathered our bats and balls and started to leave, the gang of kids slowly surrounded us. Then their leader, pulling a switchblade, told us to hand over all our money, bats, balls, and gloves. There was mild protest by Georgie Zeitlin, who was overweight but strong. He could even do an imitation of Antonino Rocca's airplane spin with Ephraim aloft on his shoulders, no less. And he loved to emulate Killer Kowalski's dreaded "claw hold" by taking his hand and plunging it into your guts until you "gave," or were reduced to a puddle of tears. But even Georgie turned over his money, and of course, the rest of us complied as well. The leader of the gang told us his terrier, still trying to snap up every last raindrop, had rabies and that a bite from her would be fatal.

As we left the park, our spirits significantly dampened in body and spirit, the gang pursued us at a dead run, shouting for us to stop. Of course we didn't stop. But their leader shouted, "Hey man, wait! I said, wait up!" So we did. We were standing on 67th and Central Park West now, and it was still raining like hell with no police in sight. These kids had taken our money, our equipment, and our pride. What more could they want?

"What the hell! You guys just robbed us," Ephraim said as their pimply leader strode up, six inches from his face. The boy was about our age, but he had the beginnings of a growth of dark moustache on his upper lip, which he licked menacingly as he spoke.

"Yeah, man. We're giving it back."

"Why?" I asked stupidly. Ephraim gave me a dirty look.

The leader pushed his hands through his dripping hair, walked up to me, and held me with two hands by my shirt: "You wanna make somethin' of it, man?"

"No," I said.

"But why are you giving it back?" Richie said. Richie later won points for bravery by informing us he had five bucks secretly hidden in his high-top Converse sneakers. He would never give that up; they'd have to kill him first.

"We were just practicing," the gang leader said. "Here—take it all back!"

He gave us back our money, along with our bats, balls, and equipment. In a matter of moments, they mysteriously vanished back into the park. We had our money back, which was good. But somehow it felt even more humiliating to be victimized as part of a dress rehearsal. I wondered how I would tell my parents, especially my father. I decided not to.

I chose to confide instead to Margaret, our maid. It was safe to tell Margaret things, because no one spoke to her, and she said nothing to anyone. She really was quite surly. On weekends, however, when my parents went out (they did socialize then, and even went dancing for a few years), Margaret turned into a different person. She made me chocolate fudge, which she served in little paper baking cups with scalloped edges. I noticed she liked watching me eat the fudge. As I ate and watched TV, I saw her look toward me and almost smile. I pretended not to see, and continued eating fudge, and drinking my milk out of a special Welch's grape jelly glass. When my parents were out of the house, Margaret sometimes even spoke to me. She was almost friendly. When my parents were around, however, she was always sullen, and never spoke to anyone—not even me.

Margaret lived in an indescribable and smelly alcove we called "The Maid's Room." It was located off the kitchen, near the service entrance where we took out the trash. Margaret's room was adjacent to where Blackie, our Cocker Spaniel, was tethered day and night, so her room smelled exactly like the urine-soaked newspaper, where Blackie, in Grandma Schvey's memorable phrase, "did his business." I wasn't supposed to ever enter the Maid's Room, and its door was always closed, so I hardly saw it. However, its distinctive odor—socks, puppy urine, shit, damp newsprint—meant that I did *smell* it. Its stench enveloped everything in that part of the house, including the kitchen.

Margaret's skin was nearly translucent. If you looked closely, you could trace a faint highway of blue veins and arteries crawling underneath her skin. In all the years she was with us, I never once saw her take one bite of anything. She never seemed to be hungry, but she always looked malnourished. You could actually see her delicate collarbones jut out above the top button of her uniform. Her uniform's whiteness only emphasized how unhealthy and sallow her skin looked by contrast.

Except for my father's closet and chest of drawers, the rest of our house was unkempt and filled with heaps of dirty laundry and Mayflower Van Lines boxes. We had moved to 86th and Madison from the apartment at 440 Riverside Drive near Columbia University four years earlier, but the moving boxes remained untouched. When my father asked Mom to get those goddamn boxes emptied and out of the house, her reply was simply, "We've only just moved in, Norman. Besides, how can anyone be expected to keep house with only one maid?" My father had no riposte; he walked away cursing my mother's family, and poured himself a large J&B and soda.

Margaret was a live-in maid in theory, but not in practice. As a "stranger," my mother forbade her access to their bedroom. A stranger could not be trusted to set foot there, let alone clean it. In an emergency, she might iron my father's tennis shorts, but that was basically it. So, Margaret didn't exist as a maid who cooked, cleaned, or did laundry; she was more of a virtual maid proclaiming to the outside world that we, like others of our class, had one. Even though we didn't.

Although Margaret served no practical purpose, she was crucially important to me. After my brother was sent to bed, Margaret and I would sit together. During the fudge making, she was all concentration, but once I sat down in front of the television with a glass of milk and fudge, we got along well. I'd make her watch old horror movies with me, movies like *Plan 9 from Outerspace* or *The Werewolf*, which Margaret hated and loved, and watched with her tiny fists clenched over her eyes like a baby. Her body actually shook when something terrible happened in the movie, allowing me to feel like her protector. I really enjoyed seeing how frightened she was, since even I knew it was only a horror movie.

Once, I persuaded her to watch me curl an old pair of dumbbells I found in the alley outside our apartment building. The dumbbells were gold colored, but the gold paint had mostly chipped off and they smelled like rust. I didn't want either of my parents to see them—I didn't let my mother know because they were literally picked out of the garbage, and even though our own apartment was full of what might be called rubbish, she would have been furious if she knew I had brought something like that home. I didn't want my father to see them because I didn't want him to know that I wanted to lift weights and become strong, much stronger than he was. Then, I thought, he wouldn't dare comment on how skinny I was or mockingly call me "Muscles" when we changed before we played tennis. So my dumbbells became a shameful secret. Somehow the fact that the dumbbells were both filthy and secret made them more precious: they were real ten-pound dumbbells, just like Charles Atlas probably used. I hid them beneath my bed, and only used them when I was alone. I could have asked for a set of weights for Christmas, I guess, but it never occurred to me. Asking for them would only prove I needed them, that I was a weakling. Once I saw a picture in the *National Enquirer* of Bronco Nagurski, a pro football star from the 1940s. Bronco was just standing there, smiling. And, perched on his upraised hand—his wife! There she was, legs crossed casually, sitting like a tiny queen, just talking to her husband. Even Dad couldn't do this! So, my plan was to become so powerful that I could hold a real live woman in the palm of my hand. I would talk to her, watch TV with her, or have her get me a Coke, and there she would be, right in my palm, whenever I needed her. I knew it would take many years to get that strong; until then, I would practice with Margaret when my parents were out of the house.

After curling my dumbbells six times for three sets with each arm, I asked Margaret to feel my bicep. She touched my skinny arm very tentatively, with the yellow tip of one skinny, tobacco-stained index finger. A few weeks after that, I asked if I could show her how strong I had now become. After considerable persuasion, she allowed me to try and lift her up in my arms. First, I raised her by her bony hips, and managed to hold her in the air for a few seconds. Despite her tiny size, I had to struggle to lift her without dropping her. As I held her in my arms, I smelled the foul odor of the Maid's Room, which clung to her uniform. But I didn't mind. This became a weekly ritual for us, and in time, I grew to love that filthy smell. Once I dropped Margaret, and she lay there on our dining room floor for one awful moment before I helped her to her feet. She brushed off her uniform and practically crawled back to her room. It was as though the world had stopped rotating for one horrible moment. I felt terrible, principally because I felt sure Margaret would never let me lift her again.

Then I wondered if she would inform my parents about what I had been doing with her in secret? I felt that there was something terribly private about what we were doing, something dirty even. Would she tell my father about our secret life together? Or reveal the two rusty dumbbells hidden under my bed? If she had broken an arm, it would all come out. Even Blackie, who was leashed to the kitchen doorknob all day, and never allowed freedom around the house, whimpered and strained to see what the matter was.

Standing outside her door, I shouted, "Margaret! I'm very sorry." I added, "I'll make it up to you ... I'll make you fudge!"

Eventually, Margaret emerged with something close to a smile, the first and only one I ever saw. I kept my promise and never dropped her again. With practice, I was eventually able to lift her quite easily and parade her around the living room. When I did this, Margaret, who when my parents were around was a virtual mute with a sullen air, transformed into a giggly Irish schoolgirl with a crush.

"O, Jesus, Mary, and Joseph, but the lad is strong! How does he do it—how? Feel that arm, will ya'? How can he carry such a heavy load as meself? And how old are you now?"

"I'm eleven, Margaret," I announced proudly, trying to prevent her from noticing the peculiar wet stain near the fly of my pajamas.

"Strong as an ox is he! Let me feel that muscle." And I'd lift her again, and while I held her aloft, she'd press her fingers down on my skinny arm, following the slight curve of the bicep. Again that funny, indescribable tickling feeling came upon me, after which I had to suddenly set her down.

Before too many months had passed, I could carry Margaret in a single arm, as she quietly moaned and ruffled my hair with her fingers. "My Gawd, he did it! Look at him; look at what he did with just a single arm! Put me down, oh, please put me down now!" But I didn't put her down, and I knew she didn't want me to.

When I finally set her down as gently as possible on the couch, we both collapsed red-faced and sweating in front of the TV, my little circumcised dart of a penis struggling to free itself. What did that mean? I didn't have any idea, and Margaret either didn't notice, or pretended not to. Afterwards, Margaret brought me fudge and cold milk. She never ate with me, of course, but I did notice she watched me chew and swallow every bite. I wondered if Margaret had children back in Ireland, but never asked. After I had eaten my fill and could walk again, I brought her my Dad's cigarette box with the Empire State Building printed on it, and she took a single one of his Kents and poured herself a thimble-full of J&B with no ice. Afterwards, she took the glass and my father's Stork Club ashtray, and washed and replaced them both exactly where they had been. When my parents returned from their party or dancing, Margaret limped back to the fetid Maid's Room and turned back into her sad, mute, surly self again.

Although she never used her Master's in Education from Columbia to teach, my mother was always interested in childhood education, especially what she called "The Gifted." Obviously, she claimed that my brother and I were gifted, and read us stories from Dickens and Shakespeare at a very early age. She exaggerated our every accomplishment, however pedestrian. In time, she believed her own hyperboles, including a story that, upon seeing *Peter Pan* I speculated aloud whether Tinker Bell would be represented by an actor or just a beam of light. Or that when I had my I.Q. tested, I asked the administrator why she had dumped out the pile of blocks if all she wanted me to do was put them back. Most impressive of all, she insisted to everyone that I had miraculously toilet-trained myself at six months, and brooked no contradiction or discussion on this crucial point.

She even took me to audition for *The Quiz Kids* television program as a child. Although I was eliminated in the second round of auditions and never appeared on the program, my mother told people it was because the interviewer didn't understand the word "paleontologist," which is what I had told them I wanted to be when I grew up. The ignoramus, she said, kept me off the show out of spite. Over time, she embellished the story so much that she said I actually *did* make an appearance and would have won thousands had the host realized that my claim that diplodocus—not brontosaurus—was the largest dinosaur was indeed accurate. I listened to Mom explain this to her friends, claiming that because the diplodocus was the *longer* dinosaur, I was justified in my answer even though brontosaurus was the heavier of the two. Of course, the moderator was simply too ill informed to know about this distinction between diplodocus and brontosaurus. For this reason, I had been unfairly cheated out of the fame and fortune which were rightfully mine.

I was present when she unfurled the story of my magnificence to Dr. Florence Brumbaugh, then principal of the Hunter College Elementary School, and author of several books on gifted children. She insisted I skip first grade, claiming I was reading at a third grade level. Since my mother had actually graduated high school by the age of fourteen, it was hardly surprising to her that I must skip a grade as well. The point of insisting on my supposed gifts was, of course, to shed light on her own. Perhaps we are all guilty of this—often to the detriment of our children. In my case, however, since I never believed in my own "giftedness," her assertions had the strangely perverse result of making me want to fail.

The growing tension between my parents during my early childhood affected my personality as well. My relationship with my brother (never close because of the six year gap in our ages) became overtly hostile. My feelings of rage were exacerbated by the fact that my mother (aware that both her marriage and any shred of domestic stability was slipping away) insisted that my brother and I share everything as equals; in order to be "fair" to both her beautiful, gifted children, I was sent to bed at the same time as Bobby—although he had just turned five.

"You see that little hole in the wall up there above your bed?" I said to Bobby at 8:30 p.m. as we lay on our twin beds one summer evening after I turned eleven. I promised to tell him a story, but I hated being stuck in there. My parents were at some kind of PTA event (despite their building hostility, they still did things like that), and I wanted to be in the living room watching a movie with Margaret. I was so angry that I had to make him pay for my humiliation.

"Do you see it or not?" I said.

"No I don't."

"If it was during the day, you would. You'd see a little thumbtack-sized hole up there in the wall right above your head."

"Yeah … I guess."

"Well, once upon a time, a whole family lived in there." I said this matter-of-factly. I was torn between wanting to tell him a story that would get him to sleep so I could sneak out, and one that would terrify him so much that they would never make me go to bed at the same time with him again.

"Wait! What do you mean? Where?" He suddenly bolted upright in bed.

"Right inside that wall; right above your head," I said. "A whole family was once imprisoned in there." I heard my brother scoot his chubby, ungainly body so far away from the wall he almost slipped off the bed onto the floor.

"No they didn't!" Bobby whimpered, "You're just trying to—"

I raised my arm above him, threatening a blow. "I'll give you a real reason to cry!" Although he hadn't actually started crying, I couldn't wait to employ this phrase—one of my father's favorites. "I happen to know that there was a family that lived behind that wall. It's a well-known fact." I hated every second I was trapped in there with him. Tormenting him was the only thing that made it bearable.

50

"It's impossible," Bobby said, wiping his eye.

"What?" I said.

"Th—that a family—could...."

"Why is it impossible?"

"People don't live trapped inside walls of houses."

"Oh, don't they? You're how old?"

"Five."

"And me? How old am I?"

"Ten."

"WRONG! I'm eleven, you idiot! You don't even know how old your big brother is. I think I know a little bit more than you about what's possible, don't I?"

"I guess."

"You guess?"

"You do."

"That's right; and I say a whole family did live trapped inside these walls. The father was called Jimmy Fuzzie, and the mother's name was Lizzie Fuzzie—"

"I don't believe it. How could they breathe in there?"

"Breathe?"

"There's no oxygen; how could they breathe inside a wall?"

"Difficult, but possible," I said. "I learned about it from ... Mr. Wizard. And someone else."

"Who?" he demanded. Why couldn't the kid shut up, or die? He spoiled everything. I really wanted to scare him, but he was tormenting me instead.

"I just told you—Mr. Wizard. God, you're stupid."

"You said there was somebody else, besides—"

"George. He told me. Our apartment was haunted, he said." George, our doorman, would presumably be knowledgeable on such things as tiny people living inside the walls.

"Oh."

"Do you want me to go on or not?" I said. "'Cause if you keep on interrupting, I won't tell you how it turned out."

"Okay, go on," he said.

"You know what?" I said. "It sounds like you're doing me a favor by listening. Good night." Now I hated him even more than I wanted to scare him.

"No, please go on."

"That's better. All right, I will."

"Well, like I said, the father was called Jimmy Fuzzie, the mother was Lizzy Fuzzie, and he had a really nasty habit."

"Fuzzie's a made-up name! It can't be real."

"You can believe it or not; it's up to you. Besides, it's no stupider than 'Bobby'."

"Yeah … well, what was it, the habit, I mean?"

"Oh, nothing much. But whenever there was someone who he didn't like, Jimmy Fuzzie would take his right hand and punch it through the wall … and … give them a gigantic nougie!" I grabbed him by the collar of his Flintstone pajamas and rubbed the knuckle of my middle finger into his scalp.

"Hey, leggo!" he screamed. "That really hurts! I'm going to tell Marg—"

"All right, maybe that part's not true. I was just kidding around." Then, out of the blue, I said, "Bobby, did you know the cops were here again last night?"

Late night police visits were becoming more frequent.

"Were they?"

"Yes, and this time they came because the neighbors complained."

"Oh no."

"One of the cops said, "That maniac's really going to kill her some day." This time I wasn't trying to scare my brother. I heard the cop say it myself.

"Who did he mean?"

"Who do you think?"

It had taken a while, but I had finally succeeded in terrifying my brother—with the truth.

"Mommy—Mommy—Mommy!" Bobby was screaming and crying now.

Margaret opened the bedroom door. She must have been smoking a cigarette, because her specter hovered in the doorway like a ghost. "What in Jesus's name is the trouble now, boys?"

"Margaret, please don't let him kill her!" he said.

"Ah, the bairn's havin' a bad dream! I'll just fetch him a glass of warm milk."

"I don't want milk. I want my mommy!" screamed Bobby.

"No, everything's all right, Margaret," I said, digging my thumbs into his wrists. "Isn't it Bobby?" When he didn't answer right away, I exerted more pressure, "Well, isn't it?" He whimpered miserably, and Margaret grudgingly shut the door.

"Don't worry," I whispered to him, "he probably won't actually do it. And it won't do either of us any good to cry about it," I added. "You sound like a little baby. Besides she isn't here; they're both out tonight at a meeting, so everything's okay. At least for tonight."

Bobby didn't reply.

I didn't want to hurt him any longer. I felt sorry for him. And I despised myself for the gratuitous cruelty I had shown. "I'm here with you. You're safe now."

"No, I'm not. You're not a grownup. You're just eleven." He flung those words with utter contempt across the dark room. And it hurt.

"Listen, let's forget all about the Fuzzies. I'm sorry I told you any of it. It wasn't true, you know, none of it. I was just teasing."

"I know."

"But you're still afraid?"

"Yes. But not of your stupid story. I'm afraid of what the policeman said."

"I was just exaggerating. Nothing's going to happen. Just go to sleep now."

"No, I want my mommeeeee … *Mommeeeee*." The words bubbled softly and plaintively through his lips.

"Go to sleep now, Bobby. I'm sorry I scared you."

Bobby refused to shut up. "*Mommeeeee … Mommeeeee*."

Maybe I was more my father's son than I imagined.

I had tears in my own eyes now. I buried my head beneath my pillow to keep from hearing his sobs.

What if I grow up and become just like him, just like my father? I thought.

I climbed out of bed and reached up to the spot in the wall where I had just told Bobby the Fuzzie family dwelt. I put my finger on the spot. There was chipped paint and a small hole there, just as I had said. What if there really was a family trapped in there? I wondered. What if I made up this crazy story and it was all true?

4.

The oversized, seven-foot tennis racket leaning against the wall in my father's apartment wasn't just a gag gift. It said something essential about who he was. Tennis was not a game for him; it was his passion. Aside from his work, it was what he lived for. I longed to be part of it, to be asked to come along and play with him on his weekends. Unfortunately, I was rarely included. I wanted to learn to play myself, of course, but more importantly, I wanted to experience the pleasure of being with him, watching him out there on the courts. Even well into his sixties, with a substantial belly, there was something inspiring about the athletic way he raced about the court. His movements and shots were different from the way other older men played. My father played with a kind of swagger which wasn't like an old guy; he was Errol Flynn brandishing a tennis racket instead of a sword. Unlike his middle-aged partners, who hit the ball boringly back and forth over the net, content to keep a rally going and not make unforced errors, Dad played every point like it was his last. He went for daring winners down the alleys, or clever drop shots that left his slower friends either panting helplessly or impotently riveted to the spot. Unlike the other men who wanted to keep points alive, my father invariably tried to conclude each rally with a spectacular shot. Like he wanted to kill it. Sometimes he failed; but more often, he would zing one down the line, or unexpectedly smash a forehand at one of his opponents standing defenselessly at the net.

Between spring and fall, he played doubles with friends at Leonard Rosen's gorgeous home in Scarsdale, where Len had built his own clay court. Len was a cheerful, red-faced, bald man, a diametric contrast to my father's saturnine energy. Len always seemed happy.

My mother's explanation for this was simple and succinct. "Why shouldn't he be happy—the man inherited a fortune!"

Len was married to a woman named Lucinda who was beautiful and had the blackest, thickest hair I ever saw, and was always nice to everyone. Len always kissed his wife, and I couldn't help notice their open affection with one another, so different from my parents. I couldn't imagine Len taking a strap to his son or daughter, and it was inconceivable that he would strike or humiliate his wife the way my father did.

On the extremely rare occasions when I was invited to go with my father up to Scarsdale, he asked his friend, Sy, to bring his son Alex along, too. We drove up to Scarsdale in Sy's white Eldorado, and Alex and I sat in the back and played Baseball Initials.

I liked being around Alex, but I didn't really like him. Actually, I think I preferred being around Alex's father more than I did Alex, because his father had a calm I had never witnessed in another adult before. My mother told me he was a Jewish Cary Grant. He was the antithesis of my father: forgiving and patient, with a dry wit. Sy was a doctor, and when he died a few years later, I was really sad. He had his own tragedy, too, my mother said, when I told her how much I liked being around him. Don't say anything to anybody, she said—your father would kill me if he knew I told you—his wife Rebecca is very sick.

"What do you mean, sick?" I asked.

"She has agoraphobia," my mother said in hushed tones.

"What's agoraphobia?" I whispered back.

"Agoraphobia's when you're afraid to go outside your own house or anywhere else. She can't even walk across the street. She's mentally ill."

When we arrived at Len's place, Alex took off running. After being cooped up in the back seat of Dr. Friedman's car for an hour and a half, we were anxious to move. We grabbed our rackets, and took off on an impromptu race across the freshly mowed lawns of the Rosen estate down to the clay court. I was faster than Alex, and would certainly have reached the court first had I not heard my father's voice boom, "Where the hell do you think you're going?"

I pulled up lame, and remember feeling like Mickey Mantle must have when he twisted his knee on the drain embedded in the outfield grass during the 1951 World Series. I walked back to the car dragging the head of my Slazenger through the fragrant grass. I thought about what The Mick might have accomplished, if only he had remained healthy. When I got back to the car, I was informed it was my job to carry both my father and Sy's tennis bags (each with two rackets and accessories) to the court. I wanted to ask why Alex didn't have to do this too, but didn't. I lifted both bags out of Sy's trunk, and saw my friend already warming up and practicing his serve.

In between the men's matches, Alex and I were permitted to hit a few balls, either by ourselves or with the grownups for half an hour until they were ready to start the next set. Occasionally, we would be paired with one of the older men for a game of doubles. The crunch of red clay underneath my feet felt wonderful as I strode happily onto the court. I had felt sluggish sitting around all that time while the adults played, but it was worth it as soon as I stood up and walked on the clay court. I unscrewed my wooden racket from its press and began swinging to get limbered up while the grownups swallowed salt tablets from a large glass bottle. It was early fall and leaves were beginning to fall. Soon they would need to be swept off the baselines so as not to interfere with the match. Soon, too, it would be cold outside. This was probably one of the last times we'd be able to play until next spring. I wore my white tennis sweater with the maroon stripes along the V-neck. Grandma had bought me that sweater. Usually I hated getting clothes for my birthday, but this was different. It came in a robin's egg blue box from B. Altman's.

"Where'd you get those sneakers?" my father asked harmlessly. I swung my racket round and round in a circle like a windmill.

"Gimbels? I don't know—Mom got them," I said, and tossed an imaginary ball in the air and slammed it over an imaginary net.

"I'm asking because those don't look like tennis sneakers—they're basketball. Lift up your feet—you can tell by the tread. Yup—tennis shoes don't have a tread like that. You can't wear those on clay. You'll ruin Mr. Rosen's court."

As I bent over to look at the soles of my sneakers, Alex's first warm-up serve hit me in the ass on a fly. I looked up and saw Alex. He was laughing, so I tried to laugh it off, too, although it hurt just a little.

"What can I do about it now?"

"There's one thing you can do, young man. Take off those basketball sneakers and put on your tennis shoes."

"But I don't have another pair here."

"Norman, what size does the kid wear? Maybe we have—" Len suggested, his shiny head growing red. "It doesn't really matter about the surface."

Whether he heard him or not, my father ignored Mr. Rosen's suggestion. He simply looked at me and said, "I guess you should have thought of that before you left home."

"So should you … if you think it makes that much difference," I shot back.

"Look, Norman, leave it—besides, the court is covered with leaves, it needs to be rolled and swept anyway when we're finished," Len said, reddening some more.

"Henry—come over here," Dad said.

Dr. Friedman motioned for his son to stop serving and join him by the water cooler. I glanced over at them, and thought I heard Alex whisper something to his father; I wondered if they were talking about me. When I looked back to my father, he smacked me soundly across the face. The shock of being hit so unexpectedly, and in public, was worse than the pain.

"How dare you talk that way to me?" he hissed. "Get off this court this instant, you little bastard. Now!"

"But I didn't say anyth—"

SMACK.

"You're a liar." My eyes filled with tears, and I caught sight of Sy interposing his body between Alex and me. "You can just sit down. I'm not going to have you ruin the court. We three can play Canadian Doubles. Come on, Alex, serve 'em up."

Dr. Friedman crossed over to where my father was standing, motioning for Alex to wait by the water cooler. After a few minutes of low conversation, my father turned back to me. "All right, Henry, get back on the court."

Humiliated, I wanted to refuse. But I couldn't. Why couldn't I refuse? I walked back on the court, smiling a stupid, goofy smile borne of my own embarrassment and humiliation in front of all those adults, and Alex.

I was teamed with my father against Sy and Alex. Dad served first and we won the first game at love. Dr. Friedman won the next. Then it was time for my serve. My first serve was a clean ace to Alex, right down the middle and absolutely unreturnable. I hated him for the sin of having Sy as his father, hitting me in the ass with the tennis ball, and most of all for being there to witness my shame. I hated everyone there, just for being alive. All that hatred went into that one perfect serve. That one clean ace.

Then I served to Dr. Friedman. It was just out, and the second hit the net and bounced back for a double fault. Fifteen–All. Then back to Alex. I was going to ace him again, the little shit. My toss was slightly behind my head, but instead of just letting the ball drop and starting over, I tried to hit it anyway. The ball hit the edge of my wooden racket and sailed far over the fence. I smiled the same ridiculous smile and pretended it didn't bother me at all. My second serve went long: Fifteen–Thirty.

Now behind in the game, I tried to hit the first serve with more direction, but slammed it into my father's calf as he stood with his back to me at the net. He turned slowly and glared. "Jesus Christ, Henry!" Shaken, I babied the second serve into the net. At Fifteen–Forty, I let up on the first serve and sent it into the wrong box. My second serve, now a foregone conclusion, was another double fault. I hated everything about tennis now; I just wanted to get back home to Uncle Lee. And now my father, having been hit once, decided to turn around and glare at me while I served, instead of facing our opponents at the net. The ultimate humiliation.

After losing the set, Dad turned to me with clenched teeth and said, "You make me sick. Absolutely sick."

I smiled, a combination of defiance and shame, and took my tennis racket with two hands like a baseball bat and slammed a tennis ball as far as I could, far over the fence.

"Now get both balls you hit over the fence, go to the car, and don't ever show your face on this court again. You're finished, mister."

Before he said it, however, I'd already decided never to play tennis again.

Not long after that, it was time to begin preparation for that sober and inevitable rite of passage nearly every Jewish child must undergo on his thirteenth birthday: the bar mitzvah. For my parents, as for most of their contemporaries, the bar mitzvah itself did not involve either intellectual demands or religious observance. I was to celebrate my special day with little effort at Rodeph Sholem, the gorgeous, austere synagogue on 83rd and Central Park West where we "belonged." With a minimum effort, my coming of age would be celebrated with a lavish party, primarily for all my father's business associates. In return, a substantial amount of cash and U.S. Savings Bonds would be deposited in a savings account in the Chase Manhattan Bank. I wouldn't be able to spend any of the money, however; although it would be "mine" in the sense that it would be put in the bank accruing interest for college.

On Saturday mornings for the past several years at Rodeph Sholem, I had been instructed in the art of sculpting dreidels out of clay and learning to fry latkes without getting scalded by spattering oil. I had been spared learning Hebrew or anything much about the Old Testament, other than a few Bible stories and the memorization of five of the Ten Commandments for Mr. Brilliant. We memorized five, and then at the next class, we were told a quiet, shy boy named Eisenberg (who sat by himself at the back of the classroom) had died of leukemia. The previous class, I had seen Eisenberg sitting by himself, quietly sobbing, and wondered why. That very next week, we were informed of his death. The week after that, Mr. Brilliant suffered a nervous breakdown and never returned to the class.

My mother ordered expensive invitations from Tiffany's, booked the Sherry-Netherlands Hotel for the party, hired an exclusive caterer—and then, out of the blue, I decided to spoil everything.

I had learned from Ephraim (whose parents were deeply religious) that there was another kind of bar mitzvah; it involved learning Hebrew, singing, and chanting something called a Haftarah portion. I told my parents that I wanted to learn Hebrew, and that I wanted to be bar mitzvahed as a Conservative Jew, not according to Reform Judaism, which was less onerous, assimilated to American traditions, and (in those days) didn't involve learning Hebrew. This, however, would mean having my ceremony at a different synagogue.

"I have absolutely no idea where he got this crap," my father shouted when I floated the idea. "You can be damn sure it wasn't from me."

"Why are you accusing me?" my mother shot back. "My brothers weren't even bar mitzvahed since there wasn't even a temple in Philipsburg where we grew up. And anyone can see how they turned out!"

Her statement floated in the air for a moment like a rather large bubble waiting to be pricked. "Yes … they can," my father said, deftly inserting a pin.

"Very funny, Norman," Mom said, but there was even a hint of a smile. I almost thought she enjoyed my father's joke at her brothers' expense, since for once it was delivered without excessive malice.

However incomprehensible it might be, it was difficult for my parents to refuse a whim as harmless and idiotic as my insistence on a more rigorous training in Hebrew. Until that time, my only exposure to Jewish ritual were the High Holy Days at Rodoph Sholem with my father and the bleak, humorless Passover Seder conducted annually by Grandpa Schvey, punctuated by cruel sarcasm (and in a perfectly exaggerated accent) on the weight and density of Grandma's matzoh balls.

"Knives and forks ve'll need for dis soup, Birdie. Spoons you better can save for de tziken," provided the only brief moments of levity at the dark, gloomy Seder held annually at my grandparents'.

Perversely, I imagined bar mitzvah lessons as a form of escape from the dreaded High Holy Days with my father, where, imprisoned in my uniform of navy blue suit, starched white shirt, and silver tie, I sat immobilized for hours wearing a tallis and yarmulke. The incomprehensible letters on the Hebrew side of the page transformed themselves into weird Jewish devils with heads of rams, cloven hooves, and pointy tails. I sat beside my father, who never opened his mouth, refusing to join in reciting prayers with the rest of the congregation, let alone sing the traditional songs, but jabbed me repeatedly, insisting I do both.

I decided that my father was present for only one reason: to ensure I never moved for an entire day. I rose when bidden, muttered meaningless prayers in stilted verse, sat, stood, sat, and stood again. If I so much as adjusted the fringe on my tallis, I received a withering glance. Thankfully, this only occurred a few times each year. But the anticipation, especially knowing my every movement would be monitored, filled me with dread.

Since I was prohibited movement of any kind, sitting in the sanctuary did force a kind of communion with things divine, and I prayed fervently for the end of services, either by unlikely natural disaster, or for the Rabbi to be stricken down, a regrettable but necessary means of liberation. As the congregation rose as one, I imagined Rabbi Plotnick with his neatly groomed salt-and-pepper beard and fixed, benign smile, clutching at his breast and collapsing on the Bimah. I imagined I heard the majestic sound of the shofar, with hundreds rushing to his aid, and I would sneak out the back and spend the rest of the day playing ball with my friends. In the midst of this pleasant reverie, however, my father would give me a stare which reminded me that he would certainly not rush to Rabbi Plotnick's aid, and would make sure I kept my seat while a yarmulke and tallis-clad EMS team arrived on the scene.

Each year, these visits to temple were filled with anxiety, beginning with the inspection of my shoes, suit, and hair. The friction of my tie being yanked back and forth under my collar, the button-down shirt so tightly buttoned against my throat that I gagged, the veins in my neck throbbing like tiny beating hearts—these were the sounds and images I associated with the High Holy Days. So, it was odd that I chose a more rigorous form of observance that might actually force me to learn something. However, I was inspired by a naïve but genuine sense of rebellion against what I considered a meaningless, stupid ritual, which neither of my parents actually believed in, but forced me to undertake for my own good. Plus, it was something I thought I could get away with.

After months of trying to teach me the meaning of the words I was required to chant at my bar mitzvah, Cantor Vogel gave up on me. Realizing I would never progress fast enough to actually comprehend my Torah portion in Hebrew, he decided to make a phonograph recording of my Haftarah, so I could simply memorize the words and melodies, instead of having to learn what they meant. This shortcut was necessitated because of the self-destructive turn my childish rebellion had taken.

At our first tutoring session, I noticed that Cantor Vogel's mouth came to a small but definitive point in the middle of his upper lip, and somehow this led me to the conclusion that the secret behind his beautiful voice was that the old man actually *was* a bird. He fluttered his liquid blue eyes, opened his mouth, and warbled ancient melodies that left us both transported. Sadly, after we had drifted back to earth, he returned to face a young man with a poor voice and no aptitude whatsoever for learning Hebrew.

"Boychick," the Cantor mused one day, "if we make it by June for your bar mitzvah, this will be my masterpiece; more likely though, my Masada. What's that—you got ants in your pants, Hennik Itzhak? Never before in all my life have I seen a youngster so restless. Never."

Cantor Vogel called me by my Hebrew name as a motivational tool; however, except for the times when his lips parted and he began to sing the blessings to me, my concentration was non-existent. When the Cantor sang, his tiny apartment, filled with plastic lawn furniture, dissolved into a world of ancient tapestries and Torahs decorated with silver. But when he stopped singing, the boiled cabbage smell returned, and I was back on 118th Street and Riverside Drive, sitting on mismatched chairs at a table of grasshopper-green Formica.

When I woke on the ill-fated Saturday of my bar mitzvah, I felt my gorge rise from nervousness and swamp me immediately. I put on my navy suit and silver tie, but my father insisted on "inspection" before leaving for the synagogue. I had chosen the wrong shoes and was returned to my room. Holding one of the offending shoes aloft like Mr. Wizard conducting a science experiment, my father observed, "Only someone from your mother's side of the family could have chosen these shoes to wear to his own bar mitzvah."

I think my father may have been secretly pleased about my decision to follow a more onerous path to getting bar mitzvahed. He showed his support that day by announcing that he was going to prepare breakfast for the family, something unprecedented. Oatmeal with heavy cream, brown sugar and raisins, orange juice, toast and butter were all brought out to the table in steady waves. I, of course, felt so nervous I could not imagine opening my mouth, let alone swallowing. Nevertheless, we sat down to breakfast as a family for the only time I can ever remember. As we ate, I spotted a cockroach in the corner. Although my parents fought about nearly everything, their most violent arguments were about the cleanliness of the house.

The cockroach was a particularly ominous sign. I decided that he was merely waiting for us to finish breakfast so he could take over and have his own meal. I prayed my father wouldn't see it, as it would have instantaneously begun another fight between my parents. Bobby had made his bed and dressed himself. He was importunately calling to Dad to come in and acknowledge that he had mastered knotting his own tie. He knew he had, but he needed my father's approval.

"Shaddup, you brat!" Dad shouted as he brought out another plate of curled Wonder Bread toast, soggy with butter. Bobby, who by now had given up waiting for Dad to come to him to supervise the tying of his tie, stuffed his shirt into his pants and ran into the kitchen to show Dad, stumbling headlong onto the kitchen floor.

"Get up and eat your toast, Bobby," I said yanking him off the ground. Since he loved to eat, I was trying to fob off as much of my food as possible on him. The more he ate, the less I was responsible for.

"Why, what's wrong with it?" he asked suspiciously. Since my story about the Fuzzie family living in the wall above his bed, he understood the depths of my deviousness and cruelty. I was well on my way to becoming my father's son.

"Nothing. Dad made a lot. Just eat as much as you can."

"Mom, did Henry spit on the toast again?"

"What a terrible thought! Besides, it's his bar mitzvah." I supposed she meant that on a normal day, spitting on the toast would have been at least plausible.

"Wow!" Bobby observed, now distracted by something else.

"Yes, isn't it wonderful?" Mom said, observing the platter of toast my father produced from the kitchen with apparently more on the way.

"No—not that. That!"

"What is it, dear?" said Mom in her happy sing-song voice.

"I've never seen one that big before, have you, Henry?"

"What?"

"That cock-a-roach—it's huge!"

"Shut up, you stupid idiot!" I said between tightly shut teeth.

Dad entered with yet another plate of toast, raising his orange juice in a toast. "Look, Henry has become a man!"

"Not yet! He still has to recite his Haftarah," Bobby said. "He won't be a man for a few hours yet, and maybe someth—"

"Shaddup," Dad shouted, before adding, "All right, everybody eat up, we have to leave soon. Bobby, that's enough toast for you." Then turning to my mother without lowering his voice, he continued, "Jesus, that kid's a fresser; the spitting image of Leon."

"That was quite uncalled for, Norman. The child heard you. Look—now he's crying! Is that what you want? Besides, Dr. Anfanger said it's baby fat, and he'll grow out of it. You know that." Bobby was whimpering in a corner, now compulsively devouring buttered toast in between sobs.

"Aw, just kidding, Bob," Dad said to mollify the situation. "How about some Cream of Wheat? We still have time, I think."

"I only eat Cream of Wheat when I'm sick! Everybody knows that!" Bobby clumped heavily back to his room and slammed the door.

"Jesus Christ, Robert. Stop that crying, Robert or … I'll give you a real reason to cry."

As I chewed yet another piece of the toast, I felt a rush of something hot in my neck, surging up into my glands. I was about to throw up. I knew the risks involved, and I had to act decisively. I also couldn't allow myself to ruin my new Best & Co. suit on the way to the synagogue. With everyone else momentarily out of the room, I took the soggy, masticated ball of toast from my mouth and tossed a thick wad behind the radiator. I imagined the roach scurrying under the radiator to get the toast, thus killing off two problems with one wad of toast. Then I threw another piece over the radiator. And another.

Rabbi Epstein conducted the beginning of the service with terse formality. I sat in a pew with my family, desperately wanting to peek over my shoulder to see who had decided to come to witness my disgrace, but Epstein's rabbinical scowl made that impossible. Finally, it was time for me to rise and step up to the bimah to recite my Haftarah. The synagogue was now full. Besides my grandparents and Uncle Lee, all my high school friends were nudging one another, making jokes, pointing and laughing. Cantor Vogel was there, too, obviously terrified and chewing his bottom lip.

I sang the short prayers without difficulty, having memorized them with the help of Cantor Vogel's record. I then realized that since no one was actually listening, it didn't matter what I sang. If I performed with confidence, I could have been singing my favorite hit, Del Shannon's "Runaway," in my patented falsetto to the congregation. People seemed to believe I knew what I was chanting. I scanned the sanctuary from the bimah, and realized that perhaps only a dozen or so temple "lifers" realized how inept I was. Armed with this revelation, I sang as never before, although I noticed Rabbi Epstein tearing at his tallis with his thumb and forefinger like a gunslinger preparing to spring a gun from his holster.

At the end of the service my Grandma and Grandpa Schvey came forward. Grandpa, who never seemed to know precisely who I was or acknowledge that I might actually be related to him, stood up. He gave me the most painful pinch on both cheeks I have, or ever expect to receive; a pinch so hard it made my eyes water. I can almost feel the pain of that pinch today.

I caught Cantor Vogel's eye as he left the synagogue and ran up to him.

"Well, boychick, you sure pulled one over on me. Who knew you could sing so good?"

"Not me, Cantor Vogel. But I was taught by a master," I said. "But do you think they noticed all the mistakes I made in my Haftarah?"

"Only Rabbi Epstein, boychickel, only the Rabbi," he said, licking his pointy upper lip with his tongue. "But that might be enough for Epstein to scratch at my hemorrhoids for the next 120 years." I didn't understand this, but it was delivered with great earnestness, and I nodded.

Cantor Vogel smiled at Rabbi Epstein, who glared back at us as though he was considering litigation for perpetrating this hoax upon the congregation.

"Don't worry, Hennik Itzhak," he said. "He'll get over it someday. I hope. Now go, have a good time. You earned it, and I earned at least a month in Miami Beach."

"But you're coming to the reception, aren't you?"

"Well, boychick, I can't ride on Shabbat, so maybe I'd better take a skip. The synagogue is way up here on 87th, and your party at the Sherry-Netherlands is all the way down on 59th. That's a long way to walk." Then he kissed me on the top of the head, and covered my right hand with both of his. "Mazel Tov, Hennik Itzhak, I'm very happy. Who knew you'd teach me something?"

"I taught you?"

"Of course, you taught me never to judge by first impressions." Then he paused and continued. "Today I learned even a *schlimazel* once in a Purim can get lucky and shoot his peepee straight into the toilet. This I learned from you today, young man."

65

I allowed this praise to wash over me, and then said, "Thank you, Cantor Vogel. But I do hope you can come to the reception."

In the car, I celebrated becoming a man by announcing I was not attending my own reception at the Sherry-Netherlands. After a brief but meaningful silence, my father pulled the Oldsmobile 88 against the curb.

"Let me get this straight," he said, shifting his weight against the vinyl front seat and turning ominously, "What exactly did you say?"

"The boy's tired, Norman," Mom said, anxiously. "And don't forget how well he did. All that Hebrew!"

"I don't give a shit about Hebrew or his bar mitzvah; I always said he was a Lerner through and through, and this proves it. You're going to the party, and you're going to have a good time, you goddam son of a bitch!"

"But Cantor Vogel told me he can't come; he can't ride in a car on the Sabbath, and—"

"Why can't he ride in a car?" asked Bobby, puzzled. "Everyone can ride in a car; maybe he's too old to drive, but he can ride in one."

"It's against his religion, Bobby dear," Mom answered sympathetically.

"I thought Cantor Vogel was Jewish? Isn't he Jewish?" Bobby asked solemnly.

"Yes dear, he is. But there are different kinds of Jews, and some of them have strange practices. There are Reform Jews like us, Conservative ones like your brother, and even Orth—"

"I don't give a good goddamn about Vogel or his Judaism. He did what he was paid to do—tutor the boy. He doesn't have to come. You, on the other hand, do. This discussion is over."

At the Grand Ballroom of the Sherry-Netherlands, a bunch of sad, old men in fire engine red tuxedos sat on folding chairs, playing popular tunes, including the Everly Brothers' "All I Have To Do is Dream" and Chubby Checker's "The Peppermint Twist". They sat there, vacant and bald. I watched my cousin Scotty dance the twist with Goodie Schuman, my first love. I hadn't seen Goodie since I had graduated elementary school, and she still had those bangs like little Rhoda Penmark, the girl in *The Bad Seed*, but at the back, her hair hung loose down her shoulders. At thirteen, she was a young woman now, whereas I was … bar mitzvahed. I could see tiny cups pointing their way through her chiffon dress. I wanted to go up to her and chase Scottie away. It was my bar mitzvah—Goodie ought to be dancing with me!

I sat on a chair in the Men's Lounge, thinking about Pinocchio and how he became a real boy at the end of the story. I was waiting for the miracle that would make me a real man. I heard a group of my friends looking for me outside: Ephraim, Pete, Georgie, and Richie. They seemed to be having fun, and came in to the lounge. Before long they all loosened their ties and tossed their jackets on the floor. Somebody rolled up one of the linen napkins and we all started playing catch. From there, the game metamorphosed into tackle football in the spacious lounge, while outside the music and dancing never stopped. The game only stopped when Grandma entered.

"What are you boys doing?"

"Playing football!"

"This is a bar mitzvah, not a football game."

"Just five more minutes, Grandma … please."

"Your father better not find out."

An old man who wanted to use the Men's Room walked in, saw the game, and turned around, muttering "Shande … shande" to himself. Then Grandma left, clicking her tongue. "Remember—your father."

The other kids left a few minutes later, and I was left alone in the bathroom. From inside one of the stalls, I heard someone enter the Men's Room; he was panting and sighing softly, muttering something incomprehensible. I peaked through the crack in the door. It was an elderly man with a red face, a beak for a nose, and an upper lip that came to a sharp point. I wanted to say something but couldn't. The old man slowly took off his spectacles, folded them, and shook his head. Then he unbuttoned his jacket and vest, and splashed his face with water. He stared at his reflection in the mirror for a long time. I was transfixed, watching, unable to speak. There was something I wanted to say, but I had no idea what it was, so I kept silent. Then he wiped off his spectacles with his tie and replaced them, put on his jacket and vest, and licked his pointy lips. He walked out of the lounge, still shaking his head in disapproval.

Why couldn't I speak? I finally left the bathroom, but I couldn't find him. I never saw Cantor Vogel again.

On Saturday mornings, Bobby and I enjoyed watching television together. Sitting in front of the TV was one of the few things I actually did with him, since he hated baseball, football, and basketball, and there was a six-year age difference between us. Occasionally, in an attempt to provoke his interest, I made him stand beside a chalked-in batter's box at PS 6 on 81st, holding a broom handle, while I fired tennis balls high and tight trying to teach him not to be afraid of the ball. Almost all these sessions ended with him running home to Mom, crying.

Oddly enough, we liked the same TV programs: *Rocky and His Friends*, *Dudley Do-Right*, *Sky King*, *Captain Midnight*, and *Winky Dink and Me*. The latter was a short-lived program that featured a marvelous gimmick. The host, Jack Barry, told all the kids to send in fifty cents, and in return you received a kit containing a pale blue magic screen which stuck right on the TV set by static electricity. With special *Winky Dink* crayons you could trace the cartoon figures right onto the magic screen, help Wink and his dog Woofer escape danger, and even receive secret messages to decode. Bobby loved anything that had to do with magic, and I thought it was pretty cool, too. After a few weeks, however, Bobby misplaced the magic screen, and that was the end of that. Or so I thought.

I didn't think twice about my father's absence when we woke up one particular weekend morning and took our normal places in front of the TV Since it was Saturday, it was normal for Sy to pick him up in his Eldorado around 8:00 a.m. He usually returned around 2:00 p.m., so his appearance just before *Winky Dink* came on was a surprise.

He walked in quietly, with his brother Malcolm at his heels, nervously smoking. The two of them walked straight back to my parents' bedroom without saying a word. The strange thing was that, as they walked past, I had my brother in a headlock, and even though I held my other hand over his mouth, there were audible whimpering sounds. Minutes before, I realized that Bobby had used his crayons on the set *without* the magic screen—and I knew there would be hell to pay if Dad discovered crayon marks on the TV.

But Dad and Uncle Malcolm didn't even seem to notice as they walked past us. They quietly entered my parents' bedroom and shut the door softly. Right after that, we heard voices rise and fall behind the bedroom door. Then they receded. I released Bobby and told him to take another look for the magic screen while I listened outside their bedroom door. After a few minutes, the sounds died entirely and I couldn't hear anything. Then I locked myself in their bathroom, listening. Their bathroom was my favorite place of refuge in the whole house, and I prided myself on my dexterity at locking the door while evading my father's pursuit. But this time, it was not a place to hide; it was a place from which I could spy on what was happening. The bedroom was silent for a long time, probably half an hour. When the door finally opened, only Uncle Malcolm emerged, dragging out the two largest suitcases I had ever seen: a matching set in ivory leather, the exact color of the tusks of the wooly mammoth in the Museum of Natural History. I noticed that each suitcase bore my parents' initials engraved in gold, along with a little brass lock. Malcolm set the two suitcases down by the door and hurried back into the bedroom. Then he and my father re-emerged carrying armloads of suits and shirts. Dad realized I was hiding inside the bathroom, but in a perfectly calm voice, asked me to come out.

"I'm leaving, Henry," he said as I stepped outside. "I can't take this anymore." His words were gentle, completely devoid of anger. He seemed more defeated than angry; then he picked up one of the ivory suitcases, tucked an armful of suits under his other arm, and quietly disappeared. Before he left, he gave me his cheek to kiss. I remember the scent of his aftershave. Then it became horribly quiet in the house for the first time ever. I didn't understand exactly what had happened, but the pit of my stomach told me all I needed to know. Life would never be the same.

Surprisingly, my mother's first reaction to my father's departure was also calm. But her silence was like the green and purple sky just before a tornado hits. Quiet filled our apartment with an ominous calm.

"Gone," she said simply.

"Yes." I didn't know what more to say.

"None of this would have happened if it hadn't been for you."

My throat was tight. "Me?"

My mind sifted through the things I had done that might have caused my father to leave us. I thought about all the lies I had told, the mess in my bedroom, my grades at school, my nails and untied shoes—even how I tried to sneak out of the house without wearing rubbers in the rain.

"Yes. He's left you."

Although I was silent, she continued as though I had contradicted her. "It's just what I said. He didn't leave me—he left you. Oh, God! I should have been the one—don't you remember? Tell me you remember! You do remember, don't you?"

"No, I don't."

"I scooped you up and took you with me to Gramsie's. You were two years old. It was right after he hit me, and I had that slipped disk and the miscarriage. We stayed there for a week. We should never have come back." Her voice remained calm and reflective. "While I was there, I asked Gramps what I should do, and he said, 'If a man is a brute, if he hurts the things he loves, it will never change. You dassent go back.'"

"We should have stayed there, Mom!" I burst out angrily, trying to take her side, fearful of what might happen next. "Gramps was right!" I thought how Gramps must have looked when he said that, and wondered if he was wearing suspenders, and if he was smoking one of those long cigars he had brought all the way back from Cuba. Then I looked back at her. But her eyes were gone now.

"Your father came up to their apartment and started banging on the door. I could see him outside through the little peephole. He begged on his knees for me to return to him! Said he would die if I didn't come back with his son."

The image of my father on his knees didn't ring true, but my mother insisted on its veracity. More important, he was asking for me.

"I locked myself in my parents' bedroom with you, and despite Gramps' warning, I felt sorry for him and told Gramsie to let him in."

"What happened then?" I asked.

"Gramsie met him at the door and told him she wouldn't let him in. He stormed passed her into the kitchen, took a carving knife from the break-front, and held it to her right breast.

"They're coming back," he told her. "And if you try to stop me, I'll slice your breast off."

And do you know what Gramsie said to his face?"

"No."

"Go ahead—cut it off! As God is my witness, that's what she said ... 'cut it off.' And then he threw the knife on the ground and started crying like a little child."

"Dad?"

"Yes, but he's not your 'dad' anymore. And just at that moment ... when I was wavering, you said—'I WANT MINE OWN HOME! I WANT MINE OWN HOME!'"

She wailed, terrifying me with her awful parody of my two-year-old self.

"Mom, I was only—"

"'I WANT MINE OWN HOME!' you screamed and kicked and made me put you down. So I listened ... so, this ... this is your fault. This is what you've done! The monster has won. I should have left. I should have been the one to leave! And now Papa is dead, and ... and—" Her voice cracked and faded away. She turned and with a bowed head walked into her bedroom like a condemned prisoner.

5.

Several months after my father left, we were evicted from our apartment. He'd refused to pay alimony until ordered by a judge to do so. We were to move into a smaller apartment around the corner from Lee and Gramsie, off Central Park West. And then, Margaret and Blackie, too, were suddenly gone. My mother told me she took Blackie to a family in Scarsdale where he would be happy. Of course I knew she was lying. But I figured Blackie would be much better off, whatever happened. A few days before he was "sent to Scarsdale," the 'whatever' nearly happened. He broke free of his leash while I was walking him. He shot back and forth across the street, narrowly avoiding the speeding cars. Standing there, I felt absolutely certain that Blackie had decided to kill himself, and had every right to do so. Being smashed by a Checker Cab would be awful for an instant, but was it worse than being tethered to the kitchen door, sleeping in his bed of urine? I respected his decision to self-euthanize.

As for Margaret, she would at last be free of the stench of the "Maid's Room." I missed watching her curl up like a little girl when we watched *Dracula*, and of course, I missed showing her how strong I was. But that was just selfishness; Margaret, like Blackie, would be better off now.

My mother arranged for me to remain at Ephraim's during the time of our move, so I was spared some of what actually happened. Once, however, when I was walking up Madison with Ephraim and a group of my friends, I saw a pile of our furniture stacked out on the street in front of our old building. I turned my head away and pretended not to see it, but Pete, Richie, and Ephraim decided to go look through it—there might be stuff we could nab. They had no idea that it was ours, of course. I just kept walking past Bolton's up Madison toward 87th, pretending not to hear; praying they would follow my lead and not see something identifiable among the debris.

Six months after we moved, our new apartment, like the old one, was still a mess. Mom refused to get rid of anything she'd brought with her from our old apartment, even though the new one was much smaller. Why should she? That would only make the bastard feel like he won. So, boxes were stacked on top of boxes until they literally touched the ceiling. The term "hoarder" was unknown at that time, but that is what my mother became. No matter how trivial, she saved it: empty Bumble Bee tuna cans, Campbell's Soup and Minute Maid tins. All were saved and placed on top of the Steinway piano. She didn't stop there. She began collecting pats of butter, sugar packets, and napkins from restaurants, and stashing them in her purse. When her purse got full, she dumped the contents on top of the piano and started over.

Worse, my mother, whom I had never even seen sip so much as a glass of wine, began drinking. I watched her carry home gallon jugs of Gallo wine in paper bags. When our eyes met, we both pretended she was carrying in groceries. Once she moved past me into the kitchen, she peered to see if I was still watching before taking a sharp right into her bedroom. She also placed three enormous Yale locks on the front door, and a fourth padlock on the door to her bedroom. When she left the house—which wasn't often—she turned up the radio full blast so the assembled thieves who were presumably waiting outside would be fooled and think somebody besides a defenseless, abandoned woman with two little boys was home. When she returned, she locked herself in her room and kept the radio blaring on maximum volume. She also began to walk differently. Instead of the stylish open-toed shoes she once favored, she began wearing orthopedic sandals, and walked with a slow, ambling shuffle. Once, when she took off the sandals, I noticed enormous bunions the size of golf balls on the sides of both her feet. Her feet had become deformed from wearing high heels for decades. But only now did her walk change; for years, she had somehow disguised her pain for appearance's sake.

After about six months in our new apartment, I came up with a brilliant idea. Since my mother was drifting away, it was now my responsibility to act. I encouraged her to get her hair done professionally. Since she stopped having it bleached at the hairdressers to save money, she colored her hair at home, and it went from blonde to platinum blonde to pink; it was now the color and texture of cotton candy. After I deliberately embarrassed her about this to get her out of the house, she reluctantly agreed to visit the salon. But this was all a ploy. While she was at the hairdresser, I decided I would clean up the apartment myself. That would cheer her up, snap her out of her doldrums, and we would become happy again. Even if we had never really been happy in the first place.

My plan was perfect. I woke up early on the following Saturday morning (I was fourteen now, too old to go with Uncle Lee to Nedicks), and as soon as Mom left the house, I dragged Bobby away from his cartoons, told him to get dressed, and marched him over to Gramsie's. I bought a giant bottle of Mr. Clean and set to work. I decided to begin by getting rid of everything I could. I threw waste can after waste can full of rubbish down the incinerator chute at the end of the hallway. I cleared the Steinway so you could actually see the mahogany again. Of course, my mother's room was padlocked, but even so, I felt I was really accomplishing something. After each trip to the incinerator, I felt better.

Then I grew tired. After a couple of hours, I began to realize that the project was far more ambitious than I had imagined. I never even opened the Mr. Clean—I looked around amid the heaps of stuff and admitted to myself that, except for the piano, nothing looked different. There was just as much crap as before. I even noticed garbage I hadn't seen previously, since it was buried under all the stuff I had thrown away. Christmas wrapping paper, Scotch tape, staplers in their plastic shields, baseball cards, phone books, the *Daily News*, Polaroid snapshots, and Welch's Grape Jelly jars with Jughead on the bottom. There was no possible way I could even make a dent in the mess before she returned. Three days wouldn't have been enough.

As I looked at our dining room, with its mix of Tiffany, antiques, and trash, idealism gave way to frustration, and then anger, as the real magnitude of the problem revealed itself before my eyes. As a child, my mother had read me the story of Philemon and Baucis, the Greek myth in which Zeus and Hermes come disguised as beggars, and ask to stay the night with the poor, elderly couple. Despite their poverty, the couple offer what little they have to the two disguised gods, and miraculously, their humble meal of bread and milk is never exhausted. Our house resembled the story of Philemon and Baucis, except in reverse. The more I threw out, the more it grew. All the garbage magically replenished itself! Despite my attempts to throw stuff down the chute, when I returned, there it was—just as much. No, there was more than before! The cleaning, begun as an act of love and concern, now filled me with anger and resentment.

Still, I thought Mom would be pleased at my gargantuan effort. Around noon, I heard her key in the lock, and raced into my room and pretended to be asleep. With my door carefully left open a crack, I saw her enter the apartment out of the corner of one eye. One by one, the series of locks that barricaded us from a hostile world clicked open. As she slithered inside and quickly locked herself in again, I listened for cries of joy. Instead, a terrifying wail like that of a mortally wounded doe reverberated through the apartment. I threw myself out of bed and ran into the living room. There she was, kneeling, her coiffed head bowed, her pale arms clinging to the massively carved leg of the dining room table. I was horrified. As she brushed the back of her left hand against her forehead, she seemed to resemble some ancient marble statue entitled *Sorrow*.

When she saw me standing in the door, her sorrow turned to hysterical anger. "Oh, how sharper than a serpent's tooth it is to have a thankless child!" she quoted from *King Lear*.

"Mom, what happened?"

"What happened? You've destroyed my life!" she keened back and forth, voice cracking. "Please, dear God above, tell me you did not throw out that yellow waste can!"

"No," I said, spotting an empty yellow pail and carrying it over to her as calmly as possible. "It's right here."

"Idiot! Not the can, you fool—what was in it!"

"What was in it?"

"Nothing, only your inheritance, your birthright! That was what was in that waste can. And you threw it out for a mess of pottage!"

"Mom, I don't know what you're talking about," I said. Then, as an afterthought, I added, "What's 'pottage?'"

"Fool! Imbecile!" she spat. Her arms were still locked around the table leg, but as she shouted at me, she uncoiled from her desolate crouch. "It's a passage from the Bible. Jacob or Esau, or somebody, sells his birthright for a mess of it. No wonder you're flunking out of school!" Then, she stood up and intoned with one outstretched finger: "You know, you gave me trouble even before you were born!"

She alluded, I knew full well, to the fact that my birth had necessitated a Caesarian section. It was something she reminded me of at moments when things got really bad. While I was thinking about this riddle from the Bible, she rushed back into her room and slammed the door. I followed her and banged on it.

She only screamed. "Nothing, nothing you can ever do will make this right. I'm going to die now, do you hear? You won't be able to do this again! Not ever! You will never see me alive again!"

"Mom, Mom, please don't!" I said. I was now near tears. "I don't even know what happened! At least tell me what was in the waste can. Maybe I can salvage it from the incinerator."

"Incinerator? You fiend! You threw that yellow bucket down the incinerator? Dear God, tell me that is not what you did."

"Yes, Mom, but there was nothing but broken glass in there."

Then, she laughed. Hysterically. And then … silence.

I pounded on the door. "Mom, don't!"

I had to do something. Anything. So I flung myself on the floor as noisily as I could, and then yelled "Unless you come out of there right now, I'll kill myself! I'm going to do it, Mom! I swear!"

I would be "dead" when she came out, unless, of course, she was already dead behind her locked door. In that case, Uncle Lee would have to figure out what to do with both corpses.

For ten minutes, I lay there on the floor, eyes closed, waiting. Then slowly, her door opened. After a minute, she nudged me with the fuzzy toe of one pink slipper. I opened one eye. Her face was still red, but her eyes were less wild.

"Do you have any idea what you did?" she said as she stood over me.

"No, how could I?"

"Oh, what a tangled web we weave, when once we practice to deceive!"

"I was just trying to clean the house—"

"Liar!" she yelled with a freshly polished forefinger stretched in my direction, but the crazed heat had gone out of her. In its place was a terrible resignation. "You deliberately threw away the crystals for the antique chandelier Papa gave me; that's what you did. It was a wedding gift from Gramps," she added sadly.

"I thought it was just a heap of broken glass."

"Why would any sane person save a bucket of broken glass?" she asked without irony. "Everyone is against me. First your father. Now you. I can't go on. Death! Death alone has the power to save me from this hell."

"Mom, listen, I'll go downstairs right now to the basement. Maybe I can salvage some of the pieces from the incinerator, maybe...." I trailed off, lamely. "I was only trying to help."

"He was only trying to help," she repeated, sarcasm dripping. Then she turned and walked back into her bedroom and locked the door.

I ran downstairs and got the key to the boiler room from the super, but of course, there was nothing to salvage. By the time I got back, Bobby had returned home in a state of euphoria from his morning with Uncle Lee. He wore a shiny black top hat and clutched a magic wand. Uncle Lee had taken him to our old magic shop.

"Look, Mom," he sang at the top of his lungs. "Look, what I can do." Lee and Bobby's return drew her back out of her room, and she even managed a weak smile as he tore up a piece of newspaper and made it reappear.

"So Mom, what do you think?" he said. Uncle Lee smiled, gently tapping on his front teeth.

She burst into tears.

"What is it, Mom? What is it?" Bobby asked. She told him what I had done, but instead of commiserating, Bobby's moon face broke out in a smile.

"That's easy, Mom—watch, I can bring it back!" He placed the empty yellow bucket upside down, tapped his new wand against the plastic, and shouted, "Alakazaam, please and thank you!" three times in a row, while Lee beamed with pride.

After I destroyed her antique crystal chandelier, my mother plunged into a deep depression. She had never shown an interest in housekeeping, and wondered how she could be expected to keep house with only one maid. Now there were none. In Philipsburg, Pennsylvania, the Lerners apparently had several maids. Her parents had spoiled her, and she was given every luxury. She was the baby sister of two much older brothers, and learned to drive, shoot a pistol, and even pilot a plane while still in her teens. But all this was in the distant past now. None of it mattered anymore.

"What's the whole life for?" Mom sighed to no one in particular. She even grew estranged from her mother and Uncle Lee who were paying our rent during this time, since my father refused to pay alimony. As far as I could tell, my mother felt abandoned by her own mother because those few people in her circle who had been left by their husbands were always sent on long cruises to the Bahamas to recover their spirits. Gramsie's idea of restoring her daughter's equilibrium was matzo ball soup and kasha.

I began losing things and walked around with my head down and shoes untied. By the time midterms came around, I received an F in three subjects, and Ds in the other two. Mom's response to my failures was curious. She never suggested the root cause of my poor performance might be my lack of studying, or even the state of the apartment, or that their failed marriage had upset me. No, she felt the source of my difficulties was directly related to the size and weight of my maroon and white Horace Mann book bag.

"Look at him, how thin he is—he can't possibly schlep all those books without stooping. Look—he's turning into a cripple!" This, she invariably addressed, not to me, but to the book bag itself. When the book bag offered no satisfactory explanation, Mom threw herself into action. I was told to order duplicates of all my heavy textbooks, and charge them to my father at the bookstore. That way I could keep a duplicate set in my locker at school and not have to carry them all home every day and end up a cripple.

I knew that this was only done, in part, out of her concern for my health, but actually was borne, in fact, out of her total sense of helplessness. When my father left, the judge refused a definitive ruling on alimony, insisting only that my father pay my tuition and all other school-related expenses, including books. By asking me to buy duplicate books, my mother was attempting to hit my father where it hurt most: in his wallet. So, I dutifully ordered duplicates of all my books even though I seldom opened the ones I had.

One chilly day as I rode the subway up to school, it occurred to me I hadn't done my homework—again. My English teacher, Mr. Ling, felt that a detailed knowledge of grammar superseded the study of literature. Glancing over the day's assignment, I knew it was hopeless. It would be easier to start devising another illness for Uncle Lee rather than to start diagramming sentences on the subway up to 242nd Street. I was no longer certain which classes I had already used Lee's congestive heart failure as an excuse for not turning in work, so I decided to abandon the whole family of cardiac illness in favor of gastrointestinal distress. It seemed plausible for a middle-aged man, who lived with his mother and gobbled Ex-Lax like candy, would suffer from something bowel related.

Late to class yet again, I feared Mr. Ling's wrath and sarcasm would be directed at me. However, to my surprise, he didn't even notice me as I slumped into my seat. Instead, he was screaming at the top of his lungs; his anger directed at someone whom he believed had deliberately trampled his flower beds. Mr. Ling was not only our English teacher, he was also the school's head gardener. Normally serene, the veins in his neck and forehead distended into thick cords, which, combined with my own guilt for being late and not having my homework done, terrified me.

Each bang of Mr. Ling's fist on the green metal desk decorated with a small bud vase and single stem made my teeth rattle. The class listened with apparent concern, but as soon as Mr. Ling turned away, I realized that everyone was in fact pleased and full of boundless admiration for the perpetrator—whoever it might be. I cast a glance at Ephraim across the aisle, nodding with metronomic regularity at Mr. Ling, while his left thumb and forefinger were simultaneously inserted deep in his nose. When I was sure Mr. Ling wasn't looking, I nudged Ephraim's less-engaged right hand, raising my eyebrows to ask if he knew who had done the deed. Words were not exchanged, of course, but his mouthed response was all too clear: Hirsch.

"This is an outrage which I tell you has moved me to tears," Mr. Ling cried. "Yes, boys, tears—and I'm not ashamed to admit that! But they are tears of sorrow as well as rage." He shut his eyes for a moment of meditation before continuing. "I am certain that someone in this room knows who committed this atrocity—yes, boys, atrocity! And I do not use the term cavalierly. Why? To murder a tender plant in its bed is for me tantamount to maiming or killing an innocent child. How could one of you, born into supposedly good families, families of wealth and privilege, be guilty of such horror? How could anyone with all your advantages—how could you choose to commit such a desecration?" Mr. Ling said this to us all, yet it seemed as though he was pointing at me for not doing my homework. I couldn't help myself, and guiltily squirmed lower in my seat.

I glanced over to where Hirsch sat, a tall, pimply boy whose sunken cheeks and striped tie gave him the look of a freshly paroled criminal at sixteen. Last term we'd read *Julius Caesar*, and it was clear to everyone in the class that Hirsch was born to play the role of Cassius of the "lean and hungry look." Yet here was the perpetrator, smiling angelically, while I was innocent, yet trembling before Mr. Ling's rage. I looked more closely, and saw his pockmarked face beam up at the teacher in ecstasy. Not Cassius, but St. Theresa of Avila had taken possession of his soul.

"I'll say no more about this, boys," Mr. Ling said, pausing just long enough to catch his breath and continue, "but I want you to know that I shall never forget this feeling of loss in my breast; nor shall I rest until this criminal is apprehended."

There was a moment of silence; then a hand shot up. It was Hirsch's!

"Yes, Mr. Hirsch?"

"Should any of us manage to identify the culprit, will we be able to reveal his identity anonymously?"

The class collectively held their breath at the boldness of his ploy. The audacity!

"A fair question, Mr. Hirsch. I understand the consequences of being considered a 'snitch' toward one's classmates, and I want you to know, that, despite my personal antipathy in the matter—which would incline me to have said individual 'unseamed from the nave to th' chops.' Ah, good, I see at least a few of you boys recall that deliciously memorable phrase from The Scottish Play. I do intend to act with discretion, as will Headmaster Gratwick. So, Mr. Hirsch, you may deliver the name of that detestable coward in confidence without fear that your identity will ever be revealed."

"Thank you, sir," Hirsch said with perfect equanimity. "Thank you very much, sir."

The class watched Hirsch's performance with reverence. Despite his pimply complexion, he wore the mask of purity to perfection; so confident was he in his parents' wealth and his own unassailable privilege at this elite preparatory school. By asking so brazen a question, he had eliminated himself from suspicion, and intimated that he might be prepared to deliver up someone else's name—an act of terrifying audacity at which we (petty criminals who thought mightily of ourselves for sneaking into the school cafeteria on a Sunday to steal ice cream sandwiches) could only gape with wonder.

Mr. Ling paused, and again I began to dread his request to turn in our homework.

However, he had another surprise in store for us. "I trust you all understand why, as school gardener, this pains me so much. Now, I must tell you that there is another matter that concerns me, and it is even more serious than the trampling of the flowerbeds outside Tillinghast Hall." He paused slightly and said, "I want you boys to take out your *Norton Readers*, please." This last was said with a frozen smile, which made my blood run cold.

"It has come to my attention by sheer chance that a few of you boys here at the Horace Mann School for Boys have apparently found it amusing to decorate—I should rather say, desecrate, your textbooks with Nazi swastikas. I want you to know that such action will not be tolerated—ever. Don't sit there gape-mouthed. Take out your *Nortons* … immediately!"

The classroom filled with the sound of book bags unzipping and pages turning. Mr. Ling stalked slowly up and down the aisles, searching book after book, but to no avail. As he came down my aisle, however, I began to sweat. Not only had I not done the sentence diagramming, but I realized that I had left my own battered, second-hand Norton at home, and had instead grabbed my spare copy—still in its manufacturer's shrink-wrapping from the bookstore—and taken it to class. Mr. Ling was now one aisle over from me and tripped over someone's book bag, nearly falling.

"Assassin!" he shouted at the boy who'd carelessly placed the bag in the aisle, before continuing his search for incriminating evidence. As Mr. Ling glanced over my shoulder, he seized my textbook. When he held it up above his head to display it to the class, light gleamed off its cellophane wrapper. I mumbled, "I've only just bought it, sir." A comment which not only failed to mollify, but produced a contemptuous snort since we were well past the midway point in the term.

Mr. Ling's fury at the desecration of his flowerbeds was now topped by his outrage toward "a pupil who has the temerity to come to class—not merely with his homework unprepared, but his textbook unwrapped!" At this point, the class's relief from Mr. Ling's menace found its outlet in laughter.

"Boys, it was doubtless my fault," he said acidly. "Why, you ask? Well, I never included instructions informing you how vital it was to actually unwrap your books before reading them! How could Henry then possibly be faulted for not opening his *Norton* when he was never specifically instructed to remove it from its cellophane? Henry, for your benefit we will in the future include a pair of scissors in your list of required school supplies." I was frostily told to remove myself to the hallway and use the momentary solitude to "crack open your textbook for the first time, and contemplate perhaps the most brazen act of negligence I have ever witnessed in the storied history of this school."

As Mr. Ling's hostility reached a crescendo of sarcasm, I was simply waved out into the hall. But as I began to leave, he stopped me with a final invective: "Wait! We do not want you to leave until we have actually seen you remove your text from its virgin sheath." At the words "virgin sheath," a new storm of hilarity broke forth, and badly shaken, I fled into the hallway.

I limped out into the hall, and a tingle crept over my shoulder blades. I had the distinct sensation that my father was watching this latest installment of my perpetual disgrace. That was, of course, impossible. My father was at work at Merrill Lynch down at One Liberty Plaza on Wall Street. I was here at 246th Street in the Bronx. Yet, nonetheless, I felt his presence.

Perhaps because I was banned from speaking to him even by telephone, my father's presence in my life at this time began to assume supernatural proportions. Their divorce had not yet been finalized, so my mother felt justified in forbidding me to contact him. Nevertheless, I saw him everywhere, cursing at me to tie my damn shoelaces, shouting to put on my rubbers, tie my tie properly, or comb my hair. I headed to the bathroom to pee and splash water on my face, hoping that when I came out, the creepiness of being haunted by his imagined presence would be gone. But when I returned to the hallway outside Mr. Ling's classroom, that feeling persisted. Instead of just standing outside Mr. Ling's class, I thought I might walk down the hall and see if the school canteen was open....

And then I saw him. Outside, squinting through an enormous plate glass window maybe twenty feet away, his brows thunderously curled up into his wavy hair—my father. I wanted to run, but where could I go? Not back into the bathroom—and certainly not back into the classroom. In utter panic, I stood stock-still, hoping he wouldn't see me. But he did. Of course he did.

"What the hell are you doing here?" His shape, distorted by the glass, almost persuaded me I was hallucinating. He called out again, "Get over here!" So I walked closer to the window. Then, with predatory mildness, he said, "I mean outside—the car is waiting."

I stood frozen, unable to move. Why was my father not at work? Why was he peering through the window of my school? And why had he appeared at the precise moment I had been tossed from class? There seemed to be something deeply amiss in the world's order to cause all these things to descend upon me at once. Seeing me dither, his impatience escalated.

"Get out here now! Now! What the hell are you doing out in the hallway? They told me you had English until 10:40. Get in the goddamn car."

I left the building, ducked into his Lincoln, still not sure if what was happening was real.

"Dad … why … why are you here?"

"None of your business," he said, somehow screwing his body deeper into the plush leather. "None of your goddamn business."

"Does Mom know?" I asked as we hurtled across the Triborough Bridge.

"Know what?"

"That you came to school to get me."

"Why would she need to know?"

"Because … she has custody of me." I figured this was the best way to provoke him into communicating.

"Go to hell. Since when has her custody meant anything to you?" He knew, I believe, that my anger towards him was matched by my disdain for my mother. I hated both of them for dividing me between them like a piece of meat, and particularly despised my mother's claim of "custody," and the suggestion of ownership.

I was silent for the rest of the ride. We pulled up to LaGuardia Airport, and he told me to get out.

"Wait for me at the American Airlines commuter desk."

Instead of going inside, I stood there dumbstruck. Then, in a state of utter panic, I actually considered running away. If I ran away, he wouldn't find me. But where would I go? I couldn't very well reappear at school, and I didn't want to go back home either and have to explain myself.

Moments later, the decision about whether or not to flee was rendered moot. "Hey—I thought I told you to wait for me inside. Never mind. C'mon—we'll miss our flight."

"Flight? What flight? What do you mean? Where are we going?" I asked as he preceded me through the glass doors.

"What do you think happens at an airport? You'll find out soon enough. Tie your shoes. They won't allow you on the plane like that."

"What do you mean, I'll 'find out'? I've never even flown before!"

"Well, then, this'll be a memorable experience." His acid smile was hardly reassuring.

We walked through the terminal until I saw the sign for Commuter Flights. Previously, I had looked forward to my first airplane ride as an adventure. Now I was paralyzed with fear. Boarding a plane for the first time reminded me of the time I went swimming in a lake, when we went to pick out Blackie from a litter of puppies owned by one of Dad's business associates in Westchester. I was six, and hadn't yet learned to swim properly. I eased myself into the shallow end of a small pond, imagining I would be able to touch the bottom. But as I waded in, as I had in the swimming pool, I suddenly sank! My mouth filled with water, my arms flapping like a tiny bird. Since neither of my parents swam, I had to be fished out of the pond by my father's friend. When I emerged, coughing and shivering, I saw Mom crying and Dad laughing. Since then, I'd hated swimming.

"You sit by the window," my father said as we boarded the tiny plane.

"Why do I have to sit there?" I assumed I was being punished for something.

"Because I can't hear out of that ear." I had forgotten about his deafness in one ear, which in turn reminded me of why he wasn't supposed to swim for fear of losing his hearing altogether. It was why he couldn't have assisted in my rescue, even had he wanted to.

84

"Does Mom know where you're taking me?"

Silence.

"Well, does she?" I asked again.

"No."

"Dad, where are we going? Mom ... I insist." I unbuckled my seat belt as a show of defiance, even though the engines were running.

"You insist?" he spat. "Put your seat belt back on. We're about to take off."

Instead of sitting back down, to assert my independence, I stood up abruptly. And smashed my head into the cabin ceiling.

"Why don't you sit down before you knock yourself out?" he asked drily. Then continuing, "Since you insist on knowing, I guess I'll have to tell you."

"Where then?"

"Vermont."

"Vermont? What's in Vermont?"

"Maple syrup, mountains, skiing. Anything else you need to know?"

"Thanks. I was aware of that." Against my will, I smiled at his little joke. Why? I was drawn into his game to diminish the scope of his crime. He had kidnapped me from school, was taking me to Vermont without either asking me if I wanted to go or telling my mother or getting her consent, and I was playing along with his banter like a little kid, even though I still had no idea where or why I was going. *What the hell is wrong with me?*, I thought. I bit the inside of my cheek so I wouldn't smile. Ever again. The pain made my eyes water.

"So you're crying now?" he said, with disgust.

"No. I just ..." I dabbed at a tear with my necktie. Now that I had laughed and cried, I knew he would answer me. "Dad, where are we going? Seriously, I want to know."

"We're looking at schools. Boarding schools."

"What?"

The propellers revved up to full speed and the plane lurched forward like a clumsy dog. A few seconds later, we were rumbling down the runway; I looked out the window. We were airborne, drifting unsteadily over houses and factories and baseball diamonds.

"You heard me, didn't you?" my father said, but I didn't answer. I couldn't. I was choked with fear. Besides, I needed to concentrate, thinking that in

85

doing so, I could keep this ridiculous machine airborne. I waited, clutching the sleeve of my father's houndstooth sports jacket until I felt confident that the pilot could continue his ascent without my help.

"Wh—why are we looking at schools in Vermont?"

"Number one—you're flunking out of Horace Mann. And two, you need to get away from your mother, or she'll ruin you. You want to turn out like Scrambled Eggs?" We were still ascending, but I knew in my heart that this trip would end badly for me.

"And what about you? What do you want to turn me into?" I blurted this out, not knowing why, but somehow trying to assert myself against the inevitable. If I was going down, at least I needed to have him take some responsibility for my failure. I surprised myself with the question, and he turned his head away, muttering, "Maybe you need to get away from me, too, I don't know...." It was an extremely rare moment of candor from my father. I looked out the window, wondering how we could stay aloft against every law of gravity? And really, I didn't want to reflect on anything else.

The plane banked a turn and flew out over the Long Island Sound; I stretched my hand out nervously and tugged at my father's sleeve for support. I kept it there. It was a gesture I both regretted and needed. Even so, there was no sign my touch affected him either way.

"Why didn't you tell me about this before?" I asked, finally removing my hand.

"Would you have come with me to Vermont if I had said, 'pretty please'? Well, would you?" He smiled, and we bounced from side to side, forcing my elbow to brush against his arm.

"No. I guess not."

"Your mother and I will be officially divorced soon."

His words shocked me. I had known it was coming, of course, but hearing him say it out loud was still a shock. I turned away from him and stared out the window. My eyes burned.

After a few minutes, my father continued. "I couldn't stand living in filth any longer, and you shouldn't want to, either. As for your brother ... he belongs with the Lerners." Bobby was nine and had adamantly refused to see him. He accompanied our mother night and day, and believed her narrative ("Your father hasn't abandoned me; he's abandoned you") completely. This allegiance confirmed to Dad that he belonged with my mother's side of the family.

I, on the other hand, refused to take sides: I disliked both of my parents in equal measure. But, the previous month, I decided I ought to see my father on weekends. For the past few months, he had been trying to reach out to me, and I actually felt sorry for him. I had no idea why, anymore than I understood why I laughed at his feeble attempts to get me to laugh. When he called, my mother picked up the other phone to listen in. As soon as she heard his voice on the other end of the line, she screamed that I needed to get off and slammed down the receiver. When he drove over to our apartment to pick me up, she refused to allow me to go. These visits were invariably accompanied by screaming matches, with George the doorman as hapless referee. While I did pity my mother, who was drinking and losing her bearings in our dark apartment filled with the detritus of their life together, I also felt sorry for my father. For some reason, his violent aggression was even more sympathetic to me than my mother's self-pity. I still don't know why.

As we descended, I was jerked from my reverie by the absolute certainty we were going to crash into one of the mountains. The one thing that gave me a measure of confidence in our survival was my father's calm presence: solid, masculine, and unafraid. I slipped my hand into his. Again, he had no reaction.

"We have an interview with the headmaster in an hour," he said. "When we land, comb your hair, straighten your tie, and for Christ's sake, use your handkerchief. You look like you've been crying the whole flight. Jesus Christ!"

I didn't end up transferring. Because of my failing grades at Horace Mann, neither school would accept me unless I agreed to repeat my junior year. On the cab ride back to the airport, we hardly spoke. My father looked morose, as if his entire plan to get me away from Mom had failed. Then he asked what I thought. My response was to think of my mother, and how she would feel if her *Quiz Kid* son, her gifted genius who was toilet trained at six months and skipped first grade—was going to be held back. It would destroy her. I didn't say this; I simply shook my head at my father's silent queries.

My father, who usually communicated through angry outbursts or blows, this time, for some reason, showed restraint. It was one of the few times I can remember that he didn't lose his temper. And as he dropped me back home at my mother's apartment, we both knew that his plans to send me to boarding school would not come to pass; that I wouldn't be leaving Horace Mann after all.

The kidnapping brought about a significant change in my relations with both my parents, but it was the opposite of what I might have imagined. I now shared a guilty secret with my father, which brought us closer together. He never once told me not to tell my mother about our trip. But he knew me well, perhaps better than I admitted to myself, and knew I wouldn't snitch. Besides, I couldn't make myself tell her about it. I knew she would assume I was an all-too-willing accomplice in my own abduction. Or maybe I simply wanted to avoid revisiting the feelings of shame and humiliation I had felt about being removed from school completely against my will. Oddly, I now felt tied to my father by an invisible thread of mutual transgression. Outlaws. There would always be that special time together, never mentioned even when we were alone. The time he surprised me at school and we flew off to Vermont, just the two of us. Both terrible and wonderful. Almost like Christmas.

Mr. Herman was five-foot-three, and wore his hair clipped to his scalp in a tight black stubble. His thick, black-framed glasses were perched on his broad, flat nose. Sometimes, he wore dark glasses in the classroom. He wore this same uniform to class every single day—black suit, black tie, white shirt. I had never before seen anyone who looked like this, and to me he cut an imperious, monastic figure. The few times I actually saw him walking in between classes or to the teacher's lounge, I noticed his walk was spare, angular, and self-possessed; no wasted motion. It seemed strange to actually see him outside the classroom, so I looked away. He belonged in front of a class, seated and in control. His mind knew no limits; he had read everything, traveled everywhere, and knew every conceivable language, from Russian to Italian and Sanskrit. But more than his self-evident brilliance, there was a strange, separateness that was unique among my teachers. This distance was accompanied by a particular habit which I have never witnessed elsewhere. He might be speaking to our class about a poem and suddenly drift off mid-sentence. While he was in one of these trances, the class of fifteen or so boys just sat there, gazing ahead, afraid to utter a sound. He gazed out the window for a minute or two, then continued in mid-sentence without losing a beat or acknowledging his unexplained absence to us.

Nearly all the teachers at Horace Mann School for Boys cultivated eccentricities at that time, but none was as bizarre as Mr. Herman. We all wore ties and suit jackets to school, and we belonged to a "Form," like English public schools, rather than to grades. Combs and nail files were mandatory at all times. In this rarified atmosphere, most teachers cultivated odd tics, which would be out of bounds even a decade later when girls were finally admitted, not to mention a later age of political correctness or sexual misconduct. Mr. Reilly threatened to use his blackthorn stick on our bare backsides; Mr. Oliver, a rotund French teacher who channeled Orson Welles' deep baritone, warned of dire consequences looming above those unable to present their combs and nail files on command; Mr. Wooster actually kicked boys in the shins beneath their desks, and if they tried to evade punishment, would literally chase them around the classroom. We called our teachers "Sir," and they addressed us formally as Mister.

Even among this bizarre group of eccentrics, Mr. Herman was set apart. He alone used an ironic, contemptuous tone towards his students, suggesting he was possessed of esoteric knowledge and spiritual illumination that others were simply not privy to. If you listened closely, you might actually be permitted to kneel at the feet of the master, but never soar to his heights. Because he dwelled in some other world so obviously superior to ours, I never saw the other kids mock him the way they did lesser teachers. Who was this man? Where did he come from? No one knew, but at fourteen it seemed to me like a wonderful and exotic place to live.

Mr. Herman was just as fastidious and authoritarian about his dress and behavior as my father, but his style was monochrome black and white, in contrast to my father's taste for colorful neckwear or flowing pocket handkerchiefs. Instead of trying to obviously control my thoughts, he craved nothing; inscrutable, he seemed to pursue only solitude and enlightenment. His mind was full of poetry, exotic cultures, and cryptic myths; above all, he seemed to live for and be in tune with the great artistic minds of the ages. He showed us long lists of the greatest painters and writers, lists we were advised to copy down and memorize. Genius—that was it! Around Mr. Herman, genius was something palpable, something I felt I could touch. His class offered me what I wanted—an escape into the magical world of literature, art, and music. There were no screaming parents, no awkward little brother; in fact, there was no one I recognized. Instead, I was able to peer into the entrance of a Prospero's cave where none but the spiritually pure might dwell. One day, if I followed his lead, maybe I would be initiated, be admitted to his sublime monastery of the mind.

Forced to re-take English after getting a D in Mr. Ling's class, I found myself in Mr. Herman's Summer School class amid a group of ten or so weak students who simply needed to somehow pass and move on. I quickly came under his spell, and convinced myself I was different from the others who, Mr. Herman suggested on a daily basis, were merely taking up space and wasting his precious time. He introduced me to Shakespeare and Leonardo, Dostoevsky and Dali, and a host of obscure artists whom he alone seemed to know and admire. These great men were no longer simply names. Now they seemed like fellow travelers; like myself, they were searching for meaning in an obscure world. Perhaps one day, if I dedicated myself, I might even join their pantheon.

Now when I went back to the Cloisters, where once, in second grade, I bent down and kissed Goodie Schuman's Luden's-flavored lips, I submerged myself in the culture of the Middle Ages, imagining the sting of the Crucifixion on my own flesh. I went to the Metropolitan and the Frick museums, to concerts—always alone—but armed with a notebook to scribble down my thoughts, images, ideas. I discovered there might be a place for me, and it had nothing to do with family, friends, grandparents, or anyone else. The door to a strange, exotic cave had been prized open. I began to slowly squeeze myself through its tiny opening.

Mr. Herman mentored by example, rather than instruction. He showed his obvious contempt for the class. When one boy asked who Italian playwright Luigi Pirandello was, Herman replied solemnly that he was a Portuguese astronaut. The boy copied it down, hoping he would be asked the name on a test. He never spoke that way to me; if he had, I would have been crushed. So oblivious did he seem to what was going on around him, I wasn't even sure he knew my name. One day after a particularly inspiring class on early Renaissance art, I dared approach the master. He sat gazing out the window, hands clasped under his chin, unaware of my existence. I stood at attention beside his desk, trembling and biting my nails, realizing he was immersed in one of his trances. Although the bell rang for my next class, I chose to wait. I told myself not to glance at my watch, since even thinking about being late was a betrayal of the wisdom Mr. Herman might conceivably bestow on me if and when he awoke.

The silence lasted many minutes, until out of weakness and fatigue I rested my palm lightly on the corner of his desk. Still, he continued to gaze imperturbably into the distance while I waited patiently for him to descend from whichever mountain top he was standing upon, hoping sometime before the last subway train departed from 242nd Street, that he might acknowledge my existence. I had apparently chosen a poor time for my pilgrimage. As time passed, I thought how wonderful it would be to dwell in the spiritual palace he inhabited rather than the squalid hut I lived in with my mother and brother. To be present, yet remain absent, to the things of this world. This was what genius was—pure genius.

"Yeth? What ith it?" (the great man had a slight lisp). My body was slouched, bent over his desk—and I knew the magic moment had come and gone. But I ventured a word.

"I'm sorry, sir. I … umm … just wanted to tell you how much I am enjoying your class." There was only silence, but I bravely took things a step further. "I've know I've done badly in all my other classes … but in yours … I … umm, I would like to do better … I've never felt—er, experienced anything like … I just wanted you to know that … in spite of everything … I'm sorry.…."

"The fool who persists in his folly will become—what?" These magical words wafted up toward me as our eyes met for a split second. I shivered. "Listen closely to me now, Henry." He continued in a whisper so soft I had to bend my body almost at a forty-five degree angle. He was telling me something, but it was delivered in a kind of secret code, or a riddle like the Sphinx offers the Thebans in *Oedipus*. Damn it, I thought in a panic, I can't understand what he's saying.

91

What if I don't give the right answer, then what? He'll think I'm stupid, like everyone else. Why else would I be in summer school? He'll lose interest. All the teachers know what kind of a crappy student I am—word gets around. What if I make something up and it sounds ridiculous? What if I pretend to understand what he's saying when I obviously don't? Oh, God! That would be the unforgivable sin. It was best to confess my ignorance. So, raising back up, I said, "I don't know, sir."

"The fool who persists in his folly will become … wise!" he shouted grandly.

What can he be talking about? I wondered. But it was too late; his gaze had gone and he was out the window again. This was going slowly, it was true, but at least I had determined that Mr. Herman knew my name, my first name. That was something; no, more than something—it was an enormous validation.

Then he spoke again. "'Everything possible to be believed is an image of truth.' This is one of the 'Proverbs of Hell' by William Blake. Have you heard of him? Of course you haven't. How could you? Go, go and read *The Marriage of Heaven and Hell*. Immediately! Then come back and see me." He waved me off. "Now go!"

"Yes sir, I will sir. Thank you, sir."

As I moved toward the exit, he jumped up from behind his desk, startling me. I stopped and turned around. He began to recite—shouting the words—as though the words were printed in flaming letters at the back of the classroom:

Hear the voice of the Bard!
Who present, past and future sees
Whose ears have heard,
The Holy Word
That walk'd among the ancient trees.

"Blake, sir?" I asked from the doorway.

"Of course, William Blake. Think about those divine words, my dear."

"I will, sir. Thank you, sir. I'll go to the library right now, and read everything I can about Blake, sir. Thank you very much!"

I was drenched in sweat, head spinning as I closed the door. The Great Man had spoken, knew my name, even called me "dear." Maybe he had given me some sort of blessing. In any case, it was something to hold on to.

I cut my next class and took the subway downtown to the Donnell Library on 53rd and 6th to find out who this Blake fellow was. But while I was sitting there staring, trying to make sense of Blake's weird prophecies, the thought kept pounding in my ears: Mr. Herman knows my name. He called me Henry. Mr. Herman said "dear" to me.

It was a revelation.

Looking back now, that crazy moment probably salvaged high school for me. It gave me a sense of burgeoning self-worth. It made me think that maybe, just maybe, someone could see in me something beyond failure, something beyond a D- student without skill or prospects, who bit his nails and couldn't keep his laces tied, who lived with a mother who lived in a locked bedroom filled with boxes of garbage, and a father for whom money and power were paramount.

Maybe I could become an artist. Mr. Herman had said: "Hear the voice of the Bard!" Why had he said that to me? Someday I might write something that would live on, even if whatever I wrote would be less incomprehensible than William Blake's. I read *The Marriage of Heaven and Hell*, and tried to read *The Book of Urizen*. It made no sense at all to me, but that didn't matter—the book's prophetic tone was proof of its profundity! I had been chosen. Delivered from slavery. Of course, I would work to become an artist.

I began to read everything I could get my hands on, and spent my evenings reading far more than I was capable of understanding. But had I not been given a sign? A promise? Yes, the great man intimated that one day I might evolve into a different sort of human being from the abject failure I knew myself to be. My mother chastised me for "escaping" into literature and taunted me with the name "Holden Caulfield" in reference to Salinger's hero. I had asked him, and Mr. Herman told me that there was nothing wrong with escape. Escaping into a world of books, he suggested, was far better than the "reality" of one's miserable life, wasn't it? True greatness involved relinquishing lesser concerns, removing lesser people.

"Why did Hamlet feel no remorse about the deaths of Rosencrantz and Guildenstern?" he asked. I did not know. "The elect need not concern themselves with such things," he said.

It was rumored among the boys in the Upper School that Mr. Herman had inappropriately close relationships with a few of his favorites. Why wasn't I selected as one of the chosen? Some, I had heard, had even gone to visit him at his home—an unimaginable honor! I was never included in this elite group and remember how envious I was of those strange, brilliant boys whom Herman singled out for special attention. Many of them were from broken homes like me, and I started to notice that they even began to talk, walk, dress, and cut their hair like him! They even fell into trances just as he did! I would have given anything to have been invited into this tiny circle, to worship at the feet of this high priest. He mentioned that he planned to lead a trip of boys to Perugia, Italy, to study Italian Renaissance art. I saw my father and begged him to let me go. I cried when he refused.

Decades later, reading about the serial pedophilia that took place at Horace Mann during the 60s and 70s, it occured to me that my father's refusal to let me go may have saved my life. Who knows what happened to those "lucky" boys who went with him to Perugia? Numerous stories of Herman's emotional abuse of his students over decades have now been documented. They suggest that he deliberately crossed the line separating pedagogy and pedophilia; his need to control young minds grew indistinguishable from the actions of a predator. Now in his eighties, he still lives in a lavish home in California bought for him by grateful former students. Some of these acolytes still apparently live with him decades after they graduated. It is said that they support "Daddy's" every whim; dressing like him, drinking special cocktails, and taking their meals together. Herman's home is called "Satis House," after Miss Havisham's splendid residence in *Great Expectations*. Like its model in Dickens, this latter-day Satis House is a place where time has stopped.

After coming under Mr. Herman's influence, I chose to be alone. I avoided my friends after school, then stopped seeing them altogether. Instead of living people, I discovered companionship in a pantheon of literary figures who were more real and more interesting than anyone I actually knew. Foremost among these was Holden Caulfield, of course, whom I began to imitate by popping up the collar of my jacket, and flinging a long muffler over my shoulder. But in addition to Holden, each week brought on some new, fantastic identity. I copied down Mr. Herman's eclectic suggestions of what I should read in a special notebook. While I now avoided homework as mundane and beneath me, I scrupulously embraced these titles, and saw in their heroes more interesting versions of myself. I took these treasures with me to the wooden benches of Grand Central Station, where I sat among bums and drunks, reading *Crime and Punishment* or *The Castle* until late into the night. Then I walked home to my mother's apartment to sleep.

Due to my new feverish interest in literature and art, I started doing better in English classes and was able to pull up my average to a C. I didn't have to repeat classes at summer school as I had in previous years. I wanted to be as far away as possible from my parents and Horace Mann until I had to return next fall. My father found me a job as an assistant camp counselor upstate in Cold Spring, New York, sixty miles from the city. I would have time to read, be far from home, and even earn some money. I had no idea how it would change my whole life.

The basketball court, of all places, was where I first met him. I had given up sports as not befitting my new artistic vocation. However, during the first week of orientation at Surprise Lake Camp, I observed counselors playing half-court pick-up games of two-on-two in the evenings. The courts were lit, and the weird yellow glare on the smooth green surface of the courts gave the pick-up games a glamorous theatricality. I watched the other counselors play, but chose not to participate, Herman Hesse's *Siddhartha* tucked firmly into the waistband of my shorts.

As I stood by watching these middle class kids from Long Island trying to play ball, I noticed one boy who obviously knew what he was doing.

Instead of just chucking the ball up and waiting for the rebound to clang off the rim, he remained under the basket waiting for his teammates to shoot from the outside. He knew how to box out his opponent, and put back the rebound for an easy layup. His game was disciplined and physical. Finally, someone around here knew how to play basketball.

During the break between games, I carefully placed *Siddhartha* on a small patch of grass, and started shooting around with the others. Seeing that I was no worse than most, I was asked to join in a makeshift tournament. I said no, until the boy who had so impressed me with his physical presence and determination looked in my direction and encouraged me—then I said "yes." We were about the same height, but he was a few years older and maybe twenty-five pounds heavier. He introduced himself as Adar. It means "Noble" in Hebrew, he said to me.

In the glow of the floodlights, there were perhaps a dozen counselors watching our game, but it felt like I was at Madison Square Garden warming up. The game began and I was on fire, hitting virtually every outside shot I took. Adar and I worked together like a machine, beating team after team, sometimes with cleverness and passing, other times through my outside shooting or his rebounding. After hitting one long jumper from about twenty feet, I turned and watched Adar smile. That said it all: we could win, and we would win the tournament. We were a team. I saw Adar tear his shirt off at the start of the next game where we were to be "skins," and held my breath: sweat trickled in rivulets down the line of hair on his bronzed chest toward his navel. His muscular body seemed like that of a man—not skinny, undefined, and hairless like mine—and it was with difficulty that I tore my eyes away.

After we won the tournament, we talked and realized we had more in common than just basketball. He was a painter, he said. These words, delivered with absolute certainty and purpose, ripped through my body like a jolt of electricity: a painter! I told him about my love of art and my solitary afternoon visits to the art museums in the city. He was from Brooklyn, and had never been to the Frick. This emboldened me to talk about how much I knew, then to confess something I had never told anyone before: I hoped one day to become a writer. Saying those words aloud was like tasting a magic draught—bitter and strange on the tongue. I swallowed, and the utterance was now inside me! Saying it aloud to Adar—his very name suggested strength—made it seem that much more real. Maybe I could become something other than Norman and Rita's idiot son, a failure in school, losing things, a boy shuffling through New York City tripping over his laces—maybe one day I could possess the kind of greatness that Mr. Herman had told me was known only by the truly great: Shakespeare, Michelangelo. That night our friendship began; we stayed up all night talking about Nietzsche's idea of the Superman; about great, tormented artists; about Van Gogh, Beethoven, and Dostoevsky. About where our dreams would take us, and where we would take our dreams. By the next morning I felt I already was a writer, just as he was a painter. The following day he introduced me to his favorite: Ayn Rand and her philosophy called "The Virtue of Selfishness." He leant me his copy of *The Fountainhead*.

"The people around us are all so small," Adar said extending a tightly muscled forearm. "We must never allow ourselves to become diminished." I instantly thought of Mr. Herman, and what he had said about Hamlet's indifference to sending Rosencrantz and Guildenstern to their deaths: "The elect need not concern themselves with such things."

"From what you have told me," Adar said, "I know you are far more than the sum of the inferior people who gave you birth," he said. "And as you grow into the person you are destined to become, this gap will only grow wider and more visible." He had never allowed his parents to control him, he said. Since he had been a child, he had gone to work. Even now, at Surprise Lake Camp, he was working to pay his tuition for art school in the fall. I was ashamed that I went to a private school like Horace Mann, and even more ashamed at never having to earn a cent in my life. I couldn't imagine having to work at a job to pay for my education. It was always a given that I would go to college, and that it would be paid for by my father. That was how things worked in my world.

Talking with Adar gave me a sense of my latent power, yet our conversations also filled me with a sense of my own weakness and dependence compared with his. He never said it in so many words, but it was implied: I was the spoiled child of wealthy parents; I never had to work or fight for anything, even my own freedom. As he said, "You have not yet begun to take responsibility for yourself; and if you don't, you can never become an artist. Or a man." The words stung. But they also thrilled with promise.

One night after he put his campers to bed, we walked for a mile or so to be alone, away from the camp. This was technically against the rules, but what did we care about rules? At the edge of a field, Adar stopped. I did the same. I assumed he wanted to sit down, so I sat on a tree stump circled by sweet-smelling grass. Adar, however, maintained his upright position.

"You're their creature, you know," he said, towering above me. His eyebrows were dark, much darker than the color of his sandy hair, and they nearly met in the middle of his forehead. His face had a gravity my contemporaries lacked. "Until you're financially free, you'll never be emotionally free," he said with certainty. "You will remain enslaved." His words had an Absoluteness to them, which was terrifying.

"You don't understand," I said feebly, looking up. "It's not that easy...."

Adar shrugged. "What is true is never easy," he said, walking ahead of me and flinging the words back over his shoulder.

I scrambled to catch up.

By the time we returned to our bunks, I realized how dependent I was on my parents to provide not only food and lodging, but even a weird kind of security. That was why I was a slave. Until I was truly free—economically and emotionally—I would never be able to create.

It didn't take long for me to confide in Adar about my parents, including the physical beatings I received from my father throughout childhood. I told him about my father's belt buckle, which had scarred my thighs and bottom so visibly I was ashamed to undress at Phys. Ed. I even told him about my abduction to Vermont, which I had sworn to myself never to tell anybody else as long as I lived. Before we had known one another two days, I had unearthed all the secret places of my heart. I told him about Mr. Herman, and the discoveries I had recently made. Night after night we expressed our amazement at the depth of our friendship, and how superior we were compared to others, not only to the shallow counselors at Surprise Lake, but to people everywhere. If we remained true to ourselves and our mission, we were destined to become the leaders of an artistic revolution! As soon as I began writing, I would share my work with him, and he would show his paintings to me. We would visit museums, go to movies together. The future, which, until very recently seemed non-existent, was now filled with exciting possibilities. There was no limit to what we could achieve.

In the midst of dreaming about our "Union," as Adar aptly called it, we dismissed our mundane duties as camp counselors. Being older and having been at Surprise Lake before, Adar's duties were far more onerous than mine. I was only a junior counselor. But we both dismissed the irksome reminders of our delinquency as beneath us: what were a bunch of spoiled, rich kids compared with the bright, new world unfolding around us?

A reprimand was delivered from the camp director that we had been reported absent from the campgrounds. We joked about the director's pompous tone, his typewritten message on Surprise Lake stationery. Then a personal message came, threatening Adar with dismissal, and me with suspension. We were summoned to meet with Mr. Meyer, the camp director.

Mr. Meyer was wearing a Surprise Lake Camp staff T-shirt and matching shorts, like we did, only he wore socks that went up to his knees like a scout master's. His cabin had real furniture in it, not just stacks of bunks. He even had a window air conditioning unit. There were framed photographs of smiling campers dating back to the 1930s. He smiled and offered us a seat on a couch, and as we sat, a Negro woman who worked in the kitchen came in and passed us a plate of chocolate chip cookies. I took a cookie; it was still warm from the oven.

"No thank you," Adar said abruptly. I quickly put my cookie back on the plate. I wasn't going to have a cookie if Adar didn't have one, too.

Mr. Meyer addressed himself to Adar. "You boys seem to be getting along well. I'm pleased to see that. We like our counselors getting along; it's a part of the Surprise Lake experience to make us all feel like one happy family." He smiled and paused. "But our first responsibility is and must be to our campers; our second is to their parents; and only the third is to ourselves. What concerns me here is that you boys seem to have forgotten those priorities, and placed your friendship above your responsibilities as counselors, for which you are being paid. Mr. Bornstein, you have now received two warnings about not properly monitoring your campers, and I trust that there will not be need for a third." A lengthy pause followed during which I grew increasingly nervous. Where was this heading? I looked at Mr. Meyer; then back at Adar. Should we apologize? Or should we just hang our heads and return chastened to our cabins?

To my surprise, Adar said nothing. From where I sat, he seemed to be glaring at Mr. Meyer with smoldering brows and clenching his powerful jaw muscles. I was frightened by the heavy silence. It reminded me of my father's tone, and as a child, I knew what was required. When Mr. Meyer's eye turned to me, I stammered that I was sorry—it would not happen again. Mr. Meyer seemed pleased and stood up.

"Well, that's it, boys. I'm glad to see you both understand, and that this transgression will not be repeated." Mr. Meyer held out his hand, and I stuck out mine to accept his handshake. The cookies were still there by the window.

Adar, however, did not. He continued to sit there on the couch, glaring at Mr. Meyer. He then said something I would never have dared utter to an adult: that we had nothing to apologize for. We hadn't gone off camp grounds, we had just taken a short walk while his campers were asleep. They were not in danger, and he resented the implication that he had been derelict in his duty.

"Mr. Bornstein, I decide—not you—what constitutes our campers' well-being at SLC." Mr. Meyer's voice was now raised, and I noticed that the plate with the chocolate chip cookies was gone. "If I can't trust you to be responsible when you are on duty, to make those campers your first and your only priority, well, you are not the counselors I thought you were." There he paused slightly to give us a chance of expressing real contrition. "I have a right to be concerned. You see that, don't you?"

"No, Mr. Meyer, I don't." said Adar. "And since I don't, I'm afraid I'm going to have to tender my resignation."

"What?" said Mr. Meyer, his voice unexpectedly cracking. "How am I going to find two new counselors now?"

"That's not my responsibility," Adar said, standing up. How could he say this to a grownup? Wasn't he afraid?

"I had been hoping to make this right, now I see that's impossible." Adar was silent. "What about you, Henry? You've only just begun working here at SLC. I took you on as a last minute favor to your father; I can't imagine he'll be happy to find out you left after just a little more than a week. Good luck trying to find another job."

I reddened, shaken by Mr. Meyer's sudden invocation of my father. Then I thought of Adar. I told myself it had been a matter of principle; we had been unfairly accused. Then I mumbled, "I'm resigning, too."

"I didn't hear that, Henry." Once I repeated it a bit louder, he continued. "All right, boys, since you have both apparently made up your minds, I guess that will be it. I'm very sorry that this had to happen. I had high hopes for you, Henry. Adar, you would have been up for promotion to senior counselor next summer with a significant pay increase. Sam will drive you to the train station." He held out his hand for me to shake a second time, but Adar stepped between us.

"That won't be necessary, sir. We'd prefer to walk. We'll make our own way back from Cold Spring."

I had no money, but I assumed Adar must have resources for us to take the train back to Grand Central. Otherwise, why would he refuse a lift to the station?

As we were leaving, Mr. Meyer pulled me aside. I told Adar I would join him in a second.

"I apologize, Mr. Meyer, but my decision is—"

"This is not about Surprise Lake. It's about him."

"Who do you mean?" I asked knowing full well.

"There's something wrong with that boy. The anger inside. I'm worried about him ... and about you."

Adar had no money for the train either. It was a matter of principle, he said, not to ask for help from Meyer or his staff. So, we gathered our duffle bags from our bunks and began the sixty-mile trek back to New York City. We passed through little towns like White Plains, Harrison, Rye, Mamaroneck, Larchmont, and New Rochelle. On one occasion, a police car pulled us over and two officers got out and asked us to come along with them. The thrill of being threatened with arrest! But in the end they did little more than warn us about our safety, asking for our names and addresses and whether our parents knew where we were in the middle of the night. Then they let us continue on our way. We slept in sleeping bags in deserted fields under the moon and stars. We found some fresh blueberries, corn, and cherries—how wonderful it all tasted there on the side of the road! We even discovered an old pump that miraculously produced fresh water like it did on *Lassie*. As Adar pumped, he had his shirt off, and I saw his bronze triceps dance with the exertion. I wanted to brush against him accidentally, touch his body just once. When he finished pumping, he stood there with his hands on his hips in the moonlight and smiled. I felt a strange feeling rise that was completely new to me. What was it?

The nights were glorious, and felt like something out of *Huckleberry Finn*, one of the few books I actually completed in eighth grade English. But instead of floating down the Mississippi, we were walking along dark country roads in search of a way back home. On our odyssey, we got to know one another in a very different way. There were no interruptions for campers, laundry, or even basketball. I felt an intimacy I had never shared with anyone else before.

I found out things about Adar I would never have suspected. He lived in a high-rise building in a section of Brooklyn called Canarsie. He was considering becoming a vegetarian. More than that, he had a whole philosophy about food. After walking several miles, we came upon an old-fashioned country store. They sold sandwiches, vegetables, and fresh fruit. With the little money we had, Adar bought some fruit and cheese, and I bought a ham sandwich and a bag of Wise potato chips. We sat down beside the road together to enjoy our meal. I looked around at the lovely view and began eating my sandwich. I don't think I'd ever felt so happy or contented as I did at that moment. My parents had vanished; I was with someone whose soul I shared. I looked over at Adar, smiling, but there was no question about his expression—he was disgusted.

"What's wrong—what is it?" I asked.

"How can you ... put that filth in your body?"

"Filth?"

"That ...," he said, his mouth frowning. He picked up a pebble and flung it into the distance.

"I didn't know you kept kosher," I said. Then it occurred to me that the camp served only kosher food, and I felt embarrassed at my own tactlessness. "If I had known—"

"I don't keep kosher either, but there's a reason why the Bible has a prohibition against eating cloven-hooved animals," Adar said, his voice firm with conviction. "And it doesn't have anything to do with religious belief. Muslims don't eat pork, and they don't keep kosher, do they?"

"I guess not," I said.

"Have you ever watched a pig? They actually swallow their own feces. I think that, as much as anything else, is why the Old Testament speaks against eating the flesh of the pig."

I had taken a big bite out of my ham sandwich, but now I put it away. I still had a small piece of hard gristle in between my teeth; I couldn't swallow it, but was afraid to call attention to it by spitting it out. It would have to wait until I could dispose of it unseen. I wrapped up the rest of the sandwich. "I'll finish this later. I'm not too hungry right now," I said.

Adar continued, "The thing to remember is that whatever you put in your body becomes who you are. If you put that in your body, that's you. That's why I've decided to become a vegetarian. I only eat pure things. You'll notice that I do eat fish and cheese and eggs. Eventually, I intend to cast these things off and reduce my food intake so that only pure fruit juices enter my body. What do you think of that?"

I'd never heard of such a thing, and wasn't exactly sure how to answer. "I think that's ... great."

Adar bit into an apple, and I watched his jaw muscles grinding the fruit into pulp with mechanical precision. Unlike me, he was dark complexioned, with powerful arms and legs. His face looked like it might be carved out of stone. His voice was quiet, even soft; but everything he said carried weight and authenticity.

He swallowed the bite of apple, and then continued. "My goal is to eliminate food altogether. Abstinence. I want to reach a level of spiritual perfection so that all food becomes superfluous. Does that sound incomprehensible? I can read faces, and yours says you think it is, but I believe it's possible. First, I will do without fish, then cheese. Then eggs. One day, no more bread, rice, or potatoes. No dairy. Only fruit juice. Then one day—nothing, nothing at all."

"That's impossible!" I said, much too loudly. Then, recalibrating: "How is that even possible?"

"I've been studying *The Fountainhead*," Adar replied, "and I believe that one strong, deeply centered, supremely selfish individual can remake the world in his own image. The world around us is diseased and impure—look at your home if you need an example. We only heal it by purging ourselves of our impurities. This means not only cleansing the body, but purifying mind and soul. The body is important as a place to begin. And finally, of course, we purify ourselves of other people too."

"Other people?" I shuddered with fear and excitement. Here we were, in the middle of nowhere changing the world, purifying ourselves, doing

103

without others. "Do you think this is something ... I might be able to do, too?" I asked.

"Do you feel you have the calling as well?"

"I've never heard of anything like what you just described. I've never heard anyone speak so beautifully of ... it's ... I don't know. Noble. Something to aspire to...." It was like a wave breaking across me, this conviction. "I would like to take this journey with you."

Adar smiled gently. He was subdued, supremely confident that I would accompany him on his great quest. I wanted him to embrace me, or at least clap me on the shoulder to congratulate me. But Adar's belief in himself and the inevitability of his choice made it inconceivable that I would choose any other path. "You know, there are many religions which believe in self-purification. Most are eastern religions," he said, voice lowering. "There is something else I have come to believe that I hesitate to tell even you about. You might think I'm crazy."

"Crazy! Of course not! How could that be, Adar? Tell me about it, please." My heart was bursting against my chest.

Adar took a few steps away as he began. His walking away at that moment reminded me of an archer, the muscular strain of pulling hard on the taut bowstring the moment before release. "Well, once you've reached the point of complete spiritual independence, complete purification of both body and soul, you acquire certain ... I don't know exactly how to describe it. I call it the Law of the Spirit. It's amazing the things the human spirit is capable of when freed of its earthly constraints. Things you would not believe possible."

"What things are they? I want to know, Adar!"

"I'll tell you only if you promise not to dismiss it or discuss it with anyone else. You are the first person I've ever told this to. You must first promise never to repeat this to anyone unworthy of what I'm going to tell you right now."

"I promise." I felt like we were about to become as close as two human beings could be: Brothers of the Spirit.

"Well, once the body has been freed from its earthly dependence on food, it is possible to become entirely free of the earth that holds us back; what I mean is, it is possible to do anything. Anything." Adar was sitting beside me as he said this, but I wanted to see him, to turn and look into his eyes and watch his lips formulate whatever it was he might say next. As I slid around to face him as he spoke, my body shivered as though touched by something cold in the small of my back. But there was nothing but the electricity of our words and bodies in close proximity.

I was facing him now. "What do you mean by 'anything'?"

His voice was soft against the purple sky; I had to lean over to hear, my face inches from his, my knee brushing his. "Levitation," he whispered.

"What?"

"I mean that it will be possible, in time, to learn to levitate the body; to fly unassisted!"

"What!" I said again, unable to keep the incredulity from showing on my face.

He rose from the ground, jaw muscles working again, this time in anger. "I knew you wouldn't believe me, not even you. I knew it! But I meant what I just said. Once people are freed from appetite and the dependence on physical matter, they can live in a different sphere. Anything is possible, even flight without the slightest benefit of machinery or assistance of any kind. However, that's not what I'm doing this for. It's really not that big a deal."

"I can't believe what I'm hearing, Adar."

"I told you, this is not a journey that is for everyone. This is only for the few, the elect, Henry."

It was like being in Mr. Herman's class at school, only this was not high school, this was friendship. This was love.

I stood up and studied the night sky. I thought about what Adar was saying—the impossibility of it, the unimaginable difficulty. About being one of the elect. I thought about what it would mean if I were not one of this few—if I were to go back to my old life, my prison of self-loathing and fear. To my mother and Bobby and Uncle Lee. A world of empty tuna fish cans and boxes. I bent down and laced up my shoes.

Ever since Mr. Herman began fueling my interest in art, I visited museums whenever I could. Instead of seeing friends, I coveted my solitude and ran to the Metropolitan Museum, the Guggenheim, the Whitney, and the Frick Collection. The Frick was a particular favorite; in time I found myself contemplating the subjects of the paintings in this intimate collection as though they were real people with whom I could share my deepest thoughts and dreams. I even communicated aloud with some of these works as I stood before them. Nevertheless, the paintings at that isolated (but never lonely!) time in my life, along with my books, completed my acquaintance. They were important to me for different reasons: Titian's *Man in a Red Cap* seemed to mirror Mr. Herman's own aloof manner and expression; the dimly lit interior in Georges de la Tour's *Education of the Virgin* blended the quiet homeliness and transcendent spirituality I longed for; Giovanni Bellini's *St. Francis in the Desert* suggested the very religious ecstasy I myself awaited; El Greco's brooding, ascetic *St. Jerome* seemed to conceal a profound secret; Rembrandt's *Polish Rider* mirrored my own adolescent quest, depicting a shy, sensitive youth upon the back of a white horse drifting toward who knew where.

One day, I stood in front of a painting by the sixteenth-century Italian painter Agnolo di Cosimo di Mariano, also known as Bronzino. The painting was of a young boy around my age (sixteen) with pale skin and heavy-lidded eyes topped with delicate, arching eyebrows. He was dressed in a black doublet with white sleeves and stood in front of a background of different shades of green. In his left hand, he held a pair of leather gloves; in the other, a small cameo, which I assumed was a portrait of his beloved. The extraordinary thing was that no matter how hard I looked, I couldn't make out the image on the cameo; its face was deliberately covered by the boy's right index finger.

When I told Mr. Herman what I had seen, amazingly, he knew exactly which painting I meant. He ordered me to go look at the painting again. I did, of course, but told him I still felt confused. He told me I wasn't looking hard enough, to go back again. This time I noticed that the boy's hands were separated by an elaborate silver codpiece. I did notice that his right hand formed a "V" between his right index and middle finger, and was pointing upward toward his heart, while the left hand holding the leather gloves was directed down toward the codpiece. Suddenly—I understood! The painting was a kind of allegory, a dialogue between his heart's desire and what my mother would have called his baser inclinations.

"Bravo! Bravissimo!" Mr. Herman said, rolling his R's like he was speaking in Italian, a language he spoke fluently, of course. He looked at me deeply. "A noble response. The slaves and peons who surround you would never have noticed such things. You have discovered much." Then he told me that the young man's name was Lodovico Capponi, and that he had fallen in love with a girl whom the Duke Cosimo had intended for his own cousin. After three years of vain pleading by Lodovico, the Duke relented and let the boy have his desire, with one proviso—he had to marry her in the next twenty-four hours! And he accomplished his goal; the boy's love had been vindicated! And, if I looked closely, Mr. Herman said, I would notice the word "sorte" written just above the obscured face on the cameo, signifying that the boy's fate was to search for—and find—his heart's desire. I was deeply moved by this story, and returned the next day to find the magical word engraved in the cameo precisely as he said I would.

While I told Adar the story, he moved toward the painting, so close he nearly brushed it with his cheek. I was afraid one of the museum guards would see him and would ask us to leave. Then Adar muttered to the boy in the painting: "You're smarter than the others; they who don't understand. Just keep following the Law of the Spirit, that's all."

As I listened to Adar's words, I felt chills. I was moved by his passionate response, but also a little frightened. *The Law of the Spirit.* The words spilled from his mouth like gold coins. He could do anything, and with his blessing, I could too. It was an honor to be one of the chosen. Maybe I, too, could become one of those superior beings who did not need to conform to rules like other people. I looked closely into Adar's eyes as he spoke; they were exactly the same shade of emerald as the velvet background in Bronzino's painting, and they flashed with fire.

When my father left, my mother stopped reading (except for the Bible and *The Daily News*), and spoke mostly in proverbs, usually by Shakespeare. She was able to spout a saying for nearly every occasion. When she found out I had returned early from Surprise Lake, she quoted Walter Scott, "Oh, what a tangled web we weave when first we practice to deceive." I wasn't sure

107

exactly which deception she thought I had been guilty of, but assumed that if I did ask, I would only be answered with additional quotations from the classics.

My return proved conclusively to her that I never should have taken the job in the first place. Why did I need to traipse upstate to pick up after a bunch of sweaty Jewish kids since Bobby was right here at home, wasn't he? And if I absolutely needed a job (although she couldn't see why, since my father was still obliged to pay for tuition and school supplies), I could work for Uncle Lee at MacLaren's Men's Wear.

"Charity," she quietly pronounced as though coining the phrase for the first time, "begins at home." It was a saying she quoted enthusiastically, along with "Many hands make light the work!" Her favorite to me, however, was "To thine own self be true, and it must follow as the night the day ..." That seemed a good fit for nearly every occasion. She never asked me for the precise details of my departure, or how I had managed to return home from Cold Spring. Normally, I would have felt relieved at the absence of an interrogation; now, however, it was further evidence that her sense of reality was slipping.

My father's response was different. He had moved into an apartment on East 56th near Sutton Place, and when he learned I had suddenly quit my job, I received a summons to meet him at his apartment at 7:30 a.m. sharp on Monday, before he left for work. I arrived at the appointed time and rang the doorbell. To my surprise, it was not my father, but his brother Malcolm, who opened the door.

Malcolm, an ear, nose, and throat specialist, answered the door with an unfiltered Pall Mall dangling from his mouth and offered me his freshly-shaven cheek. He wore a gray tweed sports jacket with leather elbow patches, a checked button-down shirt, pink tie, and a pair of gray Hush Puppies. As he turned his head to receive my kiss, Coke and chipped ice sloshed over the side of his highball glass.

"Hello, Henry, come in."

Grandma often described her younger son as a genius, and indeed Malcolm was likely to go off on lengthy uninterrupted diatribes about nearly anything. In particular, he loved to opine on contemporary race relations—how "the Ethnics had taken over the city." He had an extremely lucrative otolaryngology practice on Park Avenue, along with an appointment at

Columbia University's Presbyterian Hospital. I had no way of knowing that one day Malcolm would lose his practice for inappropriately prescribing and dispensing controlled substances—and practicing medicine while impaired.

"Your father's in the bathroom," Malcolm said as I walked in. "You know how long he takes in there primping; he'll be out in a minute."

"This is some building," I said, searching for something to say, looking around in vain for something which would remind me of our apartment on 86th. "The doorman practically frisked me before he would let me up. It was like the Spanish Inquisition."

"I guess it depends on how you're dressed," boomed my father unexpectedly from the bathroom. "That's what they get paid for—to keep out the riff-raff." The toilet detonated on cue like an exclamation point.

"Come in, sit down, he'll be right out," Malcolm repeated. He twitched, and the long ash from his Pall Mall dropped onto a Persian rug unnoticed.

"What are you doing here, Uncle Malcolm? Aren't you working today?"

"Of course," he replied, "but your father asked me to come over here while he talked with you."

I knew when I was asked to come over early, that I was in trouble. On a positive note, Uncle Malcolm's presence might be read as being to my advantage, since he lacked my father's violent temper. On the other hand, the fact that Dad found it necessary to send for his brother at all was a troubling sign that this meeting was more significant than I had anticipated.

"He'll be right in. Any moment now." Malcolm's nervous agitation was another bad omen.

Yet another hint that this encounter wasn't going to be pleasant was when I casually asked how things were going and he pulled out a revolver.

"Jesus Christ! What the hell's that!"

"A .38-caliber," Malcolm said between laying one lit cigarette on the side of the ashtray and lighting another. "It's so I can park at Columbia Presbyterian without being robbed by the Schwartzas. I didn't even repair my car after the last break-in; as soon as they see you've got plates with an M.D., you've had it. Drugs. At least I improve my chances a little by driving a Buick that looks like shit."

Malcolm stood up and shouted in the direction of the bathroom, "Norman! Jesus Christ, aren't you done in there yet?"

Grandpa and Grandma Schvey and their sons, Norman (left) and Malcom.

Norman Schvey, as a young boy
with his pet squirrel.

Henry's grandmother,
Birdie Rosen Schvey, in 1921.

Norman Schvey, Henry's father, circa 1947. A rare photograph taken at the Lerner's apartment at 101 Central Park West.

Rita Lerner Schvey, Henry's mother, circa 1946.

Henry's parents, Norman and Rita, at their wedding in 1947.

Henry's father, Norman Schvey, at 4 years old

Henry Schvey at 2 years old

Henry with his Lerner Grandparents outside their home at 101 Central Park West
Easter Sunday, April 5, 1953.

Grandma and Grandpa Schvey outside their apartment building
(The Eldorado) at 300 Central Park West.

Jay Nathan Lerner (Gramps) and Henry's mother in Central Park, c. 1950.

The Cantor chanting the blessings at Henry's bar mitzvah, 1961.

Norman Schvey, Henry's father, at the height of his power at Merrill Lynch in the 1980s.

Henry directing a play during the time he lived and worked in the Netherlands (early 1980s).

Packaging Profits by Offering a Little Certainty to Investors

SUMMARY: Few people outside Wall Street know who Norman Schvey is. But many people have been buying what he makes. His unit investment trusts — packages of securities broken down into units and sold to investors — not only are generally considered to be good values but have proved a bonanza for his employer, Merrill Lynch. His unit trusts cover a wide range — from foreign currency to mortgage securities to municipal bonds. He even put AT&T together again.

Ask Merrill Lynch managing director Norman I. Schvey what he does, and he will say he is a manufacturer. In a sense that is true. He has been manufacturing unit investment trusts — distant cousins of mutual funds — for 20 years or so, currently at a rate of four or five a week.

The vast majority of Americans have never heard of Schvey, of course, but a great many of them have been buying what he makes.

The trusts, or UITs, essentially are portfolios or packages of securities bought with Merrill Lynch capital, broken down into units of $1,000 each and sold to individual investors. Unlike mutual funds, unit investment trusts are not managed; since the same securities stay in portfolio, there is nothing to manage.

The business has grown steadily, reaching 100 unit trusts in 1979. In the '80s Schvey has structured as many as 218 such trusts in a single year, he says, and "in a

slow year, 175." Since 1971, in fact, he has turned out 1,747 trusts with portfolios of securities that add up to $71.7 billion. For Merrill Lynch & Co. Inc., whose own brokers as well as others peddle the trusts (charging investors on a sliding scale depending on volume up to 4 percent for each $1,000 unit they buy), his prolificacy has created a bonanza. In two decades he has generated hundreds of millions of dollars in revenues for Merrill Lynch and a handful of other firms that sell the trusts, as well as revenues from buying and selling unit investment trusts in an aftermarket Merrill maintains for trading them.

Schvey does not say how much money his Unit Investment Trust Division generates for Merrill but admits "it's among the top earners." His innovativeness and drive have been transposed into so much personal

Praised for his innovativeness and for structuring good investments, Schvey is practically a legend on Wall Street.

First page of three-page article on Norman Schvey in *Insight* magazine.
Written by Christopher Elias, publication date June 22, 1987.

Adar's pencil sketch of
Henry at age 17

Patty and Henry at the
University of Wisconsin, 1967

Then he turned back to me. "I'd forgotten how long he stays in there. I guess that's the nature of life on Wall Street. All about competition and appearance. In the hospital, as long as I don't go on rounds with my underpants on my head, nobody says boo. And at Columbia—well, you know professors dress like slobs. Where was I?"

"Something about a Buick."

"Oh, yeah, if I drive a crappy car, the Schwartzas are much less likely to break in and look for drugs. I didn't even replace my radio after the last break-in. Why bother? With a radio in your car, you might as well hang out a sign that says, 'Mug Me!' But when the race war begins, I'll be prepared. That's why I don't use banks, even though your father thinks I'm crazy not to invest in the market. That's what we were talking about before you got here."

"You were talking about the stock market?" I asked hopefully.

"No, race war! It's inevitable, in my opinion."

"What does Dad think?"

"He thinks I'm full of shit. But I'm trying to convince him to invest a few thousand with me just the same."

"But you just said you didn't invest in the stock market.

Malcolm smiled at my simplicity. "No. Not the market. These." He took out a blue velvet case from his jacket pocket and twitched again. Inside was something that looked like a gold doubloon from a pirate's treasure chest. Or maybe Hannukah geld.

"What's that?"

"The only safe currency in the world: the South African Kruegerrand. Pure gold. Here, don't be afraid—touch it." I did. I lifted the coin out of its snug blue velvet case; the metal felt heavy and cold.

"You mean this is safer than banks or the stock market?" I asked.

"Of course. When the race riots start, banks are always the first things to go. Gold holds its value, and Johannesburg is the only place left that's safe."

"Don't they practice apartheid there?"

"Bingo!" Malcolm said with a smile. There was a flake of tobacco on his front tooth. Another swig of Coke washed it away. Finally, he replaced the gun in its holster.

"That isn't loaded, is it, Uncle Malcolm?"

"Not loaded?" he said with a cackle, pulling it out again. "Of course it's loaded! What the hell's the point of carrying a .38 if it's not loaded? No, if you carry one of these, you'd better be ready to use it."

There was another loud flush, and my father appeared, dressed in a dark pinstripe suit and pale blue shirt with a white spread collar. There was a mauve silk handkerchief flowing from his breast pocket. He smelled like Pinaud, and while his cheeks seemed unusually rosy, it could have been red from the sting of the aftershave. It didn't necessarily mean he was in a rage.

"Late as always," Malcolm said, smiling, as my father came into the room.

"All right—what the fuck is going on?" Dad shouted on entering.

His entrance was meant to throw me off guard, and it succeeded.

But I was still full of Adar's bravery and confidence. "Aren't you going to ask me how I like your apartment? I haven't seen it before," I said, brazenly. "It's a very nice apartment, Dad. Congratulations. I think that's how we ought to begin."

"Don't be a smartass, Henry."

"I'm not."

"You know exactly why you're here!" he snapped.

"How could I?"

"You do, and don't think you're too big for me to take your pants down right here in the living room and strap you right in front of your uncle."

"Perhaps you'd like to try?" I asked defiantly.

Dad unbuckled his belt and made a strange humming sound. It was a sound that I hadn't heard for a while, but remembered only too well. When I heard that hum, the sound of leather whishing through belt loops inevitably followed.

Malcolm interposed. "For Chrissake, Norman, this is why you called me to come over at 7:00 in the morning—to watch you take a strap to a sixteen year old?"

"All right," my father said, buckling his belt again. "Now I want to know what's happened, and I want the truth. Don't lie to me." As an aside to Malcolm, Dad said, "By the way, Malcolm, the boy's a congenital liar." Then he turned his attention back to me. "How did you get fired after less than two weeks at camp? Two weeks! I want to know what happened up there, and I want to know exactly what happened on the way back."

I had walked into a trap. In an instant, all my bravado vanished, and my body went limp. Why hadn't I anticipated where this conversation was going to go? I should have known. But now, it was too late.

"There's really not much to tell. I was at camp, I left, and now I'm back. That's basically it."

"That's not basically it, you goddamn son of a bitch. How the hell could you get fired? Your first job, too. Jesus Christ!"

"I didn't get fired, not exactly … I … we resigned. We were accused of leaving camp grounds, but it wasn't really true. We never left. So the honorable thing to do was—"

"Honorable? In a pig's eye! You hear that, Malcolm? Honorable! Now tell me why you got fired!"

"I just told you."

"And I say you're lying. I happen to know the truth—Meyer called me. He said he suspected you and another boy were involved in doing something strange together. Something morally wrong. He said you and this other boy who was older and responsible for a whole cabin of kids, went off together one night. He got fired for neglecting the kids under his charge, and you went off with him. Is that true so far?"

"Yes and no," I said, hesitating. Then, after a short pause, I added, "No, it isn't."

My father scoffed. "You see, Malcolm? You see the shit I get from him? 'Yes and no'; 'no and yes'. Well 'yes and no' ain't going to hack it, goddammit. I want the truth!"

Malcolm stepped in again. "Henry, your father deserves an answer. He won't tell you this, but he was really worried when the police called saying they found you in the middle of a field near New Rochelle."

"The police?" It never occurred to me the police would contact my father. I felt trapped. I felt like I was going to pass out.

"Okay, so this is what happened. Me and this guy I became friends with spent a few hours talking late one night. He was supposed to be in his bunk inside watching the kids, it's true, but they were asleep. Anyway, we walked for a bit and talked. Then we stayed outside, only a few hundred yards from his cabin where his campers were sleeping. He was accused of 'dereliction of duty', and I felt the right, the proper thing to do was to stick by him and leave, too. That's it; that's what happened."

Talking about what actually happened with some fluency restored a bit of my self-confidence. I was explaining things as best as I could, finding words that conveyed something like the truth.

"Then what?" Dad asked.

"What do you mean, 'Then what?' I just told you what happened."

"What happened after you and this friend left the camp together. That's what I want to know. Meyer told me he offered the two of you a ride to the train station and you refused it! Started off on your own. On foot! That's what he told me, and I know it's true. So, how the hell did you get back to New York? The camp's in Cold Spring, goddammit—it must be fifty miles away! And how did the police happen to get involved? I already know everything, so don't try and lie your way out of it."

"If you know everything, why do you need to ask me? And by the way, it's actually sixty miles away, not fifty."

"Look, you little snot-nose, answer me back one more time like that and I don't care if Malcolm's here or not ..."

"Look," I said, "is there anything else you want from me? 'Cause if not, I have to get going."

My father turned to his brother and said, "He wants to know if we're through with him? Ha!" Then he turned back to me and said smilingly, "Oh, we're just getting started. We still don't know how you got back and how the police got involved. You didn't know they contacted me after you were stopped in the middle of nowhere, did you?"

"Look, Dad," I said, trying to remain calm, "I sincerely apologize if I caused you any concern. The reason we didn't accept the camp's offer to take us to the station was because of the way things happened—they didn't even ask his side of the story, so we didn't want their charity. Once we got to the station, we thought it would be fun to walk the rest of the way."

"Fun? Look, I hope you know that that was an insane, abnormal thing to do, walking home all that way. You do realize that?"

"Yes, Dad, I do. And I'm sorry."

"Good," he said, "okay." And he lit a cigarette. Lighting one of his Kents was always a signal things were calming down. Even at his worst, when he came after me with his belt and I had to lock myself in my parents' bathroom for an hour or more, the click of his lighter and the smell of a Kent meant the coast was clear. I felt a lot better now that he was smoking.

"Next, I want you to tell me about your relationship with this boy," Dad added, almost as an afterthought. He took a deep drag of his cigarette.

"What's his name, for starters?" Malcolm joined in.

"His name's Adar."

"What?" Dad was deaf in one ear from childhood complications of mumps and measles, but I didn't think his hearing was a factor right now.

"His name's Adar—it means 'Noble One' in Hebrew."

"Yeah, right. His full name," Dad asked.

"Adar Bornstein."

"And where does he come from?"

"Brooklyn."

"What section of Brooklyn?" my father asked, still on the attack.

"What difference does that make?" I said, knowing the name of the town would not play well with either my father or my uncle. But how could I not tell them the truth? I backed down almost immediately. "I think it's called Canarsie."

"Evidently from a fine family," my father said, sarcasm dripping.

Malcolm wrinkled his nose and sniffed. It was a habit he'd always had, but now I understood what it meant; he was about to professionally diagnose my problem. "How old is the boy? I understand he's older than you. What does he do? Is he in college?"

"He's nineteen, I believe."

"You believe? Or you know?" Dad interjected, leveling his cigarette at me.

"He's nineteen years old, sir!" I saluted in mock-military style. I thought it would make them smile. It didn't.

"Is he in college?"

"He's studying art at Hunter."

"Now we're getting somewhere."

I wondered where we were getting, and fretted about where all these questions were leading, but didn't ask.

"Now, your uncle wants to ask you something. Go ahead, Malcolm … ask him."

"Well," he sniffed, "the reason your father told me to come over this morning was to ask you—"

"What?" I felt a wave of heat like lava rise in my chest.

"If you and this nineteen-year-old boy, whom you were with for several nights alone and unsupervised, were ... if you and he were ... Did he touch you in any way?" Malcolm sniffed and glanced over at his elder brother for reassurance. Then he drained a last swallow of his Coke. He betrayed some nervousness as to just where this line of questioning was leading him. "So, what I'm asking you, y'understand, is this: did the two of you engage in activities which in any way might be construed as illegal?"

"Illegal? What! What are you talking about?"

"He's asking if he's queer!" Dad exploded. "In case you need a fucking road map, he wants to know if he's a fucking faggot! Or if you are!" Unable to control himself, Dad jumped up from his chair, moustache twitching.

"Thank you for that nuanced clarification, Norman," Malcolm said. "Look—if you want to deal with this issue in your own way, why did you ask me to come and talk to the boy?"

"You're here as a physician only, Malcolm. Remember that," Dad snarled. "I only want to get your medical opinion as to what is going on here underneath all his lies."

"What lies—why are you asking me this?" I blurted, outraged and horrified. "What business—how dare you? How dare both of you!"

"How dare I? *How dare I?* I'm your father, that's how dare I, you pervert!"

"I'm perverted? How about you? How about you and Mom? How about that whip I found in your closet after you left? A red whip from Mexico, wasn't it?"

"Come over here, you little bastard!"

"Have a nice day at work—I'm leaving," I shouted. "I'm not saying another word about it. To answer you would defile what Adar and I have together."

"That's exactly what we want to know—what you two have together," Malcolm said.

The next thing I knew, my father had grabbed me and spun me around. He slapped me hard across the face, and I felt myself being pushed to the ground. I caught sight of his mauve handkerchief fluttering down as I lay there with him crouched over me.

"You're the pervert! You're the pervert—not me," I said, shoving him off me and scrambling to my feet. I tore out of his apartment and down the hallway to the bank of elevators without looking back. I watched the buttons light up as the elevator began its lazy climb from floor to floor. The elevator moved so slowly, it actually seemed to mock my fright. I wondered if my father would suddenly come charging out of the apartment to pursue me with his belt. I had flung open the door when I left, and it was still ajar. *Come on. Come on. Come on.* I considered taking the stairs and running down to the street, but decided not to. You're not that much of a coward, I said to myself. Think of Adar. What would Adar do? The EXIT sign beckoned, but I forced myself to stand there by the elevators. Meanwhile, I kept pressing the "Down" button as hard and as often as I could. I would not walk down the ten flights; that would be weak. It would mean I did not even deserve to be free. If I ran now, I would always be my father's slave. And if he came after me, so what? But where was that damn elevator! Finally, the doors opened, and a few moments later I was back out on 56th Street and walking toward the East River.

But though I tried to revel in my hard-bought triumph with my father, as I walked away, I kept looking over my shoulder to see if he was following. I couldn't help myself.

As I limped in the direction of the East River, for a reason I understood all too well, I kept thinking of a giant framed poster of *King Kong* in my father's bedroom—a parody of the classic 1933 movie poster with a snarling King Kong astride the Empire State Building, swatting at airplanes with one paw, and holding the helpless Fay Wray in the other. In this version—given him no doubt by grateful employees after some multimillion-dollar deal—King Kong's growling visage had been replaced by my father's mustachioed likeness.

Following the confrontation with my father, I was in a kind of panic. I needed to do something, go somewhere. But I had no desire to tell Adar what happened, at least not yet. My sense of humiliation was too great. But I couldn't be alone either. As I rode the elevator up to the fifteenth floor in the presence of the eternally grumpy elevator operator, I wondered why I hadn't phoned Grandma to say I was coming. My visits were frequently unannounced, yet she was always at home, miraculously waiting for my arrival, day or night. I believed that. At some level, I needed to talk to her about my father, and perhaps even about Adar. There was no one else I could talk to.

As soon as she opened the door, she dragged me in by the arm back to her bedroom, whispering, "You can do it!" repeatedly.

"Do what? What are you talking about?" I said, although I knew very well what she meant. She was obsessive about bringing my parents back together. Any thought of sharing my confrontation fled, and I instantly regretted my decision to come over.

"Just talk to her; all she needs is to clean up the house, put proper meals on the table. It's not too late."

"It is, Grandma. It is too late. Don't you see …"

"Shah! I won't hear that! Did you know that there's never been a divorce in this family? No, I didn't think you did; and there won't be one now. Your father happens to be a fine man, a man of integrity, ask anyone on Wall Street. His reputation for honesty in business is perfect. Remember the squirrel?"

"Yes, Grandma."

"Then you know that man would never harm anybody. It's just that she can't keep house, can't cook for him like he needs. Also, who knows what she's like in bed—but that you didn't hear from me. Believe me, no normal man would stand for it, not just your father. You have to bring them back together."

"But Grandma, they're not happy; it's best if they get a divorce."

"Bite your tongue, Henry! Bite your tongue! Never say such things. Never! It's never better," she said. When Grandma got going, the resulting fountain of words was impressive. "Look at Grandpa and me. He's a man with a terrible temper just like your father. You think it's easy for me? You see how he does all the time, 'Bitch . . .bitch' under his breath. You think it don't hurt? He stays in his own room not saying a word until I want to scream—just scream! He sleeps in his own bed, locks the door to his room, gives me twenty dollars a week to buy tchotchkes when he could afford twenty times that. Do I complain? No, I don't complain. Why not? I love him; I would die without him. So help me, I would. So I get him his tomato juice and his sturgeon and Ritz Crackers the instant he comes home from the office—the very instant! And I fix him dinner every night like he likes, make his bed in the other room while I sleep in here. And what's been the result? A happy home all these years." She finally paused to breathe, and I jumped into the breach.

"But what if two people can't stand each other and make themselves miserable all the time? Screaming and fighting. You still think it's better to stay together?"

"Of course it is! Miserable? Just tell me who in this world is not miserable? I'm miserable, he's miserable. Look at yourself, you're miserable too—I can see it from the way you're biting your fingernails right now—stop that, will you—it's a disgusting habit! Everybody's miserable—you just don't see it! You think marriage is such a picnic? But I told you, two people can survive if they work at it. And you can make it happen. Like I said, it's up to you to bring them back together."

It was useless. "All right, Grandma. I'll try."

"Don't try—just do it!"

Grandpa walked in on us at that moment, lips quivering.

"Vat—vat filth you talking to the boy? More nonsense?"

"No, Harry, I was just saying if his parents are apart, it's his duty—"

"Duty? Bitch! Did you know that you are a stupid bitch?" He said the words with his teeth locked together so tight I wondered how it was possible he could even emit a sound. He took off his wire-rimmed glasses and unfolded a creased pocket handkerchief, still muttering under his breath, but loud enough for us to hear. "Oh, yes, she's been put here on this earth to give advice … all kinds of advice. She comes from people who know! People of importance! Yes, by all means listen to her, we should all of us listen to vat dat woman says. Bitch!"

Although this exchange was not in the least uncommon, it made me sick to hear it right after she had described what she had sacrificed.

"All right, Harry, that's enough now. All I said was that it was his responsibility to do—"

"Ahhh, she said, she said," Grandpa said, mimicking her in a falsetto with a Russian lilt. "Vell, dat's another matter. 'She said.' Dat I didn't know."

Grandma turned and exited the room. "I'll be back with your tomato juice and sturgeon, Harry."

"Tomato juice and sturgeon! Now dat's important, dat she knows about,

about dat, she's expert, a maven." He took me by the arm, and, looking me in the eye, completely changed his tone from savage to earnest. "Don't ever listen to her. She means well, but it's not your place to solve the problems between them. You hear me? I'm very, very serious now." His old eyes were serious, looking intently into my own.

"Yes, Grandpa. But—" He dropped my arm, wiped his glasses, walked into his bathroom, and closed the door. It was a signal he had no more to say, and that I must now leave.

As I walked back down the hall, Grandma pounced. "What did he say? Did he say anything? Or was it only 'Bitch, Bitch, Bitch?'"

"He told me not to interfere, and said—" Then, I looked down at the floor, and saw she was wearing white Keds without laces. For some reason, those white Keds sneakers, which I associated with little children playing, made me want to cry. In 1920, she had decided against law school to marry Grandpa. She had no regrets about her choice, but those Keds told me how much she had given up to be this man's faithful servant, and how ugly his temper could be—and was. "He said you meant well," I added unconvincingly.

"Well, that's something. Come here and sit down. I'll bring him his sturgeon and tomato juice and make you your steak and baked potato. Here, have some of these triangles of Gruyere cheese and some sardines and olives with fresh rye, I just got it this afternoon at the market."

"Grandma," I said, "I already ate. I think I'd better get going. I have homework to do."

"Sit down a moment! One moment. Have a snack at least. My God, you're so thin. Your mother doesn't know how to feed you. She never has. Now remember, I'm always here. Always. No matter what time of day or night, you come and I'll be here for you. And if I'm out, I'm just out marketing. I'll be right back. Just wait in the lobby with the doorman until I come." Then slyly, she added, "You think I don't know how much time you've spent on your homework? Not much—am I right?" I actually smiled that she knew me so well. "Now you sit down here and eat. I have something for you—one of those books you like, and a Hershey bar with almonds."

She brushed aside clippings from the *New York Times* and *Wall Street Journal* that cluttered the dining room table. This was her "office," the place

127

where she cut out news about stocks and bonds, how the Democrats were ruining the country. Later, at the height of Watergate, she showed her undying support for Richard Nixon by writing in blue crayon on her shopping bag: "They're hounding him out of office!" When I asked Grandpa about her political sympathies, he just shrugged: "Nixon? Nah, I wouldn't vote for him for dog catcher!"

Grandma made me sit in one of the stiff, high-backed chairs. She brought Grandpa his sturgeon, and returned to the kitchen. In the sink, she ran cold water to defrost the kosher steak. For some reason, I was unable to tell her that I had just decided to become a vegetarian; I wanted to put off that conversation with her, forever if possible. Besides, one more steak wouldn't hurt. Adar would never know.

Back in the kitchen, she put a large Idaho potato in the small, covered black pan to bake. She must have had that pan since she and Grandpa were married and moved into the Eldorado. While the potato was baking, she put the steak in the broiler. The hinges of her oven made a comforting squeak, different from other squeaks. She put in two slices of white toast; her old toaster, too, sounded different than other toasters, and the bread always came out a particular shade of really dark brown, just like I liked. When it popped out, she put a large pat of sweet cream butter on each slice and let the butter soak in. She sprinkled the steak with rough kosher salt while it was broiling. By the time it was done, the meat was tough, but delicious. You had to chew and chew until your jaws hurt; and when you cut the meat, the juice would turn the baked potato red. I ate some Gruyere cheese and giant black olives while she knocked on Grandpa's door with his tray, like it was room service. She closed the door, and I turned on the television and adjusted the rabbit ears. Petula Clark was singing "Downtown," but their yelling drowned out her voice.

When Grandma returned, I told her that I had decided to work part-time for Uncle Leon at MacLaren's. Adar had convinced me that I needed to gain my independence and get a job. If I could arrange it with Lee, Adar would have a job there as well. I chose not to tell her that, however.

"I'll tell you one thing, you work for Leon, you'll go meshuggah in two weeks—no, make that two seconds, about that I can promise!"

She sat facing me, pretending she was absorbed in cutting out newspaper clippings from the *Wall Street Journal* with blunt scissors that might have belonged to a five-year-old child, along with those white Keds. "Why, that Leon, his mind's completely gone! Ever since they dragged him out of Harvard Law to cut pants, there hasn't been a clear thought in his head." She sat watching me eat, and stirred a tall glass of milky brown coffee with a long teaspoon. "Poor Leon, it's no wonder that shiksa ran away from him on his wedding night, wearing only a mink coat."

"Grandma, please. I hate it when you talk like that. Besides—"

"Eat, Henry. You want some cottage cheese? I got some today, fresh. Sealtest. Fortunately, I already did my marketing before you came. You ever think of calling to see am I home first? I might have been marketing on Columbus Avenue and no one's home and then what? God knows your mother don't provide. But that's another story... ."

"You're right, Grandma; that's another story."

"You mean I should shut up, right? Okay, so I'll shut up. But if she made a proper home with regular meals for him, things might have been different."

"Sounds good," I said, dipping rye bread in sardine oil and swallowing the soggy crust.

"What?"

"You shutting up," I said. "You know I don't want to talk about bringing them back together, and that's where you're heading. Again."

"Okay, so we won't," she said firmly. "What makes you think you want to work for Leon? Does he still wear that awful rug?"

"It's called a toupee or a hairpiece, not a rug. A rug is something you put on the floor. And you know why he wears the toupee. He had Scarlet Fever. That's how he lost all his hair, like Andrew, the tall boy in that picture you have."

"Scarlet fever *mein tuchus*!" she exploded. "Is that what they told you, the Lerners? You know that's not true. His wits turned to chopped liver the day that little tramp ran off on their wedding night. Some wedding night. She ran out of the Waldorf Astoria screaming and—okay, I see I'm making you mad—I'll shut up. But God only knows what the putz did to her. You know he wears a size thirteen shoe—what does that tell you about their marriage, Henry?"

"I don't know—what does it tell me?" I said drily, sopping up more sardine oil and studiously avoiding looking at her. "Obviously, it tells you a great deal."

"Nothing. All right, nothing."

"That's right, Grandma, nothing."

"Nothing … all right." She paused only for a moment. "Why has the boy lived alone with his mother ever since? Tell me that! Is that nothing? And why hasn't he ever dated another girl? Explain that to me, Mister Sherlock Holmes. We have a real good expression for momma's boy in Yiddish—you wanna know what it is? It's called a *faygele*—"

I jumped up. "Grandma, I hate it when you're like this. You know what I think? I think you're jealous because of all the attention he gives his mother, while my father treats you like his maid, coming over to drop his laundry off and doing you a favor by picking up a roast chicken once a week, or maybe— if you're lucky—he takes some kreplach off your hands. He treats you like dirt, Grandma—"

All the color drained out of her face, and there was a long moment of silence.

"I won't hear another word—I'm leaving!" And with that, she did. Grandma ran out of the dining room and shut herself inside the cedar closet in her bedroom.

Sighing, I pushed my chair back from the table and followed her to the closet. I leaned my head against the door and spoke to her. "All right, Grandma, please come back out. You know, between you and my mother, I always end up talking to people barricaded inside rooms or closets." I thought the comparison with my mother might shame her into coming out.

"No," she responded angrily, "I won't ever come out." Then after a pause, she said tearfully from within the closet, "He's not a bad man, really he isn't. If she had his dinner on the table when he came home, and maybe his J&B and soda, if he has his tennis things and his shirts ironed, the boy is gentle as a lamb. All he needs, all any man needs, is a clean house and a good meal. That's the secret to a good marriage. Instead, he comes home every day to a double helping of *mishegoss*. I feel sorry for the boy, I really do."

I felt sorry for him, too, in a way, and couldn't help thinking about my mother's pantyhose and girdles draped over the shower curtain, the cockroaches scurrying around the kitchen when you flipped on the lights. I thought of my father's starched shirts and folded handkerchiefs. But there was another memory that flashed before me, from the time before my brother Bobby was born. I'd been scared of something in the night, and my parents let me sleep in their bed. Then out of the blue, Mom was screaming at the top of her lungs as she hurled a saucepan of ice cold water on Dad and me. I remembered the feeling of waking to her screams and the shock of that freezing water soaking through my pajamas and onto my bare legs, still warm from sleep. Moments later, I was curled up on the only dry corner of their mattress, watching him throw her onto the floor, and drag her by her blonde hair. Mom screamed and was reaching toward me, clutching the air like she was drowning. I was too frightened to reach out and grab her hand; I only remember clutching the "UNLAWFUL: DO NOT REMOVE!" tag on the mattress, not wanting to be tossed overboard onto the floor myself. A few days later she went to the hospital with a slipped disk. And a miscarriage.

For several seconds, on either side of her closet door, Grandma and I were silent while we each reflected on our respective memories and marshaled arguments to help explain the nightmare of a marriage that once must have seemed ideal—the union of two wealthy, prominent families. How could any of this have happened?

"I know he has a temper," she admitted from within the dark closet. "He always did, even as a little boy. Inherited it from his father maybe. You think I don't know what's what? You think I don't see how he spoils his mouth when he snarls that way? I see it, of course—" She broke off suddenly. "But there is never, ever any excuse for being disrespectful to your father, Henry. Maybe he saw some things at home … things he shouldn't have."

"What things, Grandma? Please tell me so I'll know what—"

"I will not speak ill of your grandfather—not for anything in the world, not even for you." Her voice trailed off and the closet finally opened.

"O.K., now let's get to work and see how we can bring them back together." She meant every word. She brought out a battered coin purse and handed me five dollars.

"Don't look at me like that; it's not a bribe. I want you to try to do your best to bring them back together. Try."

"Grandma, I have to go."

"I asked you to try—"

"Grandma, I can't—"

"Please. For me."

"Okay. I'll try."

"That's all I ask."

"I know."

"You are a good boy. My favorite."

I laughed a little. "I know, Grandma, but there's only me and Bobby."

"Watch out for him—that boy doesn't bathe, and he always goes for the gold," she said mischievously. "You listen to me. Anything you want, anything, take it. You want my heart, my lungs—you want my liver?"

"Grandma, I appreciate the offer, but I've had enough red meat right now. Besides, I'm thinking about becoming a vegetarian, and your liver wouldn't be ..."

"Freshpot!" she said. "Wiseguy!" and pushed a forelock from my eyes. "You know what I mean. I'll always be here for you."

"I know, Grandma."

"Unless, of course, I should have a stroke ... the blood vessels in my brain could burst at any second ... in that case I won't be here."

I walked out to the foyer to wait for the elevator, utterly exhausted, her voice still following me. "Wait! I forgot. I forgot to give you this fresh Jewish rye and the rest of the sturgeon. Also, I have a can of Campbell's tomato juice like you like. Just wait here a few seconds...."

I was in the elevator now, and old Stanley pretended he hadn't heard her yelling for him to stop. He shut the brass grate with a clang, and we plunged back down to the lobby. My stomach churned as floor after floor whizzed by. As I fell, I marked the floors with the names of various organs she would give to me: my heart, my lungs, my liver....

6.

Despite Grandma's warning, in the beginning we really enjoyed working for Uncle Leon at MacLaren's. We—Adar and me—chalked trousers, learned how to cut bolts of cloth, and take inventory of hundreds of Nehru suits and multi-colored Madras jackets left over from the previous season. We were both vegetarians now. At the Horn & Hardart around the corner, we ordered tiny dishes of spinach, green beans, cottage cheese, and rice by popping coins into the slots of the automat like when I was a little boy with Uncle Lee. It was fun. We would continue to work at MacLaren's for the rest of the summer, and in the evenings dedicate ourselves to reading, discussing literature and philosophy, and the Law of the Spirit.

We started working for Uncle Lee less than a month after Surprise Lake Camp. When my mother proposed that we work at MacLaren's, I was dismissive, but Adar thought it seemed like a good idea. He had lost time and money after the fiasco at Surprise Lake, and needed to work immediately if he was going to save enough money for art school in the fall. Working for Uncle Lee meant we didn't have to waste time hunting through classifieds; we could start anytime we liked. Uncle Lee met with Adar and hired him on the spot. Working together meant we could continue to see one another every day for the rest of the summer.

Then things started to go badly. We were having lunch, and I wanted to continue our discussion of Nietzsche's *Thus Spake Zarathustra*, a book which magically seemed to anticipate everything we were thinking about: the Superman who didn't need to observe society's rules. But after exactly thirty minutes, Adar stood up. He didn't need a watch to know what time it was; I was always late and didn't care. More importantly, there was an implied reproach in the abrupt way he raised his body from his chair while I was speaking. His manner seemed to say, "You can afford not to care about punching in on time—I can't!" And he was right. I had completely lost track of time. To me, if we were late, we were late. After all, we were working for Uncle Leon. But for him, this was work. He was not working for extra spending money; he was working for his college tuition. For me, our "job" was simply an older version of chalking pants with Uncle Lee as a child.

"Where is your self-discipline?" Adar said derisively. "You're treating the whole thing like a joke."

"It is a joke."

"Anything I do is an extension of myself," he said. "Anything. My job is important by virtue of its being done by me."

The words sounded oddly pompous when he said them.

"We're learning to inventory jackets and cut pants, for God's sake. You can dress it up, but it's not important, or worthy of us." I used the word "worthy" because it was a part of the vocabulary we had cultivated, and therefore one I thought Adar would respond to. Instead, it was just the opposite.

"You have no idea what you're talking about. You sound like a typical spoiled rich kid from Horace Mann." My cheeks crimsoned with shame. Then, he mollified his attack, adding, "You're not, but you do sound like one when you talk like that."

It was the first time we'd had a disagreement of any kind. I loved Adar. Not in an overtly physical way, perhaps, but spiritually. Now he had contempt for me, while I, for the first time, found him self-righteous and smug. It was not my fault he had to earn his own tuition. For the rest of the afternoon we didn't speak, and at our mid-afternoon break, he turned his back and walked away. I tried to make eye contact, but he avoided me.

After a day or two of sulking, we both decided to make up. The plan was to celebrate our friendship with a game of basketball, just like at Surprise Lake. Then we'd have dinner and see the Ingmar Bergman movie playing at the Thalia at Broadway and 95th.

"What if we have dinner at your house?" Adar asked. "It's not that far from the Thalia, and it would save us money and time."

"True," I said, all the while trying to invent an excuse. He had been up to my house once before, but it was only to use the bathroom, and my mother and Bobby were not home. While he was there, I looked around at the apartment with his eyes and felt disgust. There were soiled clothes everywhere, including a pile overflowing a white plastic hamper right beside the bathroom door. The tub and sink both had filthy brown rings. A large plastic bottle of peroxide stood on the floor, along with Bobby's magic wand and disappearing ink. Since my futile attempt to clean had ended in disaster, I had ignored these things. Now I saw them again. I had to get a stack of paper towels from the kitchen so Adar could dry his hands. I saw an empty can of Bumble Bee tuna and started to panic. All this was a betrayal of what we believed life should be. Obviously, he noticed everything (how could he not), but chose to say nothing afterwards.

Now he was suggesting a meal. Impossible. If I told her, my mother would insist on cooking for us (hamburgers?), and then the subject of my vegetarianism (which I had so far managed to conceal) would come out, leading who knew where? She would secretly blame my friend, I knew, for turning me into some kind of religious fanatic. A vegetarian—who else besides a crazy person didn't eat meat? Besides, wasn't I skinny enough already? When I went to summer camp in Maine, she ordered the camp director to make sure I was served malted milks with raw eggs in them every day to help me gain weight. And every afternoon at precisely 2:00 p.m. I left naptime with the other campers, and was forced to trudge to the dining room where I had to drink my malted. All the other kids knew about it, and, although some were envious, I was sure they all laughed behind my back at my having to be force-fed milkshakes on my mother's orders. On the return walk back to my bunk, I imagined a yellow yolk floating around in my belly, trying to squirm its way out.

It was bad enough that Adar saw my family all day at work; I hated to have him see how I lived. If that happened, all would be lost. He would see my world in all its sordid reality, and it would shame me forever. The thought of him seeing my mother's wine bottles and spouting Shakespeare was a humiliation I could not endure. Worse, my brother, always starved for affection, might be home. He would show Adar his magic tricks, or worse, his toy handcuffs and lock him in the bathroom. Or he might trot out the pack of Sygam the Great business cards Uncle Lee had printed for his tenth birthday. Adar might not show it, but any chance of convincing him of my worthiness to follow him in the Life of the Spirit would be doomed.

I convinced him to meet me instead at his apartment in Brooklyn. I had never actually been to Brooklyn before, and it seemed like an adventure to visit him there. Adar wrote out directions with a mechanical pencil on graph paper in his beautifully precise handwriting. On a Saturday afternoon in August I set out for his apartment.

I really hadn't thought much about what I would find there besides him. The important thing was not to let him see my world at close range. As I emerged from the Canarsie subway station, I was met by a tangle of green high-rise blocks. As soon as I entered his building, I felt suffocated by an overwhelming smell of cat piss. At the same time, I was furious at my own puerile response: Adar was absolutely right; I was just a spoiled rich kid. I couldn't even walk inside a high-rise without feeling faint. Where was my strength, my courage? Was this how I was going to become master of myself—by passing out? I followed a line of green ooze along the wall of his floor, which led me to his apartment. I breathed in heavily and rang the bell.

"Ya vant ta see da boy?" An old man in a sleeveless undershirt answered the door.

"Yes, please."

"Zout."

"Excuse me, sir?"

"Zout."

"I'm sorry, I don't understand what you mean."

"'Zout! The boy iz out," an old woman said, emerging from the darkness.

"Oh, I see," I said, staring.

Then she yawned loudly and stretched. "Iss so hot. Makes me sleepy," she said. Her underarms were full of dense, black hair. She wore a thin sleeveless housecoat, and carried a red ball of yarn. I noticed her legs were covered with the same coarse hair as her armpits.

"Dat's vat I told him," the man in the undershirt protested.

"I'm sorry, I didn't understand you the first time." The house stank of boiled chicken.

"You want zit down kitchen?" she said. "Zome zoup mebbe?"

"No thank you," I said. "I'll—uh—wait out here for Adar. I mean, if it's all right with you?"

136

"Ya ever see such a skinny boy?" the old man said to his wife pointing at me as though I wasn't present.

"Yah, nothing but skin an' bones," she replied. "You sure you don' wan' zoup? We got also stuffed chalupses an' kasha an' shells. Adar don't eat no meat—so the chalupses go to waste if you don't eat some."

"I'm vegetarian, too," I said proudly.

"Oy vay—not another one!" she said, "Vell, make yourself at home; he'll be back soon. You vanna go his room? Ya need mebbe use da toilet?"

"No, thank you," I said, speaking very slowly. Then, I ventured with a smile, "I didn't know Adar's grandparents lived here too."

The old woman began laughing hysterically, rocking back and forth and squeezing her arms across her bra-less breasts to keep the hilarity inside. "Heeeheeeheeee! Heeheeeheee! Ve ain't his grandparents, ve're his parents. You like my son?"

"Very much." I didn't know what else to say, or where to look. I just stood by the door, my hands nailed to my sides. For what seemed like hours. Then Adar walked in frowning, and led me into his room.

"You've met them, I see."

"Yes. They're very nice." Again, I couldn't think of anything else to say.

"What's the matter? You look pale."

"No, why would I be?" I said.

"They're very old. They had me late. After the war."

"Well, maybe they're a little older than I expected, but …"

"I thought I had told you. What's the matter with you?"

I felt nervous, like I was suddenly talking to a stranger. I changed the subject. "Sorry, I got here early; I didn't know how long it would take. I made really good time."

"Sit down," Adar said.

There were no chairs; just a small trundle bed, a bookcase, and an easel. "Where should I sit?" I asked.

"The bed, of course." I hesitated a moment, and a look of annoyance crossed his face. "Just sit down, will you?" he said irritably.

Something had changed and that change had begun to make us strangers. Seeing him in that environment affected me more than I dared admit. It wasn't simply the neighborhood, the building, his old parents, or the poverty; it was the juxtaposition between the esteem with which I held him, and the commonness of his real life. To me, he was a hero, a mentor. I was also in love. This was a young man who talked so passionately about the Law of the Spirit that he believed he might learn to free himself from the earth and fly. Yet his upbringing was as ugly as my own, although obviously in a very different way. I was ashamed of my own inability to separate the appearance of his circumstances from the reality of his being. Because he grew up in Canarsie in a filthy housing project, it didn't mean he could not transform himself into something beautiful, did it? No more than my world and upbringing had condemned me to a life of ugliness. It was ridiculous. And hypocritical.

I longed to be strong enough to rise above what I saw. I wanted our friendship returned to its romantic luster. But, it did not. Something was missing. Something neither one of us was able to admit, or articulate. A few months before, when I was reading Blake in the Donnell Library, I came across the poem, "A Poison Tree." The poem astonished me. Instead of being all flowers and clouds, this poem was simple as a nursery rhyme and night-marish as a horror story:

I was angry with my friend;
I told my wrath, my wrath did end.
I was angry with my foe:
I told it not, my wrath did grow.

And I waterd it in fears,
Night & morning with my tears:
And I sunned it with smiles,
And with soft deceitful wiles.

And it grew both day and night.
Till it bore an apple bright.
And my foe beheld it shine,
And he knew that it was mine.

And into my garden stole,
When the night had veild the pole;
In the morning glad I see;
My foe outstretched beneath the tree.

Something had come between us, but it couldn't be uttered and was left unspoken. I felt ashamed of my dear friend, unable to reconcile his spiritual questing with his common background. And Adar? Did he feel hostility and envy toward me for all the things I had and took for granted—money, privilege, education? How absurdly easy and uncomplicated my life must have seemed from his perspective! Lots of money, private schools, the assumption that I would attend college and never have to pay a dime—it must have seemed like a fairy tale! I could do whatever I wanted—except of course, I couldn't. From my vantage point, Adar's life seemed one of complete freedom—since he lacked a father bent on controlling and contradicting … no … annihilating every independent and creative impulse.

Whatever that something was that had come between us, it had borne fruit like the poison in Blake's poem. Our relationship had, I thought, been predicated on complete honesty—yet, I was unable to share with my friend any of my true feelings. As a result, I became a colder, calculating, and above all, more secretive and evasive person. My father always said I was a congenital liar. Now I discovered he was right.

During the days that followed, we pretended to communicate with our old intensity—Ayn Rand, vegetarianism, painting, the Spirit—but our former authenticity was missing. We went through the motions, but it was a parody of what we once shared. We continued to be friends. But previously, we had been something much more than that.

One morning, I woke up gasping, unable to breathe. I felt hot and clammy and threw the covers on the floor. I felt like I couldn't spend even one more day working at MacLaren's. Then I realized it was not the job I had to leave—it was Adar! I could have managed to put up with a boring job a few weeks more until school began, but what I could not accept was that our friendship, our "Union" as we called it, was not what I thought it to be. I had sworn such loyalty, such devotion. Now everything was swirling around: love, anger, guilt, and betrayal, until I was suffocating.

I called him at work and said I had the flu. My hands were trembling. There was silence on the other end. Did he suspect something? Probably.

But I wasn't lying, not really. I couldn't have gotten out of bed even if I wanted to. I watched cartoons, like I did when I had to stay home sick when I was a kid. Mom even brought me a tray with Cream of Wheat. She put a pat of butter in it like she did when I was home sick as a child. For lunch I had Campbell's Chicken Noodle Soup and saltines. For dinner, she made me her special "Egyptian" eggs: a sunny-side up egg served underneath a slice of fried bread with a hole cut in the center. Then, she put the missing hole of the bread back on top of the "eye" again. I hadn't had those since I was five or six. I even asked her about my favorite children's book, *A Touchdown for Doc*. She thought I was joking about the book, which of course she never could have located anyway, and went back to the kitchen. I wasn't joking. But then I remembered my father had taken the book and ripped it up years before during one of his rages when he caught me reading instead of doing homework.

My grandparents vacationed at precisely the same time each year. In winter, they went to The Breakers in Palm Beach; in summer, they went to the Mount Washington Hotel in New Hampshire. As with everything else, including eating and sleeping, they operated on separate schedules: Grandpa flew; Grandma took the train.

It was late summer and I had just turned sixteen. I couldn't go back to work. I had no intention of living at home with my mother, and I couldn't confront Adar about my changed feelings. So, in the middle of the night, I grabbed a few things and, without a word, decided to head to New Hampshire. I didn't even flush the toilet for fear it might wake Bobby. If he knew I was leaving, he would wake Mom and ruin everything. And if she woke up and found out what I was doing, she would call the police to stop me. I managed to lock the front door as I made my getaway. Feverishly, I walked all the way down to the Port Authority terminal from 72nd Street. I thought the walk would refresh me. It didn't.

The Port Authority Bus Terminal was filled with flying hotdog wrappers and unshaven men. The waiting room stank of sweat. An old woman cooed, pushing a small baby carriage across the floor with a smiling doll tucked inside. I had a Pan Am Airways bag with me, a jar of Skippy Peanut Butter, saltines, underwear, socks, and a flannel shirt.

The Greyhound for New Hampshire left at four in the morning, and as we pulled away, I slumped down, imagining the police were after me. I was also terrified I would see Adar. I found a copy of *The Daily News* on the floor, wadded it up, and wedged it between my head and the window-pane for a pillow. I ate nearly the whole jar of Skippy, scooping it up with my forefinger without crackers, and fell asleep. I woke up suddenly with terrible diarrhea, and barely made it to the little toilet at the back of the bus. The toilet was more comfortable than my seat, and I stayed in there a long time. When I staggered back to my seat, I noticed that the bus was empty. I walked up to the front and terrified the driver, who had no idea anyone was still left on board. He told me we had passed Mount Washington, and dropped me off at the next rest stop.

The mountain air was freezing cold. I pulled on my heavy shirt, and ate the saltines with a half bottle of fizzless Coke someone had left behind. That settled my stomach. I had no idea where I was, or how far from Mount Washington I was, and didn't really care anymore.

Outside the truck stop in the middle of the New Hampshire mountains, I watched cars flash by like monsters with yellow eyes. For the first time in my life, no one knew where I was. Not my parents, not Adar. If I died, no one would care. I might be missing for days, weeks ... my body would turn up somewhere.

"Sixteen Year Old Discovered! Face Mutilated by Animals," would be my epitaph, along with my limbless picture on the front page of the *National Enquirer*. I thought about Adar, and how just over a month ago we walked sixty miles back to New York together. How long ago that was! How shallow and superficial I was to have thrown that away! My father was right—I would never amount to anything. I sat by the side of the road, holding my knees, rocking back and forth. Then I began to scream, the helpless rage of an abandoned child.

After a while, I felt like I was watching one of those old horror movies with Margaret. She had thrust her tiny fists into her eyes, and I told her, "It's only a movie." I knew everything would turn out all right in the end, even if it seemed impossible at the moment. And it did.

"This is me speaking, Grandma. Henry. I'm calling from a truck stop here … somewhere in New Hampshire. Please don't cry—"

She stopped crying and began to scream. I took the phone and tucked it under my ear, shoving my hands inside my pants to keep warm. I knew I had to wait for her shrieking to subside, so I remained patient while her wailing shook the glass phone booth.

"OH MY GOD, OH MY GOD, IT'S HIM! WAKE UP, HARRY! HAAAAARRY!—HE'S ON THE PHONE! WHO? HENRY, THAT'S WHO! Where are you calling from? New Hampshire? HE'S CALLING FROM NEW HAMPSHIRE! I'm gonna have a stroke! What's he doing to me? How did you get here? By BUS? YOU TOOK THE GREYHOUND BUS ALL BY YOURSELF? Don't you know Stanley, my nephew, he took the bus at night and was mugged and ended up in the hospital; they said he had BRAIN DAMAGE!"

"Stanley has brain damage, Grandma? I didn't know—"

"No, they think he's okay now, but is that what you want for yourself? It serves you right! You think our kind of people take the Greyhound bus at night? Only Goyim! You think the Jews survived Dachau and godknows-where so you could ride the Greyhound to New Hampshire in the middle of the night? Do you? There are all kinds of sick, deranged people on buses. Tilly Goodman, she plays canasta with me, had her purse stolen on a bus. What's that? No, the 86th Street Crosstown, but it's the same thing. Thank God nothing happened. It's—what time is it? Omygod, you're in some sort of trouble, aren't you? HAARRRY, get out of bed and get in here right away, something's wrong! I knew it, I told him I didn't want to go this year. Get in here! No, I'm not joking! It's him!"

"Grandma, listen. Please, calm down. I'm fine. Really. Fine. I just wanted to talk to you and Grandpa."

"He just wanted to talk … so he rode all the way up to New Hampshire by Greyhound in the middle of the night—to talk! They don't have phones, anymore, at your mother's?"

"I wanted to talk in person. Visit you here."

"Do they know you're here, your father and mother?"

"No."

"OHMYGOD HAARRRY, Norman don't even know he's here!"

I heard the familiar "Bitch … bitch … bitch" as Grandpa snatched the receiver away.

"Now be calm," he said softly, but firmly.

"I am calm, Grandpa," I said. I really did feel strangely calm.

"Not you. I was talking to your grandmother. Hold on a sec. She's lying over here on the floor with a washcloth soaked in vinegar, crying. Calm down now, Birdie, I say! Look, tell me where you are and we'll pick you up."

"I don't know where I am, Grandpa." As I said this, I felt an indescribable sense of shame. How could I call them without knowing where I was?

"You don't know where you are?" There was an infinitely long silence on the other end. "Okay, that's okay. Now check with somebody who does know, and I'll hold. But for god's sake don't hang up."

"All right, I won't. It may take a minute." I went inside the truck stop and got the address.

"Okey-dokey, you wait right by that phone booth and don't go off anywhere else. You understand?"

"I understand."

"I know the place; it's about half an hour. As soon as we can. In a taxi. If dey have such tings in New Hampshire."

"Okay, Grandpa."

I started to hang up, and heard him do something completely out of character: he began to sing!

"I'll be down to getcha in a taxi, honey … better be ready 'bout half-past eight. Don't be late … Gonna be there when the band starts playing …"

"Grandpa? Are you all right?"

I heard the phone crackle as he came back on. "Just trying to cheer her up a little, your grandmother … I think she might have passed out."

I had never heard anyone in my family sing besides Mom, and the only thing I could remember her singing in years was Tony Bennett's "I Wanna Be Around." Now, here, in the middle of a freezing New Hampshire night, my grandfather was actually singing.

I stood by the side of the road stamping my feet for a half hour or so, until I saw the approaching taxi. Grandpa and Grandma were inside, and it looked like a silent movie: two people yelling, gesticulating, mouths moving, but no sound. Grandpa got out and pinched me on both cheeks, and every-thing became less surreal. I climbed inside where Grandma was waiting to kiss me. She was apparently under strict orders not to say anything. She saw my Pan Am bag, and turned to ask Grandpa where the boy's luggage was. Grandpa shrugged. "Birdie. Remember what we agreed. Tomorrow is time enough."

We drove back to the Mount Washington Hotel in silence.

The Greeks had different rivers in Hades: Mnemosyne and Lethe. If you drank from Mnemosyne, you remembered everything; if you drank from Lethe, you remembered nothing. The week I stayed with my grandparents in New Hampshire was just what I needed. After we got back to the hotel, it was still dark outside and I wasn't sleepy. Grandma told me to take a bath. I never took baths anymore, and was going to tell her no. But for some reason I listened. I felt as though someone had dipped me gently into Lethe. I remem-bered baths Grandma used to give me when I was a little boy. I always hated it when she wrapped me up so tight I couldn't move my arms or legs in the white terrycloth towel—her towels felt so soft, and smelled so different than the ones we had at home—but by the time she lifted me out and rubbed me with Johnson and Johnson's talcum powder, I loved the feeling.

After the bath, I slept until evening of the following day. I knew that they must have called my parents to tell them I was okay. But they never mentioned it, and neither did I. There was an unspoken understanding that no one would mention how I ended up in New Hampshire.

Each new day at the hotel had the same routine. At 7:00 we went down to breakfast, just the three of us. We each were given a little card with a golf pencil to mark down what we wanted, and every morning I ordered exactly the same thing as Grandpa: first, oatmeal with brown sugar and raisins and heavy cream, which you poured from a miniature sterling silver pitcher. Then a poached egg in a special cup. I'd never eaten a poached egg before, and didn't want to even try it because of my experience with the malteds in camp I was forced to drink with a raw egg to fatten me up. But now I found I could eat a poached egg and like it. While I waited for my egg, the waiter always brought fresh orange juice in a tiny glass, a basket of fresh salted rolls, and a tray with individual pats of butter. He put two gleaming pats of butter on my plate with a tiny pair of tongs. I buttered a roll and dipped it in the egg yolk. I even finished breakfast with pitted prunes and a cup of instant Postum like Grandpa. I tried to melt into their ordered lives, and it worked. After breakfast, Grandpa went back to his room and put on a pork-pie hat, and we were on the putting greens by 7:45. After lunch, from 1:15 to 2:15, Grandpa took his nap, and I played Gin Rummy with Grandma. Then, we did crossword puzzles or read the two-day-old *New York Times* when it finally made its way up to the hotel. Not once did Grandma tell me how I needed to bring my parents back together. Not once did either of them ask me how I ended up there in the middle of the frozen night.

After a week, Grandpa asked how I felt about returning to New York. I told him I was fine with that. My final weekend there, I felt good enough to try tennis again. Grandpa was napping and Grandma was playing canasta, so I went out and looked for the courts. I had not played even once since my father had left, but it seemed like it might be fun to try again. I felt so healthy and rested, and everything seemed so different now. I borrowed a racket and balls from the pro shop and walked bravely over the perfectly manicured fields to the courts to begin practicing my serve. And it did feel good to be on a tennis court again. I opened the can of balls, listened to the hissing sound of gas escaping from the vacuumed tin, and inhaled the delicious aroma of brand new Slazenger tennis balls.

But as I tossed the fuzzy white ball up in the air and followed its arc up into that flawless blue sky, my mind flooded with so many images that I couldn't even swing the racket. All those times I had gone with such enthusiasm to play tennis with my father at the Rosen's in Scarsdale and come home filled with shame, came rushing back in the seconds between tossing the ball aloft and its return. The ball plopped at my feet, and I followed it until it stopped bouncing. Then I walked away. I left the racket and can of balls lying there, too.

When I returned to the city, New York felt like a tomb. Of course, the streets were full of people—the last gasp of the summer tourist season, businessmen in seersucker suits and straw hats, women clicking around Fifth Avenue in high heels—but it felt completely deserted. I looked over my shoulder constantly. For Adar. Sometimes I felt he was there, spying on me and watching me from across the street. Other times I knew it was my imagination. Even so, I wondered, was Adar deliberately toying with me, sadistically waiting to take revenge, intruding himself into my thoughts? Uncle Lee told me he had worked two more days after I left. Then he quit without saying a word—not even a goodbye to Uncle Lee. His final paycheck was still waiting for him; did I want to deliver it to Adar myself? I told him to forward it to Canarsie.

There were only a few weeks of summer left, but something remarkable happened nevertheless. My father came over and my parents actually spoke to one another civilly a few days after my return. In the living room. My mother hired a handy man to move all the boxes into her locked bedroom. I don't know what they said, but the outcome was that if I expected to go to college (assuming Horace Mann let me graduate), I would need to see a psychiatrist. They were afraid I would commit suicide. I saw Dr. Irving five times per week. He said almost nothing. My recollection of these sessions was that we simply stared at one another for forty-five minutes—then I left. I called him Dr. Steelcase because he looked just like one of those filing cabinets: gray hair, gray suit, gray tie. Even his notebook was gray. In my imagination, his wife and children were gray, too. Even though I hated seeing him, after the allotted time, he told my parents that he felt it was safe for me to attend college in the fall.

Horace Mann took pity on me, and allowed me to graduate. However, only one college accepted me: the University of Wisconsin. Wisconsin had two features that appealed to me: it was a long way from New York, and they had lost the 1963 Rose Bowl game. I watched the Rose Bowl on television, and never forgot how Wisconsin, led by star player Pat Richter, stormed back from a huge deficit to make the game heart-stoppingly close. They lost by a final score of 42–37, and I wept at the game's final seconds when the outcome was decided. Had Wisconsin won, I wouldn't have applied. Losing gallantly made it seem a school where I belonged.

As my mother read the acceptance letter from the Director of Admissions, her hands trembled and she began to sob uncontrollably. "Those are tears of joy, aren't they, Mom?"

"Joy? Of course, they're joy," she said. Tears still shone on her cheeks. "What mother wouldn't be overjoyed to see her son ruin his life?"

"What are you talking about?"

"Where you attend college determines your future, and 'it must follow as the night the day, thou canst not then be false to—'"

"Mom, stop quoting Polonius—he deserved to die, stabbed behind that arras in *Hamlet*." Her days of studying Shakespeare with Joseph Wood Krutch and Lionel Trilling were never far from her, especially if they contained a lesson she could cram down my throat.

"How can you say such a thing? That's cruel. Polonius was a good, kind man," she said sadly, "like my Papa, or your Uncle Lee."

"He was nothing like Gramps; he was a snoop. What was he doing snooping there in the first place?"

I began walking feverishly around the dining room table. This was something I had wanted to say for years, and now I had a perfect excuse. The characters from *Hamlet* had sprung to life in my mother's mind, and had become metamorphosed into people from her family: my father was of course, Claudius; she herself was Gertrude; I was Hamlet; Polonius could be either her father or Uncle Lee depending on the situation. My view was that if Uncle Lee happened to get stabbed listening in on my conversations (as happened more than once at Gramsie's house where telephone conversations were never private), he deserved what he got.

"Polonius was there to help protect Hamlet's mother," she said, defensively. "A woman alone, attacked by her son ... it was unfair. What was her name again?"

"Gertrude, Mom. How could you forget her name? I thought you were such a brilliant student? Unlike me." My sarcasm was modulating into anger.

"Of course, Gertrude. I remember attending Mark Van Doren's lectures on Shakespeare at Columbia ... such brilliant men. I have my essays from those courses somewhere ... did I ever show them to you? I got straight A's from both Professor Van Doren and Professor Trilling. And they never, and I mean never, gave A's." She gazed towards her bedroom where the essays were buried in one of her countless boxes.

"You've shown me the essays." I said.

"Oh. Where were we?"

"Wisconsin," I said. "I was admitted there, remember." My anger was growing in direct proportion to her obliviousness.

"Yes, I remember, and I won't sit back and see you ruining yourself by going to a state school."

"It's a terrific school, Mom. My college counselor says it's one of the top schools in the Midwest academically. Besides, with my grades and SAT scores, I'm lucky to get in anywhere."

"How dare you say that?"

"Because it's true!" I was desperate now. "It's not like I've been admitted anywhere else. I even got rejected by a school you said must have been named after a candy bar!" I was referring to Clark University. She was sensitive about this topic; she even went crazy when she once heard me humming The Beatles' "I'm a Loser" in the shower. She even refused to let me see the *Follow Me Boys* movie since Walt Disney had died just prior to its release. Mom knew those boys must be following him to the grave.

"You know how I feel about you low-rating yourself," she said. "Besides, I have custody of you until you're twenty-one. I have it all worked out. Professor Mosley says you'll be enrolled at Columbia by Christmas."

"What! What are you talking about?"

"My Hen-yie at Columbia! Won't that be wonderful? You are still my Hen-yie, aren't you?" She started calling me this childish nickname when she was wildly enthusiastic.

"Please don't take this the wrong way, Mom, okay? I don't want to go to college in New York."

"That's ridiculous! Why not?"

"Hasn't Horace Mann proved anything to you?"

"Yes—that you have a despicable, cruel bastard for a father."

"And you think it will be better for me here? Who's Professor Mosley anyway?"

"A neighbor from our apartment on Riverside Drive. He teaches History there."

"And he can get me into Columbia?"

"I'm absolutely positive of it!"

I had a sinking feeling about my mother's plan that I couldn't define, except that I wanted no part of it. My mother, however, began to gleefully fantasize about the next four years with me living at home.

"You know that President Dwight David Eisenhower signed my diploma when I graduated Teacher's College for my Master's. I was pregnant with you then, so it's almost as though you've already been matric—"

"I really think it would be better for me to get away for college—to be on my own."

"I wonder who you sound like now? Don't forget that you're gifted! It all has to do with your father. Until he left, you had straight A's."

"Mom, I never got straight A's—not since second grade with Miss Hunt; in fact, that was my high point, academically."

"Defeatist! Damned defeatist! Don't you dare say that—you were always the smartest boy in your class. Remember how you skipped first grade when you got to Hunter? You walked in, could read better than any of them … you could read at three. Doctor Brumbaugh said you were the smartest, most beautiful little boy she had ever seen—those blonde curls! And don't forget you were potty-trained at six months!"

"Mom, nobody is 'potty trained' at six months. It's impossible."

"SIX MONTHS!" Now things were serious. I had stepped on a land mine. "Listen to me, Henry. I'm talking to you. Please sit down next to me. Please."

I did as I was told.

"Now, as God is my witness you were not only toilet trained at six months, you could read at three years old. You can ask Gramsie if you don't believe me. You are gifted. And you are God's own dear child. Do you understand me?"

"Yes, Mom, if you say so."

"Don't be condescending about it."

Even if true, the correlation between toilet training and academic excellence was a principle that eluded me then, and still does. Nevertheless, to my mother, there was an inextricable link between the two. No matter who won our fights, on that one point she never wavered.

I left for Wisconsin. My mother continued to resent my leaving home, and turned her cheek when I kissed her goodbye. But she hadn't said anything about transferring to Columbia for several days, and seemed to accept my decision to fly to Madison with my father for orientation and placement examinations in French, Math, and English. In a few days time, I would begin my new life as a college freshman. I was excited to start over in a place where no one knew me, and where I could reinvent myself and become the person I wanted to be. As I sat at a little wooden desk with four No. 2 pencils and a pink eraser, I prepared to begin the first of several placement tests at the University of Wisconsin.

As I tapped the point on my pencils to make sure they were neither too dull nor too sharp, a man in a crew-cut and bowtie came up beside me, kneeled down and whispered so as not to disturb the others: "You don't belong here, son." I had just finished reading *The Trial* on flight to Madison, and my first reaction to this bizarre comment about not belonging was to believe him. The second was to mumble to myself the mesmerizing opening sentence from my green Modern Library edition of Kafka's novel: "Someone must have traduced Joseph K., for without having done anything wrong he was arrested one fine morning."

I was too nervous to speak. Finally, he planted himself beside me, refusing to go away. I clutched the yellow pencils tightly, which now mocked my abortive independence. I had been admitted, hadn't I? I had the letter of acceptance to the College of Integrated Liberal Studies in my pocket; I was about to take placement tests like any other freshman. Maybe I was in the wrong room. I got up slowly to check the room number.

"Isn't this Room 167, sir?"

"I don't think you understand," he continued gently. "You're not enrolled at all."

Trembling, I pulled out a letter. "Look at the date," he said. Then he told me that my mother had phoned, demanding my enrollment be rescinded, and the deposit refunded.

"She said you're going to Hofstra, I think."

I felt my throat constrict, and the glands in my neck go all hot and sweaty.

"Why don't we go out into the hall?" the bow-tied man said.

The hallway was dark wood, and from the ground floor I glanced up and saw an intricate staircase. But I would never be allowed to climb those stairs. I was going back to New York. I couldn't talk. I needed to run. I saw two giggling girls with hair the color of Wisconsin cheddar; they were laughing, and of course I knew they were laughing at me. I thought of my humiliation on the very first day of second grade when, embarrassed about raising my hand to ask to go to the bathroom, I went in my pants, and the whole class learned about my disgrace as Miss Hunt personally escorted me to the little boy's room. I walked away from the man in the bowtie with as much dignity as I could summon.

Once I separated myself from him, I bolted down the hallway and vomited all over the white and black tile of the bathroom floor. Bascom Hall was the central administration building and housed the Chancellor's office. It had huge white columns outside, and I wondered if the chancellor himself could hear me retching from his office. I hadn't vomited like that since I was five, and I'd completely forgotten how awful and embarrassing it was: the sounds, the sour taste, the half-digested food, the smell! I felt I should apologize to someone. But there was no one to apologize to, so I got down on my knees and cleaned up the mess with paper towels. Then I knelt down in a different corner of the bathroom, and pressed my forehead against the cold tiles.

I took a sip of water from the fountain outside the Chancellor's office, and recovered a bit. I walked back to the Wisconsin Inn where my father was waiting. Here for the express purpose of being on my own, as soon as I arrived, I had thrown up and run to my father. I hadn't felt this helpless since my bar mitzvah. I knew I would encounter either anger or mockery, possibly both, as I approached our room at the end of the corridor. How could I confess that I had not taken the placement exams?

I knocked softly, and waited for him to answer the door although I had a spare key in my pocket. The television was on and he had been watching football with a tall Bloody Mary in his hand, a stalk of celery peering over the top of the glass. I said nothing.

"Just sit down and tell me what happened," he said calmly.

"But—but—but," I stammered.

"Listen, you have to remain calm, Henry; just breathe. I can't do anything until you've let me in on what has happened." He didn't mention my tears, the disheveled state of my clothes, or the vomit stains and smells on my clothes.

"All right, what happened?" He had a way of astonishing me. Just when I thought I had figured him out, he turned into someone else. When I felt confident, he treated me like dirt; when I had nothing, he was compassionate. I couldn't understand it, but I was grateful. I stopped sniveling and kissed him. He offered me his fragrant cheek, and held me briefly in his arms as I told him.

"Sonofabitch! Goddamnsonofabitch Lerner bastard!" I felt much better at the sound of those comforting words.

What happened was this: while my father and I were flying from New York to Madison, my mother phoned and canceled my registration. She'd planned for me to attend Columbia all along. When she accepted that I couldn't get into Columbia on my own, she had made a deal for me to go to Hofstra for the fall semester, prove myself with good grades, and transfer to Columbia after Christmas. It was as good as official. I had been accepted and enrolled, without being informed, at Hofstra, a school to which I hadn't even applied.

When the Registrar called and told her about freshman pre-orientation, my mother insisted there had been a mistake. She had legal custody of me, she said, and I was going to Hofstra. She was very, very sorry about the inconvenience. She could be polite and charming when the occasion demanded it, and maintained that I would not be attending Wisconsin.

My registration was rescinded.

My father demanded to see the Dean while I lingered nervously outside his office biting my nails. He and my mother were divorcing, he said. It was really my mother who was mistaken. After all, here I was, ready to begin my freshman year and take whatever damn placement tests they wanted. He yanked me in from where I was waiting, and asked if I wanted to be here in

Wisconsin. Right on cue I nodded. Did the university require a check to cover the inconvenience? He took out his checkbook and said he would be glad to cover the costs. No, but since they had returned my tuition deposit, would he mind writing a new check out for that same amount? Of course not. As he wrote the check, I noticed the gleaming diamond pinkie ring on his left finger, his elegantly manicured and polished nails, and his gleaming signature signed with the Mont Blanc fountain pen he used only on special occasions. "Well," the Dean said, "we're so sorry about all the inconvenience. We'll get him back into the same dorm, and it will be like nothing ever happened."

"Like nothing ever happened."

Those words were from a fairy tale. I looked up at my father and he smiled down at me. We're in this damn thing together, his look said.

I'll never forget that day. It was one of those moments where a common foe led to intimacy and reconciliation. He never alluded to my throwing up or crying. In fact, he never mentioned it again. Even at his irrational worst, he never used my past failures against me. Never. Somewhere deep down, he was decent, I argued to myself. Somewhere, deep down, he cared.

Reflecting on this episode now makes me want to call him in the hospital and remind him of that time in Madison, how much it meant that he stood by me. But might he not remember the episode very differently? Somehow, I can imagine our conversation drifting from my gratitude into some fault: my ignorance about finances or the improper way I raise my children. This has all happened before. So I don't call. Instead, I think of a passage I recently jotted down from Montaigne: "We are entirely made up of bits and pieces, woven together so diversely and so shapelessly that each one of them pulls its own way at every moment. And there is as much difference between us and ourselves as there is between us and other people."

Instead of phoning him, I close my eyes. I imagine myself walking along Jan van Goyenkade, the street in Leiden where we live. I look on the seventeenth-century red brick buildings, sleeping houseboats, and peaceful canals which line our house—all of which might have been painted by Vermeer. I see myself cycling along the Witte Singel, past the bust of Rembrandt van

Rijn, Leiden's most famous citizen. Most of all, I remember that my children are safe at home, growing up in a culture so different from the one I knew. I know they are safe. More than that, they are far from New York.

I replace the telephone in its cradle.

For the first week, I was terrified of the bone-biting cold of a Wisconsin winter. But after a few weeks, I enjoyed it. I loved walking along the Lakeshore Path. Walking along Lake Mendota, the wind whipping me in the face so hard I couldn't breathe. I bought a thick blue turtleneck sweater and a pea coat at the Army-Navy store, and as I walked back along the lake at night I flipped the collar of my pea coat up, channeling Raskolnikov tramping across the Nevsky Bridge in Petersburg. I took out a quarter from my pants pocket and sent it skimming across the frozen lake, imagining I had just tossed my last roubel into the Neva. I prowled Madison's streets, but screened off the reality of a college town with its bars and Brat Haus; instead, I imagined myself swept up in the mystery and romance of a Russian winter at the end of the nineteenth century.

I was walking to the library, preparing to meet with the Director of Freshman Composition. He told me to meet him because I was flunking English I: Expository Writing. On my fall midterm exam I had left my blue-book blank—not one word, except for a strange, hallucinatory poem, that even I could not understand when the exams were returned. The graduate assistant who taught the class, Mr. Palven, told me I should immediately report to the Health Center for counseling. Furthermore, he informed Dr. Skinner that I wasn't welcome in his class anymore. Now I had to explain to Skinner why I should be allowed to finish the course—a flashback to high school. The funny thing was, I read everything in sight—I just wouldn't read anything required for my classes.

On my way to meet Dr. Skinner, I thought how poorly I was doing, not only in English Composition, but also in Chemistry, Geology, and Ancient Greek. Why had I taken Greek? Mr. Herman once remarked that every truly educated person needed to be able to read Sophocles in the original. The rest of the class assumed this was one of his typical allusions to our insufficiency, but I took it seriously. So, I signed up for Ancient Greek at 8:50 a.m., Monday through Thursday in my first semester. Unfortunately, I had neither the discipline nor the concentration to succeed. I sat in the back row of Greek class with Dostoevsky's "White Nights" tucked inside my Greek grammar, like some pervert hiding a dirty magazine on the subway.

Dr. Skinner was tall and morose, and had an Adam's apple like Ichabod Crane in *The Headless Horseman*. He took out my bluebook, and began to click his tongue and make tsking sounds. He must have sat there silently holding the exam for about five long minutes, with only the sounds of his clicking tongue to distract me. Then he asked if I was seeing a psychiatrist; if not, he knew a good one at the Health Service. When I refused, he said that if I ever turned in another exam like that (with or without a poem), I wouldn't be allowed back, and would receive an F. Because Mr. Palven refused to take me back, he was doing me the favor of transferring me into a different section.

My life at school wasn't entirely confined to Dostoevsky and skipping class, however. My friend during that first semester was Dwayne Pfefferkorn. Wearing his white-blond hair in a crew cut, Dwayne had the misfortune of being born in Brillion, Wisconsin, population 800 and something. Dwayne desperately wanted to live this down and keep his origins a secret. At our first meeting during orientation, I casually asked him where he was from, and Dwayne flushed and put his index finger to his lips.

"I'll tell you later, in private," he said. I raised my eyebrows, but let it go. Later that night, over several Old Styles obtained with his fake I.D., Dwayne informed me about his origins. He whispered that nobody knew how Brillion had received its name. Prevailing wisdom was that when the town was founded in 1855, Postmaster T.K. West proposed the name Pilleola, an acronym based on the letters in the names of his two daughters. I wondered what those two daughters' names might have been—Pilly? Leola?—but Pilleola was rejected by Mr. West's post office colleagues, and the name was changed to Brillion. Some said it was named for a town in Prussia; others after someone named Brill. No one knew for sure. But for Dwayne, this uncertainty about his hometown made him feel like a bastard and an outcast—forever insecure about his origins.

Dwayne's embarrassment about his birthplace made him feel disproportionate excitement when he discovered his roommate was from New York City. Earlier in the summer, when he received word we were going to be roommates, he wrote me a letter asking all about New York and saying how excited he was to make friends with a New York Jew. He was crushed when, after my registration fiasco, he was assigned a different roommate, and I was given a rare single room, probably in compensation for the school's embarrassment surrounding my registration. Dwayne was even more "ticked," he said, when they gave my place to some kid from Manitowac who wasn't "Jewish, Negro, or anything." Dwayne decided he and I had a special bond, and he came into my room at all hours to "kvetch" (as he put it), about Greg, his Manitowac roommate, who also had white-blond hair and looked like he might have been Dwayne's twin. Dwayne loved saying the word "kvetch" and used it as often as possible. He knocked on my door when he came back after his morning lab to see how I was doing. I was still in my pajamas, having overslept and missed Greek again. I believe Dwayne saw himself as my responsible elder brother. He worried about my being sequestered in a single—and was especially concerned about my penchant for cutting classes.

"Missed Greek again, dincha? Hey—it stinks in here! What's going on? You smokin' somethin'?"

"No, Dwayne, I don't do that stuff. Anyway, that's not what marijuana smells like."

"So what's that stink from anyway? I tole ya you're not supposed to have a hot plate in here!"

"I wasn't cooking. I was burning something."

"Whatcha been burning?"

"Nothing."

"You gonna flunk it? Greek, I mean."

"Probably."

"Then why did you take it?"

"I thought it would be more interesting than it is."

"Ancient Greek? First thing in the morning?"

"Yes, Dwayne, you're right. I was wrong."

"I really don't mind waking you for Greek class. I have Chem Lab at the same exact time. If we were roommates like we were supposed to be, I wouldn't let you sleep through classes."

"That's really nice of you, Dwayne. I can get up on my own."

"I just don't want you flunking out, okay?"

"Thanks, Dwayne. I appreciate it."

"Yeah, okay, then." Exasperated, he brushed his hand through his white blond crew cut.

Dwayne walked over to my desk, and picked up the envelope lying beside the smoldering ashtray. "Hey, this is from the Selective Service! Is that what you just burnt—your draft card?"

"No," I lied. Actually, it was more misdirection than lie. What I had burnt was a letter from the Selective Service asking to verify my student deferment, prior to sending me my draft card. Instead of sending the information back, I burnt the notice.

"Damn, why'd you do that?"

"I don't know."

"You're gonna get in some serious trouble. There's a draft on, ya know. Vietnam War and all," Dwayne said proudly.

"I've heard about it, Dwayne," I said.

"Henry?" he asked. "Are you what my dad calls a subversive?"

"I don't know, Dwayne. Do I look like a subversive?"

Dwayne eyeballed me.

"I don't know. Could be. But if you're not, why'd you burn that thing?"

"I don't know." And it was the truth. It had nothing to do with opposition to the war or even the draft. It was my way of expressing my indifference toward real life in all its manifestations.

"Wow," he said, "this is big. Can I tell Greg?"

"No, Dwayne. I'd prefer it stayed just between us. Kind of like Brillion."

"Okay, I get it," he said, all cheery acceptance. "You wanna go to Hillel Friday? You guys have services every Friday night, dontcha? Candles, wine, egg bread?"

"You mean challah."

"What?"

"Never mind."

I liked Dwayne a lot. His curiosity made me feel sophisticated and important. Like there was something incredibly fascinating about me having grown up in New York, even if I knew there wasn't.

"Yeah, I'd really like to."

"All right—we'll go," I said.

"Cool." Dwayne was satisfied, but he still didn't leave my room. He was waiting for something.

"So, I'll see you at dinner?" I said, opening the door, hoping he would take the hint.

Friday night came and I made some excuse so I wouldn't have to go to Hillel or take him along. I liked Dwayne, but I just didn't want him (or anyone else) getting too close to me. I still felt Adar's influence when I spoke to other people, and I knew he wouldn't approve my socializing with others. And other than Dwayne, I hadn't met anyone I'd felt even a little comfortable with during my first semester.

There were more than 30,000 students at the University of Wisconsin, but every one I met seemed to fall into one of three distinct groups, none of which I connected with. First, there were the angry young men and women violently opposed to the Vietnam War. Their world was a black-and-white struggle against the Military Industrial Complex, and any dissent from "Truth" as they saw it was further proof of your cowardice and acquiescence to governmental conspiracy.

The second group was much larger, but far less visible: fraternity kids who got drunk on State Street every weekend. Unlike the anti-military group, which was largely comprised of East coast kids with backgrounds more or less similar to mine, this second group was mostly made up of in-staters from Wisconsin. They were throwbacks to a more innocent time before there was a war, and seemed confused or dismayed by all the fuss on campus. If they thought about the war at all, they probably supported it, parroting their parents' views. I was much too apathetic to join the first group. I found this second group oblivious. I wanted nothing to do with them either.

The third group was comprised of artist and hippie types. The girls wore their hair long, and favored tie-dyed shirts and Indian fabrics. With flowers in their hair, they looked like characters from a children's book; the guys had beards and jeans. I should have been happy to join this group, since like me, they were indifferent to radical politics. However, their philosophy of "Peace and Love" was diametrically opposed to my own. This third group, too, was into drugs, casual sex, Bob Dylan, Joan Baez, and The Beatles. They believed in Happenings, improvisation, and collective genius. I felt art was a pure, solitary, and above all, a deeply serious calling. I wouldn't have minded the free love part, but I was too shy and afraid to mingle or even talk to anyone.

So, instead of spreading love for everyone and everything, I idealized my isolation, and, although Adar and I were no longer one, I still tried to live according to our philosophy. An artist, I felt, could not embrace a collective mind-set. So, even though there was no dress code, and I hated everything that reminded me of high school, I still wore a dark suit and tie every day to my classes, just as I did at Horace Mann. Dressing like this was a private gesture of aloof non-conformity in the face of naïve benevolence. My odd attire even raised me to the level of a kind of campus oddity amid the vast sea of hippie non-conformity.

In classes, anti-war kids raised the ubiquitous cry of "What's the relevance?" for every possible occasion. Life was boiled down to that one issue of what was happening in the war in Southeast Asia. However, instead of leading to real debate, the issue of relevance led to simplistic connections tying everything to the Vietnam War. It also led to a perverse relationship between students and their professors, in which the latter opted not to lead, but follow the prevailing political wisdom. When the teachers couldn't make simplistic connections between their subjects and the war, many abdicated responsibility, with lame apologies for the "irrelevance" of the very subjects they had earned their doctorates in. I longed to be exposed to new ideas and discuss great works of literature—to find the next incarnation of Mr. Herman—not talk about whether the university should stop teaching Shakespeare because he had nothing to say about the Vietnam War.

Everybody was so caught up in the circus of pot smoking, protesting Vietnam, banning napalm, or revealing how the C.I.A. had secretly poisoned our water, that there was no appetite for any other ideas on campus. Nobody seemed passionate about works of literature, only politics and pot—especially our professors. In Wayne's class, he told me they were discussing John Donne's poem "The Flea" when someone hurled the familiar "What's the relevance?" at the young teaching assistant for the class. He apologized for the frivolousness of the poem, and told the class he agreed with them; he was truly sorry he couldn't justify teaching the poem while Americans were murdering Vietnamese and burning villages with napalm. The class erupted in applause, and was adjourned for further discussion. When I asked Wayne what happened next, he shrugged. "We went to the Brat Haus and had a few cold ones." A few weeks later, Dwayne told me that the teaching assistant had quit the PhD program in English.

Slender, with large eyes, full lips, and a waterfall of black hair, Laura, my new English teacher was quite an improvement over Mr. Palven. She taught class perched cross-legged on top of the desk, legs encased in black, fishnet tights. Her walk—proud, athletic—with shoulders pulled back, breasts thrust forward, made her appear like a miniature lioness. I couldn't stop staring at her, and her blunt sexuality terrified me. I was not merely frightened about her somehow witnessing my excitement at looking at her; I feared the repercussions to myself. Even though I hadn't seen him for months, Adar and the Life of the Spirit were still alive inside me. He was still there reminding me of what I should think or do, scolding me when I let myself be distracted by "lesser" things like Laura's breasts, swaying bra-less underneath her sheer blouse.

A week after I transferred into Laura's section, she told me to meet her at the campus Rathskeller. I wondered what she wanted to see me about, and was both thrilled and frightened. I decided to cut my last class before our meeting so I could rush back to my room and change. I removed my dark jacket and tie, and put on instead the navy turtleneck sweater I bought from the Army-Navy store after seeing *Doctor Zhivago*. I hadn't spoken in her class yet, but I had managed to alienate the other students by my sullen silence and repeated belligerent stares when they uttered comments I condescendingly dismissed as stupid. I was more than an oddity now; I was on my way to becoming downright weird, even on a campus full of hippies and potheads.

On my way across campus to our meeting, I saw a group of students milling around the Sociology building. They chanted and cursed, holding signs and banners of protest against Dow Chemical Company, the firm that manufactured napalm. Nearby, men in suits handed leaflets to a small group of demure, in-state students proclaiming all the good things Dow Chemical was engaged in. While this was happening, protesters chanted that the Dow recruiters were murderers. Their placards depicted burned, horribly deformed Vietnamese babies who had been disfigured by napalm. I found the surreal atmosphere as mesmerizing and disturbing as a play.

When I reached the Rathskeller, I saw Laura perched in a small booth, sitting cross-legged as usual, sipping coffee. I couldn't take my eyes away from her—she was so beautiful—so I simply turned around and left! After walking away, I berated myself. This is only a meeting with a teacher, not a date. I forced myself to walk back inside. She was reading a copy of *Madame Bovary* and probably hadn't seen my flight. I stood there a few seconds and then she turned her brown eyes up towards me. Her purple top with long, flowing sleeves suggested wings; her black hair hung loose about her shoulders.

"I'm here," I said. Although I had never been, I felt drunk as I said the words. "I hope I'm on time." I never wore a watch on principle, because Adar decided neither of us needed to know what time it was. "Time is only for those who need it," he intoned. Unlike the benighted watch-wearing people of the world, we could control time by our wills. Adar was always on time; unfortunately, for me, abiding by this philosophy simply meant that I was nearly always late.

She cocked her head and studied me. "What is it? Oh—I know! You're not wearing a jacket and tie. I don't believe I've ever seen you without that uniform on."

"I-I-I thought I'd give it a rest."

"Good," she said. "You almost look like a college student. Maybe a poet, rather than a businessman."

"We had to wear a jacket and tie in high school," I said.

"You're not in high school anymore."

"No."

"In college you can discover who you are. You might even be surprised at what you find."

"Maybe I will."

I wondered how many jackets and ties I had packed with me, and how long it would take me to cut up and burn them all behind Adams House.

"Let's get down to business. I finished reading your essay on *Oedipus*."

161

"Yes?" Damn it, why did I say that? Of course she had read it—she just said she had read it.

"And, I must say, it surprised me," Laura continued.

"Oh?" Again—stupid! Why was I such an ass?

"I was surprised because you obviously have real insight into what makes good literature. You were the only one in our class who seems to have understood why that play is still so profoundly important today. I want you to do something for me."

I thought about jumping up on the wooden bench and screaming, "ANYTHING! I'LL DO ANYTHING FOR YOU!" But of course I said, "Sure." Cool as ice.

"I want you to sit at the front of our classroom, not way in the back, glaring at the other students. And stop wearing those funereal outfits. I know you've got something to offer in class. Speaking up will help you express your own ideas. Right now, it feels like you're just sitting there in judgment of everyone." She toyed with the handle of her coffee mug with her fingers.

She was right. That was exactly what I was doing—sitting in judgment of others. I realized that was what I had learned from Mr. Herman and Adar. Perhaps my father as well. An imagined sense of my own superiority as a strategy to avoid feeling like a failure. Laura's eyes locked into my own. "You'll do that, won't you?"

"Of course," I said, quietly. My voice was calm, but my body trembled with sexual excitement. The combination of her face, voice, even the sight of her fingers touching the handle of her cup was giving me an erection. She was talking to me about my performance in English, and I was becoming aroused.

"That was what I wanted to talk about."

I wondered whether this meant I was supposed to go? I rose, instantly embarrassed and wondering if she would see it, the bulge in my pants. I yanked my Raskolnikov sweater down so that it covered the compromised area.

"Where are you going?" she asked, looking at me, pinning me to the spot.

"I thought that ... our conference was over."

"If you want it to be. I'm having another coffee. Would you like some?"

She smiled. Was she really inviting me to stay there? "I'll get us coffee. How do you take it?"

I never drank coffee. Adar's black coffee tasted like ashes. My father took his with cream and sugar; it tasted like Schrafft's coffee ice cream.

"I always take it black."

"Interesting. So do I," she said. "I'll be right back." After she got the coffees, we talked about everything—I don't remember too many details, because I was too focused on the purple butterflies fluttering on her blouse.

"You remember Dr. Skinner, the head of English Composition? He told me you handed in some crazy poem and left your midterm exam completely blank. Is that true?"

"Yes."

She burst out laughing.

"I can't believe it! I wish I had been there! He's from Georgia, you know. You blew his mind. When he handed you off to me, he said, 'I have a mentally unbalanced student. I was going to fail him, but I decided to offer him one more chance. Will you take him on?'"

"What did you say?"

"I told him I would."

"Why?"

"Because Skinner's an asshole, and you sounded different from the Cheeseheads. We get a lot of them here. Pretty much all the same. I've been teaching English Comp here for three years, and you're the first to hand in a blank midterm with some crazy shit. Congratulations. But ... don't do it again. Also the fact that Skinner said you were mentally unbalanced was a kind of turn-on. I liked that."

"Really? Thank you. I guess."

Laura laughed.

We left the Memorial Union, and it was dark and nobody saw us part. I took the lakeshore path, and there in the dark I danced for the first time. It was not dancing like we did at the Viola Wolff School wearing white gloves; this was jumping and whooping and yelping in the freezing Wisconsin air—waving my arms and trying to touch the moon. It was like those happy times when I was with Uncle Lee, reaching for the real brass rings on the carousel before they stopped using them.

I danced there in the dark to express the pure, unqualified joy I felt for this woman. The lake was frozen, but my body was pulsing and warm.

"Where have you been all this time? I've been waiting for you!"

Dwayne was in a panic when I returned to Adams House. I saw his tiny shape at the end of the hallway waving at me like a maniac, but by the time I got close he only whispered to come inside his room. He closed the door and told me to sit down while he stood, rattling his keys with the huge silver keychain. "Have you heard what happened? I mean the latest?"

I couldn't have cared less. I just wanted to get into my room, close the door, and lie down and think about Laura. "No, what happened?"

"They burned down Krogers! Krogers!" he said, incredulously. "Do you realize what this means? It's all over."

"What's all over?"

"My education. If my parents hear about this, they'll make me go home. To Brillion. Geez!" Geez was the closest thing to a curse I ever heard him utter.

The police were called in to break up the riot outside Sociology. They broke it up with billy clubs and tear gas. Some students fled, but most just lay down and refused to move. They told the cops that they were political prisoners. Then the police dragged them off, and they more or less were. That's when Dwayne figured that a bunch of the other subversives must have gone to Krogers and started the fire.

"Are you sure? Krogers? I mean, it's a grocery store. It can't be a high priority target for the SDS."

"You're forgetting one thing," he said.

"What's that?"

"They want to start a revolution. What better way to make people afraid than to threaten their food supply. Geez!" Dwayne was studying Dairy Science; I supposed he knew what he was talking about.

When the phone rang, sure enough, it was Dwayne's parents from Brillion, right on cue. They had seen the riots at the Sociology building on television. I tried to sneak back to my room, but he barred the door.

After he got off the phone, Dwayne broke down. His father wanted him to come home immediately. His mom was terrified; sending him off to college in Madison had been a terrible mistake. I felt terrible for Dwayne, and put my arm around his shoulder. I knew that now it would be impossible to convince his parents that Wisconsin was anything other than a hotbed of subversive radicals. We walked morosely over to the Brat Haus and had a pitcher of beer with Dwayne's fake I.D. Then another. The great Pfefferkorn experiment in liberal education had come to an end.

I fell asleep in my clothes. Next morning, I noticed a yellow slip under the door informing me that there was a package waiting for me at the post office. It was a large box, wrapped in thick twine, with the sides battered in. I saw the handwriting and knew who had sent it. Since I had come to campus, every week Grandma sent me a Care Package. She wanted to make sure I didn't waste away. This time she'd sent several boxes of kosher Tam Tam crackers, completely crushed, along with tins of Portuguese sardines, two dented cans of Campbell's tomato juice and Gruyere cheese. Only Grandma would anticipate that I might run out of cheese in the Dairy State! There were other necessaries like Man Size Kleenex, and rolls of Charmin toilet paper, which Grandma either assumed would be unobtainable, or (more plausibly) that I would neglect to buy for myself. At the bottom of the box there was something else, something to take care of another of my needs: a two volume copy of the *The Brothers Karamazov* with my name printed in bold black lettering. The letters of my name were much larger than Dostoevsky's. I still have it.

I opened the package of Tam Tams and held a few pieces of cracker in my palm. I opened the Gruyere, sardines, and tomato juice and ate there in my dorm room. Following the incident with Dwayne's parents, I felt grateful that there was at least one person in the world who cared for me, body and soul. Even if she didn't trust me to supply myself with toilet paper.

7.

Since my meeting with Laura, my work improved a bit and I began to feel like I belonged. Then, in the middle of the night, I received a phone call. The feeling of being woken at 3:00 in the morning made it seem like a nightmare. It was Uncle Malcolm, and he was crying. Grandpa had died. My father wanted me to come back home for the funeral immediately. I wanted to ask why he hadn't called me himself, but I didn't. It would have sounded selfish and like a veiled reproach at this moment of sadness. Still, I wanted to know; were the two brothers simply sharing the responsibility of calling family? Or was my father unwilling to share any emotion—even grief—with me? I dressed and flew back to New York.

Grandpa was frail and in poor health all his life. Grandma told me he came to America from Riga in 1915, already in poor health, and was convinced he probably would not live much longer. He seemed to have been born old, wearing wire rim glasses and a three-piece suit. Unlike Grandma, who was once beautiful and even seductive, I couldn't imagine Grandpa ever being young. His younger brother, after whom I was named, was a medical student who contracted typhoid while treating soldiers during the great influenza epidemic. Grandpa, the frail older brother, outlived his younger sibling by half a century. His good health was thanks to Grandma, who ministered to his every need despite his petty cruelties and mockery. He retired at age fifty a very wealthy man, and went to his office at the Empire State Building every day. Of course, he also needed to be away from Birdie. The idea of even a single day alone with her in their apartment was impossible. Yet, her devotion and care were what kept him alive.

I flew back for the funeral just before Christmas break, aware that an era in my life was ending. I had been deliberately kept in the dark when my mother's father (Gramps) died of stomach cancer, so this was my first real brush with death. I loved Grandpa dearly, especially after the miraculous time in New Hampshsire, but mostly I was sad for Grandma, and couldn't imagine how she would survive his absence. At the funeral, she saw the small, round pebbles that the mourners left on the as yet-unmarked headstone and flung them as violently as she could back at the mourners. Then she fell to her knees.

"How did you allow this to happen!" she railed at some unseen divinity above. "How can you take my Harry from me?"

She prostrated herself on his grave, screaming and clawing with her fingernails in the dirt, calling out a hostile, indifferent God for allowing this. Most of the mourners were my father's and Malcolm's wealthy colleagues and friends. No one moved or spoke a word. Her tears and her grief were without measure and without end. With a wail from the shtetl, she threw off the assistance of the rabbi's arm and refused to stand. She would not return to the limousine. She would not listen to her sons. Centuries and cultures were crossed, and no one knew where to look. Uncle Malcolm sniffled and wiped his glasses. My father seethed. His salt-and-pepper moustache twitched, but he would not stoop to raise her up. That duty fell to me. I went over and tried to reason with her—but she pushed me away, too. "I'm staying here with my Harry," she said rocking back and forth. "Go home." I looked back at my father. He glowered, teeth bared. A snarling dog.

Twenty minutes had passed since the rabbi had chanted the Kaddish in Hebrew and departed. A parade of black Cadillacs was waiting, motors rumbling. Chauffeurs scratched their heads under their caps, wondering when their shifts would be over. This was not what a funeral was supposed to look like among sophisticated New Yorkers with second homes in Scarsdale or Rye. Some of the guests began glancing at their watches. They couldn't leave—how could they—their limos were blocked! No one could leave until Grandma chose to release herself from Grandpa's grave, and that was not going to happen. Not now, not ever.

I returned and knelt beside her. "Grandma, please get up, let's go." But why should she listen to me? Why should the end of a lifetime lived with another person who was everything to her be regulated by the clock or other

167

people's expectations of appropriate grief? What was time to her? Finally, she allowed me to gather her to her feet. But as I lifted her up, she collapsed back down again! My father's look told me that this was done to deliberately embarrass him, that she was doing it for effect. I thought it must be weakness from kneeling, combined with exhaustion and not having eaten. But, whatever the cause, she could not stand. She announced to all who could hear her that she would never walk again. Malcolm and I had to lift her up and literally carry her back to the limo while people coughed and bowed their heads in both real and embarrassed expressions of sorrow.

When the seven days of sitting Shiva were done, Grandma still refused to walk. Malcolm and my father took her to see a specialist. Tests showed she was in the final stages of pancreatic cancer. A month to the day after her Harry's funeral, I returned to New York to bury my grandmother.

On the flight back to Madison after her funeral, a single image kept popping into my mind: watching Grandma being zipped into a black plastic bag. Since her cancer was inoperable and in its last stages, she had been allowed to die at home, but was in a morphine-induced haze when I arrived. We never spoke again. Once she was placed into the bag, I followed the gurney down the hallway along with two EMT technicians. We walked past the cedar closet, which still contained that musty copy of *Bomba the Jungle Boy* and the picture of my father with the squirrel, past the fruitwood telephone cabinet with its carved bust of Shakespeare and the little stool where she sat talking and giving advice to everyone about the best butcher for kosher meat on the west side of Columbus Avenue, and where she told me to bring my parents back together. The elevator doors slid open, and she was wheeled in. The elevator itself was identical to the one I used so often during the seventeen years of my existence—but no—I had never seen it before. This was the freight elevator: no mirrors, no art deco molding, no highly polished wood, just a vault used to transport the dead. Once she was wheeled inside, its steel jaws snapped shut and I never saw her again.

I phoned Laura when I got back to Adams House, just to hear the sound of her voice. I felt terribly lonely. It was the beginning of the new semester, but I still had to re-take the Ancient Philosophy final I missed due to Grandma's funeral. Dwayne was back in Brillion now—and I didn't speak to anyone else in the dorm besides him. I hadn't even unpacked my suitcase, but Laura offered to meet with me. Her Master's degree was in Philosophy, and she offered to help me with the make-up exam.

She told me to meet her on the second floor of the Wisconsin Historical Society building. I had never been inside before, even though the cavernous limestone building was just across the street from the Memorial Union where I went every day. She said we would meet at a long wooden table on the second floor. There, she said, she would tutor me on the pre-Socratic philosophers. I was exhausted from the funeral and the flight and didn't feel like studying. But I needed to pass, and she offered to help me scrape through.

When I arrived, she was already sitting at the long wooden table, going over her notes from when she was an undergraduate in philosophy. She looked up and smiled, but she was very professional and wore glasses, which I had never seen before. I sat down beside her, and tried to think about Plato. She had removed her long black coat, and was dressed in jeans and a black leotard. Between her fragrance and the silhouette of her breasts, Heraclitus and Zeno's Paradox didn't stand a chance. After an hour, I accidentally touched her thigh. I apologized and stood up, confused. I said I needed to leave. Then she rose and offered to show me more of the museum, since I had never been. She took me past the Ojibway Indians to a place with baskets and moccasins and beaded dresses encrusted with tulip-shaped flowers. I remember a dress decorated with tiny cones—"tinklers"—which the Indians had fabricated from empty snuff tins. They hung from the dress like miniature silver bells. I tried hard to look at the displays, just as I had tried to concentrate on the pre-Socratics; but Laura clasped my hand, and at her touch, my body flooded with fire.

I felt a kind of confused panic. Yes, I loved it, but this wasn't supposed to happen, not here, and not now. I had to do something to distract myself from the burning inside. I released my hand from hers and walked toward the nearest exhibit, a large display case. I came across a miniature Indian Village, which had been discovered near La Crosse more than 700 years ago. A group of longhouses, all clustered together in the form of a parabola, bore the unforgettable inscription: "Can you imagine living in a longhouse with sixty of your relatives?" I laughed out loud and looked around to share my amusement with Laura, but she had gone. I called her name twice, but there was no reply. I remember thinking that women had a habit of disappearing from my life.

"I'm close by," she whispered from somewhere.

But I couldn't find her anywhere. Then, a slender finger appeared from below, beckoning me to meet her on the floor underneath the exhibit. I took a breath filled with both joy and fear, and crawled underneath the Oneota Indian Village. There were no guards in sight, so in the glimmering light, I felt like I was entering a subterranean world: secret, damp, dark. The smell of earth and ancient trees seemed to embrace us, and by the time I crept beside her it did not seem unnatural to see a squaw breastfeeding in the opposite case. In the darkness, Laura slowly pulled her leotard over her head. I was stunned at the magnificence before me.

Her breasts were even larger than in my fantasies, and her nipples were set like garnet jewels against her ivory skin. There were clusters of fine black hairs surrounding each nipple. Strange and exotic, the sight went with the musky regions we inhabited. She gently held the back of my head and lowered me until my mouth was buried in her breasts.

I was barely conscious of where we were, but wondered: *can I remain here forever?* I had only kissed one girl previously, and I'd fumbled with the clasp of her brassiere for hours until finally I gave up and let her do it. As she unhooked the tiny silver clasp, in my mind's eye I saw Adar rub his stubbled jaw and twitch with anger. He asked me if I knew what I was doing. I knew I would never be able to levitate now. By the time she'd removed her bra, I was no longer aroused, and her gentle, forgiving smile only made me feel worse.

I never told Adar about the incident—it would have been impossible. But as I climbed on top of Laura, he was gone. My family vanished, too. My eyes were closed, and she wrapped her arms around me and transported me into an ancient world. I wanted this moment to last forever. And then, when I was certain she must stop and take us back above ground, she unbuttoned her jeans and gently guided my head between her legs. I kissed her in places I never knew existed.

Just before we re-emerged from our dim cave, she took my hand and placed it deep inside her body. I felt like I'd lost my single self and had crawled inside another being whom I would forever be part of. My hand emerged and we both licked my fingers. We walked back to my dorm along the lakeshore path, holding hands. It was late and bitterly cold. The moon was full, and added to the magic. I had escaped into a beautiful dream, better than any novel, sweeter than any fairytale. Every few steps along the way we stopped and kissed. I wanted to stay with her all night. My world had changed into something I could never have imagined, and it seemed that if we held each other long enough, our bodies might literally freeze together; here beside the lake, we might literally become a single person. Then she kissed me and put her tongue inside my mouth. She told me she loved me. I didn't know what to say to this, so I told her how funny it was that we loved one another, and I really didn't even know her, not even her last name. She dropped my hand.

"Did I say something wrong?"

We were near my dorm now, and she turned her head away.

"Why are you crying?" I asked.

"I'm married."

She was married to another graduate student. We wouldn't be able to see one another again, she said. Not like this. Then she turned around and walked back in the direction of the Union. After a moment's hesitation, I ran toward her, intending to follow, then I stopped. This was not what she wanted. I turned back. The last thing I saw was her mane of black hair waving from side to side as she disappeared back into the night.

Once she disappeared, I crawled down by the lake and clasped my knees, shivering. I made no sound. I wasn't angry. How could I be? What had happened was completely unexpected and so beautiful. But also terrible. I felt numb, like I wasn't really there, just a shadow. The freezing wind off the lake felt like it might suddenly blow me away like a dead leaf. To sail off into the night, skimming the frozen surface of Lake Mendota. Grandma was dead now. There would be no more Care Packages with Tam Tams and Dostoevsky. Laura was dead, too, in a way.

When I returned to my dorm room, my unopened suitcase still lay on my bed. Had Laura invited me to that place to study, or with another intention all along? I would never know. If only I hadn't mentioned not knowing her ... her last name. She was married and would never see me again, not in that way. I started to think that maybe the whole thing was my fantasy, except for the moon burning above me on Lake Mendota, laughing.

Second semester was nearly over when I received something that made my hands shake: a blue envelope marked with my name. Something in me knew exactly what it was and who had sent it. It was unexpected, yet in a sense, I had been anticipating it ever since my arrival in Madison. My fingers trembled, and I put it inside my thermal undershirt against my skin. The envelope seemed to possess its own burning life, like a little blue flame. I brought it back to my room, sat down at my desk, and with my pocketknife, slit it open. This was not a letter to be ripped open with my fingers.

Henry,

It has been five months since you left me. Leaving me like that, without warning or even a note, was the hardest thing I have ever had to endure in my life. I have never felt so betrayed. I even thought about tracking you down, wherever you were, and.... But I have come through it and believe the experience has brought me increased inner strength. Despite my anger, I feel as though there is too much unfinished business between us to simply forget about our Union and go on our separate paths. We need to acknowledge what happened, talk about it, and learn from it. For this reason, I am offering the following plan.

I am entitled to a week's vacation in my new job. I propose that we meet at the YMCA Hotel in Chicago next weekend to discuss things. If all goes well, I have the opportunity to spend a couple of days visiting you in Madison. If not, I will return to New York by bus.

I hope you will answer me. But if you do choose to ignore this letter, I will never contact you again for the rest of my life.

In friendship,

Adar

The bus ride to Chicago was terrible. It snowed the whole way. I had the crazy fear that the driver was drunk and we'd crash or get stuck and end up in a snow bank. The passengers would all escape, and I'd be left alone somewhere, freezing. I was really petrified about this happening, but I realized my fear was tied up with my anxiety about seeing Adar. What would it be like to see him again? What were his actual motives in arranging this meeting? Was I right to accept his offer? Part of me was excited about having a chance to make things right. Another part felt a kind of dread he might secretly be motivated by revenge. What if this was a trap to lure me back to New York? I hadn't told anyone about my trip, and suppose something did happen to me, or what if I was murdered…?

Arriving at the Chicago YMCA at 1:00 a.m. was seedier than anything I could have imagined, and made the Port Authority Bus Terminal seem like the Plaza by comparison. I checked in, and as I wrote my name in the register, a tiny eighty-something-year-old desk clerk with a mouth full of dazzling white, ill-fitting false teeth leered at me. Your "friend" is waiting for you upstairs, he said. It was all too clear what he was thinking. As I walked to the stairwell, he shouted after me, "You better tell him I get off at midnight, and he still owes me for that aspirin and shit—this ain't the Waldorf, ya know, there ain't no room service."

I knocked at the door, but no one answered. I knocked again: silence. Finally, I unlocked the door and let myself in.

He was sitting there at a small wooden desk at the back of the room bent over a piece of paper. The only light in the room was a candle on the desk, and the reflection of a neon sign outside with the letters Y, M, and A blinking in orange. The C had burned out.

He quickly turned over the sheet of paper he had been writing on as I walked in. There was something sinister about this tiny room. It was the sort of room I imagined drug dealers or whores frequenting. Or worse. Supposing you were planning a murder… .

"Henry." Adar's face remained averted, and he gazed out the window, bathed in the lurid orange glow.

"Why are you sitting over there like that, in the dark?"

"Reflecting on the past," he said, with a familiar twitch of his jaw, "and on us." I moved closer to the middle of the room, and saw by the candlelight

173

that he was much thinner and unshaven. He was sweating, and looked like he hadn't slept for days. He probably had a fever.

"Aren't you well?" I asked. He kept his face averted.

"Doing all right," he muttered. "I'm okay, so long as …"

"What?" I couldn't understand him because of the low timbre of his voice and the crackling sign outside. "I asked if you were well."

Adar cleared his throat and said something. His voice was so hoarse I couldn't hear.

"I'm doing fine," I said. I wanted to sound fine, but not too fine. "I'm a freshman at the University of Wisconsin. But I guess you knew that? I'm better now … better than before, I mean. I mean I'm doing better than when I left.…" I was nervous, and couldn't stop filling silences with the sound of my own voice. I cut myself off and blurted, "Before I say anything further, I want to apologize to you, Adar. For leaving in that way. It was a cowardly thing, unworthy of me, and—I'm very, very sorry."

Then there followed a long and terrible moment of silence, during which the only audible sound was the sign outside. Then Adar's body shuddered, and he stood up for the first time. Is he crying, I thought? Is he actually crying? I suddenly remembered his laugh, which wasn't even a real laugh; it was an old man's laugh. But I'd never heard him cry, and it made me afraid. In that moment, I had the very distinct feeling that one of us was going to die here. Why had I come? I had fallen into a trap. I had to get out!

Adar walked up so close to me so that our faces were just inches apart.

"I hate you!" His voice was now audible, and carried the threat of intense and immediate retribution. He pushed me onto the bed, and while I was lying there, slapped me hard across the face. Twice.

"You ruined my life!" he screamed, standing above me, shaking. You ruined both our lives. We were so close … had everything—our Union—and then … nothing. You hurt me. I think … I don't know what to do anymore. Abandoned me! You abandoned me!"

From towering above me on the bed, he moved to the floor, where he curled up in a corner, and began sobbing.

I had no idea how I would ever be able to extricate myself from that horrible room. He was obviously in great pain, and I had been the cause. At the same time, I knew now I had to leave. For the first time, I felt sorry for him. Paradoxically, until he hit me, I always assumed he was the dominant one in our friendship. Now that he had slapped me, I knew our positions were reversed: I was the stronger. It was he who seemed lost. Lost and sick.

Adar slowly rose from the floor and added, "I'm sorry. I have no idea where all that came from." He stood up and shuddered, then approached me again, laying his hands on both my shoulders. His hard grip felt strange, awkward, not like what I had expected. I had always wanted him to touch me when we were together before, not necessarily in a sexual way, just as a physical affirmation of what we meant to one another. Now his hands were on me—bony, an old man's touch— holding me captive, and his touch was repulsive. His face had a darkness I had not noticed before. The beetling brows, the clenching jaws, the slightly hooked nose—all repelled me. There was a weakness, a helplessness I had never noticed before. After a few uncomfortable seconds in this fixed position, the sign crackled again, and I tore myself away.

The room had only a sink, a miniature Ivory soap, and two dirty hand towels. The shower and toilet were down the hall. The two twin beds were metal cots maybe six inches apart. They had filthy striped mattresses, and the green walls had empty rectangles where pictures once hung. Below them there were dark red patches where bugs had been smashed against the walls. Although it was a different kind of seediness, I thought briefly of our last meeting in Canarsie, which changed our friendship.

I stayed, and we spent the night sitting on those creaking cots talking until noon the following day. Neither of us slept.

Sometime during the night, Adar asked if I was seeing girls. I was surprised at the question, and confessed that I had been seeing someone, although I no longer was.

"You felt you needed it?" he added, provocatively.

"I—I'm not sure what you mean," I replied.

When I mentioned that the woman (I used the word "woman") I had been seeing was older than me, married, and my teacher, he smiled. But it was a sinister smile—a sneer, really. He never said so, but it was obvious he was judging me for being with Laura.

Then he told me he asked because he was now free, free of sexual desire. If I was lucky, I too might reach that level of pure abstinence. After Laura, being free of desire didn't seem all that fortunate, but I chose not to contradict him. I asked about his health, noting that he looked thinner. Yes, he had lost a good deal of weight, but that was only because of the healthy way he was eating. Fish and dairy products were now gone from his diet, and he had never felt better. He was sweating, his cheeks were hollow, and he looked far from healthy, but again, I didn't contradict him. He told me about a book by Alan Watts he was reading, and said he now practiced Buddhism. He would teach me to meditate if I wanted to learn. I saw his sallow skin and tight cheekbones covered with brown stubble, and imagined I saw his skull lurking beneath his taut face—a horrible image. Was this all my fault?

He stopped painting, he said, but would return to it soon. When I expressed shock, he said he needed to earn money. He worked at Chase Manhattan Bank in Brooklyn, and although his job didn't pay much, he was trying to save money for tuition and put aside a little something each month for his parents, who were both sick. I don't know if this was said to make me feel guilty, or if he saw me avert my eyes.

I told Adar that leaving New York the way I did was shameful. I explained how impossible it had been for me to work for my uncle; I couldn't face going in there one more day. I knew he needed to earn money for his tuition, but I just couldn't go back. That was why I fled.

"I never realized you were so unhappy, so desperate," Adar said, and apologized for unintentionally coercing me to work for my uncle just because he needed money.

"That was not worthy of me," he said.

On the third day of our visit, I blurted out my anxiety about being "swallowed" by our friendship. I told him that however much I respected and admired him, it was better not to try and resume our friendship.

"I need to find out what kind of man I am, Adar." The word "man" sounded strange in my mouth. Just strange, not false. "I don't think it would be wise for you to come back with me to Madison," I said, frightened at the effect my words might provoke.

"I knew that the moment you opened the door," he said. "Even before I saw your face. I knew by the sound of your walk."

I didn't ask him what he meant.

Adar said he would remain a few more days at the Y. Perhaps a visit to the Art Institute would inspire him to paint again. I thought of the strange old man at the desk downstairs, and wondered why anyone would spend even a second more here than was absolutely necessary.

Before I left, Adar gave me a small package wrapped in a page from the *Chicago Tribune*. It was a framed pencil and blue watercolor sketch of a young man in profile. It was what he had been working on when I intruded on him that first night. I studied the face, eyes cast down, head slightly averted.

It was me, furtive and insecure, poised awkwardly in between the boy I was, and the something else I might one day become. In a few strokes, he had managed to capture who I was at that moment, at the cusp between adolescence and manhood. I turned back to express my thanks. But he was turned away again, staring out at the flickering sign. He looked like a frail, old man. I closed the door gently.

8.

According to the calendar, it was spring. Unfortunately, in Wisconsin the calendar was immaterial and spring might not show itself for months. Lake Mendota was still frozen solid. Ducks hopped around, desperate for breaks in the ice. But the freezing cold outside seemed only to whet the blazing heat of political activity sweeping the campus. A chair came crashing through a window in one of my classes, injuring a girl with broken glass. The National Guard was beginning to make its presence felt on a daily basis, and the sight of fresh-scrubbed eighteen year olds wielding bayonets outside classrooms was no longer shocking. Classes were routinely canceled. Sit-down strikes in Bascom Hall were a normal occurrence. The entire campus and the city of Madison had become a tiny fortress of radicalism within America's Dairyland. Dwayne Pfefferkorn was long gone, and he wrote me that his transfer to the University of Wisconsin's Oshkosh campus had now become official.

In my class on the modern novel, the professor was lecturing on Julien Sorel's arrival in Verriers when a small band of seven or eight radical students entered the lecture hall, mounted the little platform where the professor had his notes carefully assembled, and began fiddling with his papers. They deliberately mixed up the pages, "accidentally" dropping them on the floor, and talking to one another to disrupt the lecture. The professor kept his cool fairly well and continued speaking, but, seeing that he was ignoring their taunts, the students began to chant: "HO-HO-HO CHI MINH—THE VIET CONG'S GONNA WIN!" in counterpoint to the professor's comments on *The Red and the Black*. After a few minutes, one girl in front of me stood up and shouted at the protesters to leave. Then, several more students rose and started moving down the aisle to forcibly evict them. At that moment, when violent confrontation seemed inevitable, a squad of helmeted policemen wielding clubs and shields stormed through the back entrance to the lecture theatre and chased the radicals out.

The professor erupted into a high-pitched squeal: "PIGS, PIGS! OUT OF MY CLASSROOM! ACADEMIC FREEDOM! I MUST HAVE ACADEMIC FREEDOM!"

Nothing made sense to me. I was confused by the scene of utter anarchy that ensued with the cops chasing the protesters out of the lecture hall. I wondered about the academic's tepid response to those who had disrupted his lecture, contrasted with his violent one toward the helmeted police who had restored order.

I turned eighteen, but with Grandma dead, no one remembered my birthday but the Selective Service. They sent me a second notice to register for the draft. Again, I disposed of it, not in protest against the war, but as a gesture of contempt for politics and the crazy world spinning around me. I was not a hawk, not a dove, nor a conscientious objector. What was I?

Since meeting Adar in that Chicago YMCA, I felt purged of my guilt. Nevertheless, I tried to adhere to some of his principles of spiritual purity. I ate no meat, did not socialize with others, and generally continued to feel superior to my benighted fellow classmates. I drew the line at levitation, which was, I conceded, probably unrealistic. I was no longer in Laura's class, but despite her announcement that we would not see one another anymore, we continued to meet every now and then for the next month or two, until we broke it off entirely. The sight of her striding in thigh-high boots across campus still made me feel uncomfortable—but now we were both ashamed of our desire. We met secretively, either underneath the glass case in the Historical Society, or off-campus at the Henry Vilas Zoo where the apes and reptiles offered tropical escape from the Wisconsin cold, and we were unlikely to be spotted by her fellow graduate students, who, according to Laura, lurked everywhere. I had been so in love with her, but all that remained now was impersonal, furtive sex. I lay on top of her, and through a thrusting of her hips and pelvis, she managed to raise and lower us both, providing an anti-climactic climax. That seemed enough for a time, until it simply wasn't.

"It's time," she said simply after one of our loveless outings, and I muttered a passionless, "Okay." And that was it. I actually felt grateful that she had initiated our breakup. I never would have had the courage. She still had not told me her last name, and I never asked again.

I was still too much under Adar's influence to dabble in anything that would allow me to lose control. Unlike most of my peers, I never tried drugs. In childhood, my father exerted an unseen hand dictating all my actions; when I fell in love with Adar, another sort of authority was substituted— monastic self-absorption in a solitary palace of art. So, instead of trying any of the various opiates that proliferated, and in keeping with my self-image as a pure, solitary intellectual, I let my beard and hair grow, and even began smoking a pipe.

My father would have been displeased with the gradual changes in my appearance, but he hadn't seen me since Grandma's funeral. However, when he learned that I had not registered with the Selective Service, he was furious. The Selective Service wrote him at his home address since they received no response from me. They wrote saying I had to report to the Selective Service Bureau in New York for a mandatory physical immediately. Since I had not registered, I no longer had an automatic student deferment and was draft-eligible.

"YOU GODDAMN STUPID SONOFABITCH!" his voice boomed through the telephone. "I should let them just fucking drag you off to Vietnam. You deserve this, you idiot."

I agreed that it was stupid to fail to register and claim the student defer-ment to which I was entitled. But secretly I thought that there were worse things for a young writer than the army. Tuning out his curses, I imagined the remarkable material I would get from a tour of duty in Vietnam. I thought of Hemingway and the young British poets of the First World War. Their expo-sure to mustard gas and war in the trenches made them into great artists. Then again, I had to admit to myself that many of them had been maimed physically and emotionally—or had never returned at all.

I returned to New York immediately following our phone call. After a haircut at his barber, he drove us to the Selective Service Bureau, and explained that I was a student in good standing at the University of Wisconsin, and had never received a notice to register. The sergeant then produced copies of various notices sent to me, which I had destroyed or simply ignored. Surrounded by army posters and throngs of kids in khakis with shaved heads, I realized for the first time that this draft thing might be serious.

"Do you have proof he's full time? A transcript?" the sergeant asked.

"I assure you he's a full-time college student. He's entitled to a student deferment," Dad insisted.

"Yes, so long as he is a student and is doing satisfactorily," the sergeant answered. "That's why I need to see his academic record. What's your GPA, son?"

They both stared at me. "Umm, I don't remember my exact grade point average, if that's what you mean," I answered nervously, "but I am full time." I decided it would not be prudent to volunteer the information that I had been placed on strict probation for having a 1.9 GPA, or that I had been threatened with reduction to part-time status if my grades did not significantly improve.

"Full-time, huh?" the sergeant said dryly, and stood up. "We'll check with the registrar at his school."

"Uh, Dad ..." I started.

"Shut up, Henry!"

My father reached in his breast pocket and handed him a letter. "You might want to take a look at this before you call." The sergeant put on reading glasses and sat back down at his metal desk. He peered down at the letter, then at me, trying to correlate the two.

Suddenly, he took out a stamp and slammed it down on my draft card. "All right, he's 1-Y," he hollered, then to an unseen official, "We won't need this one unless the Viet Cong invade New York."

"What just happened in there?" I asked as we left.

"None of your goddamn business," Dad snapped, and walked several paces ahead of me.

Trying to catch up, I said, "Well, I think it is my business, don't you, Dad?"

"I told Dr. Irving to put a letter in your file describing your psychological treatment last summer, something that I could produce if worse came to worst," he said, scanning the street for something less embarrassing than his own son to rest his eyes on. "He wrote that he had treated you for severe depression and that he considered you a high risk for suicide in the military. He hates this fucking war. When that sergeant said he was going to call Wisconsin, I decided to play that card. Or do you think I should have let him check your academic record?"

"No."

"I didn't think so, you sonofabitch."

"Thanks, Dad," I said after a moment of silence. He had rescued me, possibly saved my life.

"You'd better shape up, mister."

"I will."

"Strict probation!"

"H—How—You knew?"

"I asked—they told. Your grades better improve. Otherwise there's nothing I can do."

"They will, Dad."

"They'd better!" he said as we crossed the street. "You better wake up. You just dodged a bullet, young man. You just came this close to getting killed," he said, thumb and forefinger centimeters apart.

I smiled at his hyperbole.

"You think I'm kidding?" he said incredulously. "Remember: I know you. You wouldn't last a day over there. Not ONE FUCKING DAY." He elbowed past me and walked back to his car.

With my one year of college behind me, I felt much older. I had taken a work-study job at the university's library in the spring. This allowed me time to drift through the open stacks making discoveries about what I needed to read to become the person and writer I wanted to be. And at the year's end in June, I used the money to take the Greyhound bus back to New York instead of relying on my father to fly me home. When I arrived, my mother refused to speak to me. She still held a grudge because I hadn't gone to Hofstra, and eventually, Columbia. Whenever we spoke by phone while I was in Madison, she sounded cordial at first, then found an excuse to hang up on me within five minutes. Although I knew her anger would subside if I moved back in with her, I wanted to live on my own. I found a small apartment on Riverside Drive, near where we lived when I was a child. My plan was to take one summer school course at Columbia and find a part-time job.

I had close to $5,000 from my bar mitzvah, which I hadn't touched and which would provide me with enough for rent and to live on until I found a job. When I went to the bank, however, I discovered that there was nothing left. Everything, even the savings bonds, had been cashed. When I phoned my mother to ask her how this happened, she said she had no idea. She was polite, cold, and non-committal. Mom was the only one, aside from Dad and me, who knew I had any money or where it was kept, and I knew my father would never touch it, not only because he didn't need to, but because he never would stoop that low. About financial matters he was always ethical, just as Grandma had said, even if his interpersonal ethics were manipulative and controlling.

I called my mother, whose response to why I needed the bar mitzvah money—"Hasn't your father given you enough?"—spoke volumes.

"How can all that money be gone, Mom?"

"Go ask your father, since you enjoy his company so much!" And she slammed down the phone.

When I asked my father who could have cashed the checks and Savings Bonds, he smiled. It was not a pleasant smile; it was a cold thing composed of white teeth, silver moustache, and a good deal of triumph. It was the smile his competitors saw before he destroyed them. It was the smile he wore when he hit an un-returnable winner down the line in tennis.

We went to the bank together. The manager, deferential in the face of my father's climbing stature in the financial world, presented copies of the withdrawal receipts that showed my name scrawled on the signature line. It was obviously not my writing. I was pretty sure I recognized Uncle Lee's handwriting, but I knew he never would forge my signature without my mother's prodding. His loyalty to his sister easily trumped his love for his nephew, especially since I was sure she had told him the whole Hofstra story. I also knew that in Lee's judgment, he had done nothing wrong. I hurt my mother by leaving home against her wishes. I had not been a good son like he was to Gramsie. When his parents told him to return from Harvard Law

School and help with the family business, he gave up his life and career as a lawyer unhesitatingly. I didn't.

In the end, my mother did not deny that Uncle Lee forged my signature, although she insisted the funds were, in fact, hers, since I had been under eighteen and in her custody. My father said I should take her to court and that he would pay for a lawyer. I was so angry that I seriously considered it. But then I remembered how strapped she was for money and what her life was like. Possibly even worse than before. I thought of the boxes stacked up in her bedroom, and the copy of Norman Vincent Peale's *The Power of Positive Thinking* on her bed. My father had not simply deserted her. He manipulated things so that he paid her almost nothing in alimony, and stood idly by as she was humiliated by creditors and evicted from our apartment on 86th Street. He instructed his attorneys to keep postponing hearings until she was left with nothing but Gramsie's food and Leon's loyalty. For some reason, I thought of advice my father had given me more than once in the event I was held up.

"Always fight dirty," he advised. "Find out who the ring leader is—then go up and kick him in the balls. Then start swinging your bat—wildly—that'll stop 'em."

As he told me this, I sensed the sensual thrill he got from imparting this wisdom to his son, just like the time I tried out for the basketball team and he told me the key to stopping your opponent from out-rebounding you under the basket was to "accidentally" stand on your opponent's sneaker as he tried to jump. But I couldn't do it, not even in practice. I never could.

When I went to my mother's apartment to collect my things for the move to Riverside Drive, she informed me she would be better off dead.

"What's the whole life for?" she mused, "I have only my two precious boys, and one of them has already abandoned his mother. Go to your father. You only care for him anyway. Go to him and his whores."

I remembered a particular redhead named Betty with a young son. He went to horse shows with her and had even bought her a horse. Later, there was the blonde from Scarsdale. I knew the woman, whom he addressed as "Mrs. Jeffries," and who I knew was married to one of his business associates, so what was she doing alone with him in his apartment? He did have women around a lot now; for all I knew they might be whores.

184

My brother remained steadfastly loyal to Mom, and she rewarded him with extravagant gifts she couldn't possibly afford. Whatever he asked for, she found some way to obtain. Knowing his love for cars, she acquired a Ford LTD for him when he turned sixteen. I think that what Bobby wanted was to leap over childhood and adolescence, and land directly into prosperous and sedate middle age. An LTD, the heavy, stolid car of a wealthy, middle-aged businessman, was exactly right for him. Even as a teenager.

Mom and Uncle Lee were inseparable during the year I spent at college. They were more like a happily married couple than any married couple I ever knew. Each morning, he called at precisely 6:00 a.m. to say hello and whisper, "Wake up, Beautiful!" At 10:00 o'clock at night he called again and said, "Sleep tight, Baby!" They had all their meals together and watched TV until it was time for her to walk back to her apartment on 72nd Street. They were both enamored of Norman Vincent Peale and attended his lectures and seminars. Mom felt protected and loved at last. When she spoke to me, every conversation concluded not with hanging up on me, but with the obligatory sing-song refrain: "Every day and in every way, things will get better and better."

One morning, I woke up and it was August, time to think about returning to Madison for my sophomore year. I said goodbye to my little apartment on Riverside Drive (my father "loaned" me the money, although he refused my efforts to repay him from the pittance I got from my part-time job operating a switchboard at Columbia). Sunlight streamed through the curtains, and everything felt different—I felt like a man who wakes up after having been in bed for weeks with a fever. I felt well. And the most curious thing was that I hadn't even realized how sick I had been. The illness, contracted in a particularly virulent form, was adolescence. And although I knew only too well I was not to be mistaken for an adult, something in my body told me that I had weathered a storm and survived. I was now about to start the next chapter of my life.

9.

As my second year of college swung into gear, I missed Laura. I rationalized her absence by deciding that a certain self-imposed, monastic isolation would be good for me as I pursued my real vocation, whatever that might be. I practiced the same kind of abstinence toward my love of sports. I had been drawn to Wisconsin since its football team had lost so heroically in the 1963 Rose Bowl. I could have gotten tickets to any game I wanted since the team was terrible and there were plenty of empty seats, but I never attended a single game in the four years I was there. This was not because I didn't want to watch the team lose, it was because I thought that depriving myself of something I wanted would make me stronger, and help me develop as an artist.

On Saturday afternoons I remained in my room and chose something impressive and grand from my bookshelf, while the rest of my peers, as I thought, wasted their time with something as frivolous as going to the football game, cheering "OHHHH SHITTT" as another game was fumbled away. While everyone else was at Camp Randall stadium, I curled up in my room with my penknife, a wedge of Gouda, a loaf of crusty bread, and Milton's *Paradise Lost* as company. Above the bed stood a nineteenth-century print I had found in Paul's Bookstore on State Street of a strange gypsy girl gazing wistfully into space, longing for me perhaps. Her name, I decided, was Esmeralda. On my stereo I listened to Rachmaninoff's *Second Piano Concerto*. However, since I passionately loved football, I couldn't stop thinking about the game I was missing. Unable to concentrate on Milton, I stayed in my dorm eating Gouda and listening to the game on radio. When it was over, I felt guilty, depressed, and sick from eating all the cheese.

After ending things with Laura, I resumed my uniform of black sport coats and ties and didn't participate in classes any longer, preferring to watch intently, defiantly, and above all, judgmentally. If someone said something that I considered stupid or banal, I stared at them from a remote corner of the classroom. I thought I could somehow compel them to psychically confess their folly with my disdainful glares. This, of course, never happened.

There was one girl, though. She sat across from me in my Afro-Asian history class and had long hair the color of Greek honey. I never tried to pin her down with my withering stare. Instead, I watched the way her blue cable-knit turtleneck sweater clung to her breasts. So I suppose I did stare, just in a different way. Once, she asked if she could borrow Lady Murasaki's *The Tale of Genji*, a novel we had been assigned to read for Monday. There were no copies left at the bookstore, she said, pushing her hair back over her shoulder. Her name was Patty.

It was a surprisingly warm Saturday morning in October when I walked over to Showalter dorm to lend her the book. She took it, and after a few moments of strained silence, asked if I wanted to walk along the lake. I said yes. She was animated and enthusiastic and seemed to love life. She had a crazy sense of humor, which was different from other girls I had met. She also said she had once seen me throwing rocks at the ducks on the lake one day while her younger sister was visiting.

"Rocks at ducks?" I said, reddening at being caught in the act. She knew that I wasn't really trying to hit them, of course. She said this in a way that told me she knew I was doing just that, but even though we both knew I had done this really weird thing, she didn't hate me for it. Her younger sister had seen me, too, and said I was cute, but asked why I dressed like an old man. I liked the idea that they were watching me, talking about me, and that someone thought I was "cute" even if I had been spotted throwing rocks at the ducks.

We continued walking, then headed to the off-campus Arboretum. We saw a field with apple trees, and sat down on the grass. At first we just sat; then I decided to pick the apples. I had a little penknife with me and tried to peel the skin off an apple in one go like Gramps had done when I was a child. I still couldn't do it. I sliced up one of the apples and started feeding Patty slices, slowly at first, then faster and faster. When I tried to force the last one into her mouth, she laughed. I loved her laugh. It wasn't a sultry laugh like Laura's, but it wasn't a little girl's giggle, either. It said laughter was all right; laughter was nothing to be ashamed of.

I kissed her. Her kisses felt different than Laura's, but wonderful in a less experienced way. We lay down in the field in and hugged. Then the air grew cooler and I took in the scent of the apples mixed with the honeysuckle of her hair.

When we woke up it was cold and dark. I draped my jacket over her shoulders. As we headed back, she noticed a primitive sign.

"Oh, my God!" Patty said. "How could we have missed that?"

"What?"

"That sign! Those apples were sprayed with pesticide!"

"Well, at least I've spared you a horrible death. Thank God for that. As far as I can recall, I was the one who touched the apples and peeled them, right?"

"My hero!" she swooned and fell into my arms, Camille-like, then pretended to breathe her last there upon the grass. I lay back with her and we kissed.

This was our first date. We had been together twelve hours.

When we reached the dorms, it was midnight and past curfew in the women's dorms. We knew Patty was going to be "campused," forbidden from leaving her dorm after dinner, even to go to the library. She was summoned before the Judicial Board, and told she could not leave the dorm for a whole week for her transgression. The next day I snuck into her dorm room and stayed there, pressed against her warm body until morning. We were recreating a scene from *Romeo and Juliet* with her roommate, Barb from Oshkosh, as the Nurse, posted as lookout to make sure no one saw us. At daybreak, I climbed out her window and scrambled onto the lawn and back into my dorm room without being detected.

Within a week of our first date, however, we broke up. In fact, we broke up all the time. Sometimes, our fights had to do with my jealousy; she refused to tell her St. Louis boyfriend that she was seeing me and me alone. Sometimes, I deliberately picked fights because I was terrified about the closeness of a relationship, which troubled my self-conception. I didn't exactly know what that conception was, but I knew it didn't involve dating a nice Jewish girl from St. Louis named Patty Cohn. Things came to a head after Patty confessed to an affair with her T.A. before we'd met. I exploded, neglecting to mention my own illicit sessions with Laura the previous year. After that, there was our Afro-Asian History professor who asked Patty to come to see him during office hours. Thinking it was about her work, which had begun to suffer a bit after meeting me, she complied only to be blindsided—he wanted to talk about our relationship, not her work. He said I seemed crazy, that she should stop seeing me. He told her she had "stepped out of a painting by Rubens; your sad friend out of one by El Greco. I've never seen a more ill-matched pair. That boy is clearly unstable. Is he seeing a psychiatrist?"

When she told me, I began to scream that he obviously wanted her for himself—that's what these professors do, I said. I was furious that she would even listen to that pompous windbag and stomped out, leaving her alone, crying. An hour later, I called and apologized. She refused to accept it. I called back and we made up.

Near the end of the semester, Patty surprised me by breaking off her relationship with her St. Louis boyfriend, whom everyone back home considered her fiancé. She invited me to spend time with her at her home in St. Louis over winter break. I said if we were still seeing one another by then, I would come. Christmas vacation was weeks away, and it didn't look like we would make it. But I had no other plans, and was certainly not looking forward to returning to New York at Christmas, or any other time.

On the flight to St. Louis, I fell asleep with my head thrown back against the headrest. When I awoke, my neck was completely stiff. We were met at the gate by a crowd of relatives. Patty's parents were there of course, along with her sister who had seen me throwing rocks at ducks and thought I was cute, her grandfather and his redheaded girlfriend, and several aunts and cousins.

I greeted her family with my head down, unable to make direct eye contact because of my neck. Was this new boyfriend pathologically shy or otherwise deeply disturbed? There were whispers as the relatives helped with my luggage. Still averting my eyes, I mumbled something about seeing the

Arch. Patty's ten-year-old cousin blurted out that was impossible—it must have been the McDonald's by the airport, since the Arch, recently erected in 1966, was in the other direction.

Taking our bags into the house, I lifted my head to the other position available to me—straight up. The sky looked huge. I hadn't noticed a sky like that in Madison, so it must be something unique to St. Louis. Patty led me through the door to their home since I was unable to look anywhere but up or down. On the dining room table, a lavish spread had been laid—none of which I was able to touch, given my dietary proclivities: smoked salmon and whitefish, corned beef, sour pickles, mustard, and two huge glass bowls of tuna and egg salad. I figured that I would be able to eat the pickles and mustard, along with a bagel. Within seconds, the brightly colored room was filled with life. It wrapped itself around me in a tight embrace. I kept apologizing that my neck was stiff, and no, I could not eat corned beef, whitefish, tuna, or egg salad. Patty's bright fourteen-year-old sister, Racey, kept asking why I had become a vegetarian? If I couldn't eat egg salad or tuna fish—what could I eat? Having seen me heaving rocks on Lake Mendota, she asked Patty why I was now so concerned about a tuna sandwich when I thought nothing about possibly killing ducks indiscriminately a few months previously.

After our meal, Patty's father, Max, distributed our luggage (we had to sleep in separate rooms, of course), and announced he was going to take their Pekingese for a walk. I went along. He wore a tweed cap, and we smoked our pipes. It was beginning to snow, and I glanced up at the huge expanse of white St. Louis sky. What a strange world I had stumbled into! Max walked a few steps ahead with the little dog, and I noticed his shoes were worn unevenly at the heels. Overweight and balding, his front teeth were yellowed from decades of pipe smoking. He hadn't said much until now, but as we continued on our walk, he began to open up. First, there was the snowfall and how lucky we were to have arrived before the ten to twelve inches were dumped on St. Louis. As we walked up the hill, he told me how his whole family had moved into or close by their subdivision. They all lived within a quarter mile of one another. In my family, they would have already been sarcastic and fighting. Here everyone was friendly, even loving, towards one another—amazing! He told me he had worked for his brother's printing business since high school and had never attended college.

190

"Harold handles all our accounts, bookwork, and what not," he said. "I do the printing. That's the way it's been for more than twenty years now, and I hope it will never change. We've never had a single disagreement. Not ever. Even Harold's wife Nettie and my Edna love each other like sisters," he smiled. What kind of *Twilight Zone* episode had I stumbled into? Here it was normal to have close, loving relationships. Even pets were not neurotic like Blackie—helplessly chained to his urine in the kitchen until attempting suicide. It didn't seem banal or trite—it seemed beautiful in its very simplicity. Max had no aspirations beyond working six days a week at Press-Craft, and providing for his wife and two daughters. He wasn't articulate or even particularly interesting, but he had no hate or envy and truly loved his family. A few months ago, this would have seemed pathetic, even contemptible to me. Now it appeared beautiful—the way a family should be. Perhaps my New York world wasn't the real one. Perhaps family could be more than a poison tree.

Max spoke nostalgically about serving in the Fifth Armored Division during World War II, and the camaraderie in his Intelligence unit. I couldn't imagine how this poorly educated, simple man could engage in espionage. He laughed like a little boy recounting the time he got lost behind enemy lines. They sent a whole platoon to search for him, and he suffered a demotion to Staff Sergeant. He took the pipe from his teeth and his eyes watered as he recalled his rescue. The tears were not a lament for his disgrace, they were tears of gratitude and affection for buddies who had risked their lives and brought him back alive.

I thought about my own father, how he had not served in the military, and had never confided in me a single time. Never had he shared a single moment of vulnerability or intimacy, and the soles of his shoes would most certainly never be unevenly worn. Our communication, on the rare instances when we had it, was always about my deficiencies, my weaknesses, never his. For all I knew, he had none. Despite my father's arrogance and pride—in his intelligence, his ambition, his infallible sense of what was proper and right, he had never served his country or risked his life. I couldn't help thinking that Max—so insignificant beside my father's brilliantine hair and moustache, his money and power—had discovered the secret to something about which my father didn't have a clue: how to receive love from others and love them back in return.

191

The snow was falling heavily now, and Max and I put the little dog inside the house, and began shoveling a path leading up to the door of their modest ranch house. Patty's mother opened the door a crack, and told us to come back inside. I had just flown and must be tired, she said. I told her I wasn't; I wanted to stay out there with Max and finish digging our path. We shoveled together, and I loved the exertion and the sense of Max and I doing this work together. Snow blanketed everything like a snug down comforter. After we finished the path from the street back into the house, we cleared the driveway so Max could get his Chevy station wagon out in the morning. It felt like important, useful work, and I didn't want to stop until it was complete. Finally, we tramped back inside, took our boots off, and grabbed mugs of hot chocolate and sat by the fire in the den and played Gin Rummy. Before going to bed, I inspected the little pathway we had made from the door; it was ragged, but it would serve.

Patty's mother was the soul of the family. She worked part-time as a substitute teacher, but her dedication to home was her real job. The house was spotless—but not the kind of spotlessness which is constricting. Their ranch house was modest, but it was a place where something had taken root other than anger and brutality. In the center of the living room, an enormous dieffenbachia plant rose all the way to the ceiling. On the refrigerator, I read a list of handwritten menus for the week in Edna's elegant, school-teacher cursive.

Since she has been warned about my peculiarities, a second refrigerator out in the garage was stocked with vegetables and fruit reserved for me. It was Shabbat, and the smell of homemade matzo ball soup and challah smelled so good that I decided to violate my principles. It felt wrong to eat spinach, broccoli, rice, and grapes while everyone else was celebrating together.

I tasted Patty's matzo ball soup. Moments later, I asked for a bowl of my own "if there's enough for everybody."

"Enough?" Edna laughed at the absurdity of the question. I asked for a second bowl. A plate of roast chicken and roasted potatoes followed.

Long after Patty and I were married, I realized that on that very day I began constructing an alternate family for myself. I substituted the chaos and cruelty of New York for the affection I discovered in St. Louis. Each member of Patty's family played his or her part. I understood it might be possible for me to one day build a world that was not watered by tears and violence.

This did not happen without pain. When I proposed marriage, I bought Patty a fifty dollar engagement ring with my own work-study wages. Our wedding was set for the summer of 1969. Among the few available dates was my own twenty-first birthday. We jokingly said I should choose it so I would remember our anniversary. However, I had far more personal, symbolic reasons for choosing it.

My parents knew we were dating, but were unaware of any plans to marry. We chose to have our wedding in St. Louis. I knew my parents would be violently opposed to our engagement, let alone marriage. Patty's family and their modest lifestyle made it impossible for them to support such a step. And I was only twenty years old! To spare them—and myself—I refrained from telling anyone. Nor did I tell Patty's family that my parents had no idea about our wedding.

During the two years Patty and I had been together, I became serious about my studies and was able to graduate Wisconsin with honors. My parents agreed to come out (separately, of course) for my graduation, and Patty's family planned a picnic to celebrate both our graduation and impending marriage. We were sitting at a long picnic table when Edna lifted a champagne glass to propose a toast. Everyone raised a glass, including both my parents. Then Edna added how delighted she was about our recent engagement, and how much she looked forward to greeting everyone in St. Louis for our August wedding.

My mother began to weep.

My father spat his mouthful of champagne onto the grass.

"What are you crying for, Mom?" I asked. The question was met with a withering stare. And then came this:

"Ingratitude, thou marble-hearted fiend,
More hideous when thou show'st thee in a child
Than the sea monster."

Afterwards, silence.

My father crushed his champagne flute under his shoe. "Make no mistake," he said with apparent tranquility, "this will not happen, you bastard!"

I tried to make amends, but he refused to answer. He called a cab and flew back to New York that same afternoon. There was nothing Edna or anyone could do to appease his fury, and when I apologized for not telling him about the wedding, he stared right through me. His moustache twitched, and I knew all too well what he longed to say and do.

A week later, I received an express package in the mail. My father enclosed a collection of divorce statistics for my edification. Of course, by then every member of my family (including Uncle Malcolm) had been divorced, so he had little credibility. For the next several months, I was subjected to a barrage of telephone calls from both my parents reminding me how much better I could do than marry a "fat Jewish girl" from St. Louis "by the name of Cohn." Both city and surname were pronounced as anti-Semitic slurs.

They screamed and yelled, but reluctantly my parents both agreed to come out for the wedding in August. Separately.

On the steps of the synagogue where the ceremony was to take place, my father swore at my "Lerner taste" for not knowing better than to wear brown shoes with a tuxedo. He insisted I go back to the hotel and change. I did.

Over the next two decades, as my father rose to the very top of his profession, I managed to complete my PhD and obtain my first teaching post at Leiden University in the Netherlands. He became vice-president and chairman of the Bond Funds Division at Merrill Lynch. He was looked upon as the "Godfather" of municipal bonds, and his outsized personality dominated the most profitable and successful brokerage house in the world. Not for nothing had he received that *King Kong* poster. He was widely considered a genius, someone who did things his own way—ethical, but imperious, egotistical, and unpredictable. Like everyone else in high finance during those Reagan years, he embraced the conspicuous consumption of the 1980s. Still, for all the chauffeur-driven limousines, magnums of Dom Perignon and Montecristo cigars, he retained something of the conservative child of the Depression. On weekends, he and Malcolm hunted for bargains at Alexanders. For all his ostentation, he really did not spend huge sums on himself, and he never remarried. He lived with comparative modesty. On one of my rare visits back to New York, I even saw him wearing a pair of reading glasses, darning a pair of socks.

"You look a bit like Grandma in that pose," I noted sarcastically.

His half-smile was accompanied by tapping his red swizzle stick against the side of his highball glass, followed by a deep swallow of J&B and soda. My attempt at childish malice was swatted away.

The women in his life were interchangeable: fit, young, blonde, and attractive in an outdoorsy way. None were Jewish. Jewish women, he told me in a loud voice deliberately within Patty's earshot, were loud, opinionated, and grew fat once they were safely married. He still knew how to press my buttons. Although his blondes dressed with sophistication, it was apparent that their taste was of recent vintage. I met several on visits back to New York from the Netherlands, which my father generously paid for. On these trips, which included Patty and the children, I met my father alone for dinner. When his limo pulled up at our hotel, there was invariably a laughing blonde in the back seat, applying lipstick or sipping champagne from the mini-fridge. Sometimes, she came with an attractive friend. A friend my own age. Was my father trying to set me up, tempt me to stray from Patty? It certainly appeared that way.

Just before his seventieth birthday, Merrill Lynch announced that they were shifting their corporate headquarters from Wall Street to a new campus in New Jersey. My father was indignant and refused to move. He was adamant about not leaving the city. This was followed by a proposal from the top to restructure his division. Again, this was ignored. Finally, his combination of obstinacy, arrogance, and ego led to a reduction of his role in the firm. He remained in his New York office with a small staff, but the rest of his huge division was transferred. In 1991, he was replaced as head of Municipal Bonds in favor of a younger man with an MBA. My father was allowed to retain the title, Chairman of the Municipal Bond Division, but no longer performed the day-to-day administration of the division he had created.

Rather than subject himself to this indignity, he retired. He had been at the firm for over twenty years, and was truly a legend in the world of corporate finance. Lavish parties were thrown, at which he never permitted the word "retirement" to be uttered. I returned for one of these grand fêtes, and smuggled a box of Havana cigars from the Netherlands as a gift. As I stood trying to deliver my present, one of his administrative assistants directed me to put it on a table across the room. There I saw not one, but several iden-

195

tical boxes of the same contraband Montecristo cigars. I don't think he ever knew I got him anything, or for that matter, even cared. A few weeks later, I received a thank you note signed by his secretary.

I knew nothing of my father's illness until Malcolm phoned me in Holland. After muttering some pleasantries in Dutch to remind me he was familiar with the country and remembered a few words of the language, he told me my father had been taken to the hospital, and would be there for some time.

"What?!" I was stunned. Dad had never been sick in his life.

Malcolm was annoyed by my interruption. Like Grandma, he delighted in telling interminable stories fleshed out with specific details only he could provide. I was reminded of her explanation that if I left my shoes untied, I would likely fall to my death through an open grating in front of Gristede's; or if I happened to pet a dog in her lobby, a bite and rabies would almost surely follow. Didn't I remember that Morrie's son's ear had been mutilated by some mongrel in Central Park? He needed to have it sewn back on. He would never be the same, poor boy. The world was full of incomprehensible horrors, leading to misfortune, agony, and death. Such disasters were particularly likely to befall me, she suggested, if I didn't scrupulously wash my hands both before and after each meal.

I thought about Grandma while Malcolm made his usual sniffing sound, then said, "Just a second," as he irritably let the receiver fall on a table. I heard him crumple cellophane from a fresh pack of Pall Malls. I imagined I could smell the smoke through the phone as he exhaled. A deep swallow of Coke followed, then the rattle of the chipped ice against his glass. No conversation with Uncle Malcolm ever lasted less than a half hour, but the performance could easily last much longer. Whether the subject was racial violence, nudist colonies in Spain, the impending threat of socialized medicine, or the quality of hashish at the *Nieuwezijdsvoorburgwaal* near the Central Station in Amsterdam, he was equipped with both questions and answers. At this moment, however, I was too impatient to wait.

"Malcolm—please tell me what happened!"

"Well, after he passed out, they took him to the hospital."

"Passed out?"

"He had been to the dentist with an infected tooth. When he got home, he collapsed and was taken by ambulance. Then he was subjected to a detailed blood analysis. Not the level of sophistication we do here at Presbyterian, y'understand, but pretty good just the same. I mean, under the circumstances. And I think it was remarkably perceptive of the physician to realize your father was stubborn and would just try to leave the hospital, and go—"

"What exactly are we talking about, Uncle Malcolm?"

"I want to explain this to you precisely, step by step; so just give me a chance and don't interrupt. Y'see, the problem turned out to be more serious than anything the doctors imagined. So they sent him off to the hospital. There's poison, y'understand. Poison in his blood...." His voice trailed off.

"Poison in his blood? For Christ's sake, Uncle Malcolm, what do you mean?"

"Lymphoma. Your father has lymphoma, Henry," Malcolm said simply.

"What ... what does that mean? Isn't that like leukemia?" My mind flashed back to the sound of the little boy Eisenberg crying his eyes out that Saturday morning at Rodeph Sholem. We never saw him again.

"Well, Henry, I'll tell you," he said, and began as though speaking to a slow-witted eight year old. "Lymphoma, y'understand, is one of many blood cancers that develop from diseased cells in the lymphatic system ... part of the body's immune system. The lymphatic system is important because it fights infection. What happens is, with lymphoma, one of the cells undergoes a transformation into a malignant cell, and, y'understand, it begins to grow abnormally."

"Oh God."

"There are more than thirty different types of non-Hodgkin's lymphoma, which is what he has, y'understand? These include both aggressive and indolent kinds. They start in lymph nodes or in lymphatic tissue in the stomach or intestines. Often, they spread from one site to other parts of the body. So, he might get symptoms like night sweats, coughing, fatigue, and of course, swelling of the lymph nodes."

"What's the—his prognosis?" I gripped the phone tightly.

"Well, your father could live another twenty years, or ... it could be soon. They don't know."

197

"How soon should I come in?"

"If it were my father, I'd come in yesterday."

I heard him swish the ice around in his glass, sniff, and take a long swallow of Coke.

Six months after this diagnosis, however, my father improved enough from his radiation therapy to propose taking my two daughters aged five and eight to St. Martin's for a week's vacation. He still needed regular transfusions, but was told his platelet levels were manageable. Although the thought of him with my girls in another part of the world made me nervous, it was difficult to refuse my father at any time, and particularly now at this point in his life. Who was I to say he couldn't see his lovely granddaughters? Reluctantly, Patty and I agreed, but only after he agreed to hire a young au pair whose responsibility it would be to supervise the girls. However, on the second day of their vacation, Jerusha, our eight year old, called from St. Martin to say that the sitter had packed her bags after a single day and had flown back to the States.

"Daddy, please save us!" Jerusha cried, voice quivering.

Something had obviously happened between my father and the eighteen-year-old au pair, and I asked Jerusha to put him on the phone. He calmly explained that nothing was wrong. The girl had returned to the States because of a family emergency. He assured me at length that everything was fine, that he would find someone on the island who spoke English to help out with the girls. Part of me wanted to get on the next flight to St. Martin. Another told me that what I heard was an overly dramatic child understandably worried at being left alone without her parents for the first time. Since Patty was away visiting relatives in California, I questioned myself—should I tell her what Jerusha had said? If I did, I knew she would cancel her vacation, rush back home, and insist that I fetch the girls in St. Martin. Instead, I assured my daughter I would see her at the end of the week. My father got back on the phone to tell me the kids were absolutely fine—there was no need to worry. I decided that Jerusha had overreacted to the au pair's sudden departure.

When I met the girls at Kennedy Airport, they were tanned, beautiful, and laughing; they both had their long hair braided in cornrows, and were dressed in gorgeous matching outfits acquired on the island. I was embarrassed by my excessive worry—of course nothing was wrong. I was glad I hadn't responded precipitously out of fear.

However, as soon as my father left for the men's room, the girls' expressions changed and both began sobbing uncontrollably. Jerusha whispered she had been terrified the whole time—why hadn't I come to save them? And why did Grandpa Norman always want to be alone with Natasha? Was it just because Natasha was littler and cuter? Looking over her shoulder, Jerusha confessed she was afraid to leave her sister alone with her grandfather, and had packed her suitcase to return home the very day the au pair flew home. She refused to unpack, even though Grandpa Norman ordered her to.

What had happened? What had I *permitted* to happen? As I listened to my daughter in horror, my father strode back to us smiling and humming to himself. Then he walked right up to me, close enough that the toe of his shoe rubbed against mine.

"When I get back to the office, you know what I'm going to do, Henry?" he said smiling in a breathy whisper so the girls couldn't hear him.

"No, what?"

"I'm calling my lawyer. And I'm going to have them taken away from you for good," he said.

"What?!" I said. "What the fuck are you talking about?"

"You're not raising your children properly."

"'Properly?'" I shouted. I wanted to rush and kill him, but was paralyzed, unable to move. An old, familiar feeling washed over me—trembling impotence.

"You fucking bastard!" I suddenly blurted out loud. Before I could think, the paralysis was gone, and my hands flew to the lapels of his sports jacket, twisting and grinding the silk between my fingers. Slowly, I removed my hands from his jacket and clenched my fists. It was the first time I ever raised my hands to my father, but at that moment I wondered why it had taken me so long. I was in the presence of pure evil. I didn't care if it was lymphoma, impotence, senility—whatever. He wanted to obliterate me as a human being, destroy me and my children, and I was going to have to kill him.

"There's not a goddamn thing you can do about it," he continued with a withering smile which forced me to unclench my hands. "And you know I can do it!"

The terrible thing was, I did know. Money, connections, and malice. I had no idea what had just happened, or what he was accusing me of out of the blue. I only knew that my father was threatening for some reason to take my children away and was telling me I was powerless to stop him. I had no idea why, but felt just as impotent as when he chased me round and round the dining room table with his strap.

"You thought it was all right to leave our girls alone with him—with that monster—without an au pair?" Patty said when she returned from California. "After all you've experienced? How could you? Have you learned nothing? What kind of man are you? What kind of a father are you?"

I had no idea how to respond. "If I called and told you, I knew you would come back, and … I didn't want to ruin your holiday," I offered pathetically. "He's sick. Probably dying. He seemed sincere about connecting with the girls, behaving like a grandfather … I thought—"

"Even after Jerusha phoned and told you she was terrified out of her wits?"

"I … I'm so sorry," I mumbled.

Shortly after St. Martin, my father's health rapidly deteriorated. Blood transfusions went from weekly to daily, and there was talk of a bone-marrow transplant. I heard from Malcolm that he fell asleep in restaurants, woke up with a start and began cursing the wait staff. His erratic behavior at the airport was a harbinger of physical and mental decline. We never spoke about St. Martin's again, and he said no more about removing the children. I chose to pretend nothing happened. Nonetheless, my sense of anger and guilt over the incident never left me.

It was summer, and a literary conference at NYU gave me the opportunity to visit him at Columbia Presbyterian Hospital. The first thing I saw as I entered his suite was his bloated mustachioed visage hanging above me larger than life in bright, primary colors. His nurse was blowing up an assortment of his retirement balloons with his face on them. She rubbed them on her starched white uniform to create static electricity and then stuck the balloons all over the walls. While his face was ubiquitous, he himself was absent. The nurse directed me to McKeen Pavilion on the ninth floor of the Milstein Hospital, where a green arrow led to a luxury restaurant with a magnificent view of the Hudson River.

Dad was lounging in a silk maroon smoking jacket, talking with a young blonde. He had lost weight and looked healthy. The restaurant was gorgeous, and looked more like a tearoom in a fashionable hotel than a cafeteria in a hospital.

"Ah, you must be the son," said the blonde who, at around thirty-five, was probably a good ten years younger than I. "You're on time for high tea! We're having a little tea party, aren't we, Norman?" She handed me a plate, and piled it with little sandwiches—watercress, egg salad, and Nova Scotia salmon—with the brown and white crusts removed.

"I'm Charlotte," she said. Her hands were vascular, her handshake firm. An athlete's handshake.

My father gave me his cheek to kiss. My thoughts were not about St. Martin. I thought, thank God he smells like he is supposed to: musky, masculine. I couldn't bear it if he smelled like a dying man. Since entering the hospital, my great fear was that he would carry the smell death on him. I couldn't bear that.

"Say hello to Miss James, Henry," my father said loudly, and I was nine years old again intruding on a serious conversation between two adults, not a professor in my forties with three young children of my own. I made a note to myself to stay no more than half an hour, and I was determined to make things pleasant.

"I can't believe this place, Dad!" I said with forced cheer.

"Why the hell not?" he growled.

"It doesn't look like a hospital. Or feel like one. And this food! It's high tea at the Plaza."

"How the hell would you know what high tea at the Plaza looks like? Have you ever been there?" Something irritated him; I had no idea what. "Jesus Christ Almighty. You'd think at your age, you could learn to say something that wasn't completely asinine. Christ, Charlotte, you know the boy has a PhD in something or other, but still behaves like an idiot!"

"All right," I said. I really didn't want a fight here in the hospital.

"Norman, the boy was just making an amusing observation," Miss James said benignly. She was the comforting adult; I the child. "Besides, he's right. And I have been to the Plaza for high tea! You've brought me there, if I'm not mistaken, on more than one occasion."

"Shut up, Charlotte," he said between clenched teeth. "You can go to hell, too."

I decided to change the subject by referring to my son's passion for science and space travel. "Aram got straight A's on his report card. He's going to Huntsville for Space Camp next week."

"How's his tennis?" my father instantly shot back.

"You know he's not interested in sports." Somehow, I was being drawn into a fight. I checked my watch; less than five minutes had elapsed.

"Norman, we were having such a nice time," Miss James said. "What happened?"

"Nothing."

"Then why has your mood changed so suddenly?"

"Him!" A crooked, arthritic forefinger waved in my direction.

"You're cruel, Norman. Cruel and mean-spirited. You know he came all the way to see you from—where did you say you were teaching?" Miss James asked me.

"Leipzig," my father answered.

"Actually, it's Leiden. Leipzig's in Germany." It was still fifteen minutes shy of the half hour I'd promised myself. I'd never make it. "I think I'll head back to the hotel, Dad. I'll see you later."

"No, Henry, please stay," Miss James said. "You've come all this way—from Germany, you said? Please stay with us! Especially since he's behaving like such an old fart." She said this with a smile, but my father exploded.

"Fuck you! Fuck you both! Nurse! Nurse, I'm going back to my room." A nurse appeared. But he stood up and walked back to his room by himself, the nurse pushing his empty wheelchair from behind.

By the time we returned to his suite, party balloons were all over the place, and his moustache was staring at us from every angle. My father was propped up in bed, and Miss James and I were on either side.

He turned to me suddenly. "You see that body? Jesus Christ! Even with a business suit on, you can tell she's got it." This was said far too loudly, and it was impossible to say who was most embarrassed: Miss James, his nurse, or me. He continued, however. "Look at that stomach!" He ripped the blouse up from her skirt, and smacked her bare midriff with the flat of his hand. "I'm telling you, you could bounce a goddamn quarter off that. Yup, and those breasts! Best money can buy—believe me, I know! Built like a Lexington Avenue hooker!" Miss James turned white, and I opened my mouth to change the subject. But it kept on coming. "The way she dresses ... you'd never know. I mean, you'd think she belonged on Wall Street, among the right kind of people, among people who know. You'd never think only a few years ago she jumped off a bus from Dubuque or Wichita, or wherever the fuck it was, literally begging for a job, would you? No, you wouldn't. And that once she got that job, she parlayed it into another. And another. And now—just look: a brilliant young executive at Bear Stearns!"

The nurse stole out of the room. Charlotte James walked to the window, sobbing. Smelling blood, he continued. "Breeding shows, doesn't it? Huh? Not only among cattle, but women. In their genes. Still an ignorant bitch beneath the Calvin Kleins." Then he jerked his head away as though he couldn't bear her sight. Miss James closed her eyes, trying to stand her ground, but her voice betrayed her when she finally spoke.

"Norman, you are a son of a bitch. I'm leaving."

"No, *ple-e-e-ease* don't leave! We want you to stay, don't we, Henry?" he said dripping sarcasm. "Of course we do. She brightens up the room! Like the wallpaper or a decorative plant." Miss James pressed her forehead against the windowpane. Without the window, she would have crumpled to the floor.

I had no idea where this venom came from, but I couldn't help feeling a little pleased that it was not directed at me. After this last outburst, we sat there in silence while the nurse peeked in to see if the storm had abated. I exchanged brief, helpless glances with Charlotte. We were both trapped. Neither of us wanted to be there; but my father, I knew, enjoyed our discomfort as much as we hated it—perhaps more. We were his captives, and there was nothing either one of us could do about it.

After a while, he grew calmer. He politely asked Miss James to go so he could talk with his son. She bent over to kiss him on the cheek. There was no indication in her face that she had been humiliated moments before. She strode to the door, metamorphosed into a sophisticated young woman again. She was free; I remained behind.

"Come over here. There's something I want to ask you."

In the course of our lives together we had never spoken truthfully about our relationship or our feelings. Not once. Now there was something in his changed tone that made me think such a conversation might be imminent. I moved a bit closer, expecting the Reconciliation Scene. I was familiar with this scene from novels and plays. I hoped it would give us a chance to repair the damage of a life in which neither one of us had told the truth for one minute about what we thought.

"Still bite your fingernails, don't you?" he began as I pulled my chair up to the bed.

I glanced at my reddened cuticles, then at his manicured hands. I thought *I don't think this is how this scene is supposed to begin.*

"You remember Fionna?"

"Who?"

"Don't be an idiot! Fionna, Fionna Bingley! Fionna! Fionna! Of course you remember her. Blonde—British, friend of mine, Portugal!" He was furious I could not remember her for some reason.

"Yes…." I remembered her as Fee, but never knew her first name was actually Fionna.

"She just had a baby boy. In England. I need to congratulate her."

"How can I help?" I wondered about this sudden interest in a former mistress and her infant son. Fionna must be in her early forties, close to my age.

"Go to my apartment, find the address book in my desk. Here's the key."

I took the key. I noticed his initials NIS had been scratched into the brass. "And?"

"And nothing. That's it," he said. "Find the goddamn address book with her address in it and bring it back here. You think you can handle that?"

"Yes, I think I can just about handle it."

"Don't be a wiseass. Get the address book—bring it back here. There may be other people I need to contact while I'm stuck in this shit hole."

"Okay."

"Now, what did I ask you to do for me?"

"I think I can remember, Dad, I'm forty-five years old, I have a PhD in—"

"Repeat it, I said! Goddamn it, now—repeat it!"

I tried to speak. But when I opened my mouth to try and repeat his instructions, nothing came out. It wasn't defiance. Or maybe it was. The words got caught and for three seconds that felt like an hour, I stood there with mouth open, unable to utter a sound. Then I left the room without turning back.

So, there was to be no father-son reconciliation; no epiphany. Such moments, I realized, were better left to theatre. Or grand opera.

I spent the night in my father's apartment and had a strange dream. I was in a small room at Riverside Chapel, and a funeral service has just concluded. People wander in and out, poking their heads through the black drapes to peer at me. A bald man in a white short-sleeved shirt with hairy forearms rushes in wearing a black tie and yarmulke. He snatches a sign, which reads Norman I. Schvey—Funeral, tucks it under his armpit, and starts out of the room. "I've got to change the letters," he says, asking if everything is to my satisfaction. I don't know what to say, but before I can respond, he has vanished.

There is a coffin standing on the Bimah.

I rub my hands over the bronze handles, trace my fingers along the cherry wood sides of the casket. I peer inside. It is my father all right, with salt and pepper moustache and slicked-back silver hair. He is immaculately dressed, and I am mesmerized by his hands. No longer crippled by arthritis, they are beautifully manicured and folded across his chest. His fingernails gleam. There is just the right amount of white shirt cuff visible under the suit jacket. Silver cufflinks. I recognize everything, but something is wrong. I don't know what it is, but something is wrong.

The body springs upright in the coffin.

I'm frightened. The face isn't his. It belongs to someone else … it could be my face. The mouth opens, and a scream comes out, shrill and ear piercing. It wails like a siren, drowning out everything, including the traffic down below in the streets.

I wake up screaming and jump out of bed—mouth dry, heart racing.

Three days afterwards, I am back at the hospital and find my father near death. He is unshaven and shivering, rocking restlessly from side to side. The hospital blanket has been kicked off, his hands are buried deep in his crotch. In the fetal position, it appears he is trying to dig upwards into his own viscera. His thighs are thin and weak, and I remember how he looked in the locker room after tennis—his strong legs compared to my weak ones, his thick penis emerging from a forest of pubic hair.

How do I become a man? It's not going to happen.

I watch him quiver and moan; hands ineffectually reaching for safety between his legs. It's like watching an animal suffer. I want to put it out of its misery, but I have to see it through. I cannot leave until this is finished.

Hours later I am still there. I have lost track of time. The terrible shivering and rocking has stopped. He is quiet beneath the two extra layers of blankets a nurse has brought in. I am sitting now, though I have no idea when I sat down. A physician enters. I do not see his face. He tells me my father is on morphine and in a deep coma. It is a coma from which he will likely never wake. He pronounces these precise words: "If he does wake up, your father will be a vegetable." He asks if I want to stop the antibiotic drip, and tells me, "You are your father's executor." But I hear him say, "You are your father's executioner."

A nurse brings me a paper cone of ice water.

206

Malcolm walks in with Bobby and someone else. Bobby sports a moustache. He is dressed in a dark pinstriped suit and blue dress shirt with white
spread collar. His cuffs are white and monogrammed: RMS. He wears
a plum-colored handkerchief with five points in his breast pocket. He is a
bloated caricature of my father; like one of those balloons in his hospital room.
I have not seen my brother in a decade, and he has grown obese. My father
carried his excessive weight with elegance; Bobby looks like a mafia don.

The three men do not look at my father; instead, they circle me.

I am introduced to the other man as Malcolm's lawyer. He is old, frail,
and very tall. He is dressed conservatively in white shirt and striped red tie.
Stretched out, he must be at least 6'5", but his spine is so crooked he looks
like a walking candy cane. I begin to recount what the doctor has just said,
but Malcolm stops me with a wave.

"It's bullshit. I've heard it all already."

"What do you mean?"

"The story that Norman's brain dead. I know half a dozen neurologists
here at Presbyterian who'll swear exactly the opposite, y'understand. Your
father can and will recover. His brain function will return to normal. That's
why I brought him with me—just in case." He signals Candy Cane. He bows
gravely, forehead almost touching the floor.

"In case what?" I ask.

"In case you're thinking about killing your father. Terminating life
support."

"What are you talking about, Uncle Malcolm?"

"It's not going to happen," he snarls, "so don't go getting any stupid ideas."

The three of them surround me in a tight circle.

I tell the doctor not to disconnect the antibiotic drip. Another five days
later, my father dies in his sleep.

At the reception at Riverside Funeral Chapel, an old Chassid in a
yarmulke comes up and introduces himself in Yiddish. I assume he is looking
for one of the other funerals being held on a different floor, and offer to escort
him out. He looks so absurdly out of place among the elegantly attired busi-

nessmen and trim blondes in black dresses. I try to lead him out, but he turns and waves his arms and makes guttural sounds intended to tell me something. "Machatoonim! Machatoonim!" he bleats. "Shloime! Here for you fater! You fater Nachman."

I remember my father's response to my grandmother's grief at Grandpa's funeral, and imagine what he would say to this shabby intruder. In my imagination he takes this old Jew by his scruffy velvet collar and tosses him out onto the street. But Shloime is here and will not leave. He points to his slashed black necktie, which he has cut with a razor according to Orthodox custom honoring the deceased. He is agitated and perspiring; I offer him a seat, a plate of cookies, and a cup of tea. He eats a cookie and it seems to calm him, so I ask how he knows my father. He sighs. He explains that they are—were—first cousins. Best friends as little boys. Shloime's father, Harry Schvey's younger brother, was a rabbi in Philadelphia. While Grandpa went on to become a rich businessman, his brother—Shloime's father— attended rabbinical school in Philadelphia and became a *Tzaddik*, a man of wisdom, according to Shloime. Shloime tells me his father never learned to speak English, and that the two brothers from Riga went their separate ways. And after being childhood friends, he and my father lost touch.

It is very sad, he says, and tells me he is glad to have met me, even on this sad occasion. "Vat you do?" Shloime asks in his best English. I explain that I live in the Netherlands with my wife and three children, and teach English literature at Leiden University. He is quiet for a moment, then nods impressively. "*Tzaddik*, a *Tzaddik* like mine own fater, of blessed memory," he says. I smile and tell him he is mistaken, I am not a wise man, but he is undeterred. "No! No! *Tzaddik! Tzaddik!*" he shouts. "And now you must tell me, tell me all about how Cousin Nachman turned out, yes? Come, you tell me! I know he was a great man, you fater, an honorable man in business."

I nod silently, trying to think of what to say.

"Yes, he was an honorable man in business."

At that moment, my mother and Uncle Lee walk into Riverside Chapel holding hands. Almost gratefully, I offer my respects to the old Chassid, explaining that I must attend to my mother. Her hair is a combination of platinum blonde and pink, and she is wearing Gramsie's floor-length white mink coat. Her skin is pasty and white, which makes the contrast with the unnatural tint of her hair even more unearthly. But she is pleased to see me, and seems in good health. I kiss her and tell her how well she looks, and kiss Uncle Leon. He kisses me back feelingly on the cheek, and tells me how broad my shoulders are, how tall I am. I want to tell him that I am forty-five, and am not that tall or especially well built. But he is already weeping softly, recalling how beautiful I was as a child. I wonder if he remembers the time I called him Fairy at the magic shop. I want to tell him how sorry I am for that now, that I never meant it. I want to beg his forgiveness, but I don't have the courage. Oddly, Uncle Lee looks almost exactly as he used to, although he must be eighty now. His toupee is still the same coffee-bean color it was when I watched him drape it over the phrenology head in his bedroom before we went to sleep in his room at Gramsie's house. Lee thought I was asleep, but I secretly opened one eye and saw him without it. It made me terribly sad. His skin is still alabaster, like it always was.

My mother really is looking well. The floor-length mink, however inappropriate, offers a convincing narrative: it alludes to "Papa's factories in Philipsburg," maids, and summer cottages, Gramps as King of the Jews in a town full of goyim. It says that, no matter how she looks, she was married at The Pierre and is easily the match of any of the blonde shiksas prancing around Riverside Chapel pretending to mourn. She is still her Papa's daughter, his baby. She is also Norman I. Schvey's widow with the prestige that accompanies it. She has trouble walking, and beneath the mink, I see the orthopedic shoes with holes cut into the sides to accommodate her oversized bunions. But she carries herself with the same confidence as the beautiful prodigy who learned to shoot a pistol and earned a pilot's license, who graduated high school at fourteen and college at eighteen. Later, long after her divorce, she even went back to graduate school at City College and completed all the necessary course work towards a PhD in Accounting. She's ABD—All But Dissertation—and still is hoping to complete her doctorate.

I wonder what she is thinking. Does she feel a sense of triumph at having outlived her antagonist? I doubt it. Over the past few years, they've grown cordial, and she even betrayed a strange, lingering affection toward her nemesis. She asked his advice on unusual fluctuations in the stock market, and he always told her calmly, "Don't sell, just ride it out." I overheard one such conversation, and was stunned to hear her call him "Normie" again.

There was even a hint of little-girl flirtation in her voice, as though speaking to him brought out—just for a second—the innocent she was before being crushed by life, and him. Grandma's perpetual "You can bring them back together—it depends on you!" sprang to mind. Could she have been right? However mismatched and miserable, should they have somehow stayed together? Neither ever remarried, or even had a lasting relationship since, so perhaps there was something else I could have done. It's a ridiculous fantasy, but I can't help thinking it.

My mother is still in contact with Uncle Malcolm about things medical, and calls him frequently about this and that. Right now they are whispering intimately in a corner about some new product, which is absolutely guaranteed to dissolve earwax. I hear her thank him profusely, and proclaim to a handful of mourners what a brilliant doctor Malcolm is. I turn to find Uncle Lee, and see him standing next to Shloime, silently heaping food on his plate. The two don't converse. Each is aware of the other's presence, but no one makes the first move to explain who they are, or how they might be connected to the deceased. They just stand there eating.

Bobby strolls in with his wife and two boys. The boys, aged four and six, are dressed in matching suits with matching bow ties. They look like little yellow robots. Bobby wears a gray overcoat with a blue velvet trim. He also wears a homburg, which might have belonged to Uncle Lee in the mid-1950s, and makes him appear twice his thirty-eight years. His wife is wearing chunky open-toed heels and a dress that is far too tight across the bust. She scowls; they must be quarreling again. She brushes past me without saying hello.

I hear a child crying in an adjacent room. I know that sound and rush into the room where the coffin sits. The casket is closed, not like in my dream. Charlotte James is there, her black dress setting off her toned arms and blonde hair. Natasha, my youngest child, is there as well, her tiny fingers splayed out on the sides of the coffin. Charlotte, thinking she is the only adult left in the room, attempts to comfort her.

"Stop it, sweetheart, please stop," she says. It is unclear whether she is motivated by embarrassment or genuine sympathy. She tries to lead Natasha away from the room, and points at a huge blown-up photograph of my father, elegant and smiling, standing on an easel beside the coffin. "Look, Granddad's happy in heaven—he doesn't want to see you crying."

It is a fine portrait; my father speaking on the telephone in his sumptuous Merrill Lynch office, a giant Montecristo cigar clenched between gleaming, white teeth. Behind him, the East River floats by passively, as though it, too, has succumbed to his demands. But while he is joyfully giving orders over the phone, my father takes pleasure in the photographer's attentions, and smiles broadly. It is a picture of a man in control of everything and everyone. Natasha, however, pays no attention and continues crying, her long hair delicately brushing against the casket.

"There, there," Charlotte says, "let's come away from here. Cookies and punch are in the next room. Granddad knows how much you loved him."

But Natasha ferociously turns on her. "You think I'm crying because I love him—I'm not! I'm crying because he never said he loved me, and now—it's too late."

The child's words make my heart race. What she has said is true, and I've never even thought about it. The dead man has not once told his grandchildren—or children—that he loved them. And now it is too late. The deep sadness of that simple fact appalls me beyond words. For all of us. I wave Charlotte away and move toward Natasha. When I turn back around, I see the room is empty and the other mourners have fled the apparently hysterical child. Only Natasha stands beside me, looking up, a strange expression on her face. *What is she thinking*, I wonder? That I am her father and she knows I love her? Or is she still thinking about the dead man in the box who never said he did? Or something else I am not privy to.

As the child grips my hand, her warm fingers send a thrill through my body.

"I love you, Natasha."

"I love you too, Daddy." So simple. So easy.

With these words, she leads me out of the house of death.

Alone in his apartment immediately after the funeral, I unearth the portfolio from its hidden place in my father's desk and look through the photographs again. Yes, just as I suspected, it is Charlotte. She smiles a humiliated smile. I turn the picture over and read the date. It is of recent vintage. I put it down and realize that these pictures are whispering something important to me. Something about myself. And now I understand what that is.

I walk down the hall and enter a room far smaller than my father's clothes closet. The room smells of rotting fruit, garbage, and roses. Flies buzz around charcoal-gray trash bags leaning against one wall. Inhaling the rich scent of decay, I twist the latch, open the incinerator door, and toss the portfolio down the chute. It sails from floor to floor, then—silence. I return to my father's empty apartment, and think of the time, decades earlier, when I accidentally incinerated my mother's chandelier crystals.

I know that it is time now for me to leave New York.

ACKNOWLEDGMENTS

My foremost debt is to my wife Patty, who managed to keep me (relatively) sane during the painful, solitary process of digging up fossil remains from my distant past and dredging ancient memories up into the light of day.

Additional thanks go to the many people (teachers, editors, students) who have patiently critiqued my work, and whether by instruction, example or support, helped me discover what this book was about:

Brad Cook, Bernard Cooper, Judy Copeland, Julie Schafler Dale, Nicholas Delbanco, Donna Essner, Kathleen Finneran, Cynthia Florin, Emily Follman, Gabe Fried, Laura Gyawali, Kathryn Harrison, Robin Hirsch, A.E. Hotchner, Cindy Kahn, Jane Lapotaire, Carter Lewis, Kristina Blank Makansi, Lisa Miller, Eric Nuetzel, Jane Otto, Anna Pileggi, Eileen Pollack, Aram, Jerusha and Natasha Schvey, Richard Selzer, Penny Stein, Alison Stoltzfus, Adina Talve, Elizabeth Tucker, MaryEllen VanDerHeyden, Paul Wagman, Kerri Webster, Bill Whitaker, Kea Wilson, my gifted cohorts at the 2012 Yale Writers' Conference.

About the Author

HENRY SCHVEY was born in New York City and attended Hunter College Elementary School and the Horace Mann School for Boys. After graduating from the University of Wisconsin, Madison, he received an MA in Western European Studies and a PhD in Comparative Literature at Indiana University. He worked in the Netherlands for fourteen years, during which time he taught at Leiden University and founded the Leiden English Speaking Theatre (LEST). He, his wife, and three children returned to the U.S. in 1987, where he became chair of the Performing Arts Department at Washington University in St. Louis. He stepped down as chair in 2007, but has continued to teach, direct, and write as a professor of drama and comparative literature.